Measuring Service Quality
The P3D3 Matrix

	PRODUCERS	PROCESSES	PEOPLE
DIAGNOSING	Structural analysis Check sheets Mystery shopping Internal focus groups	Graphic techniques Run charts Stratification Flow charts	Complaint elicitation Content tracking Belief system analysis Pareto charts
DETAILING	Nominal group technique Benchmarking Deleting dimensionality The as-if frame The video camera	Control charts	External focus groups Survey research Laddering Factor analysis Gap analysis Wish lists
DELIVERING	Brainstorming Force field analysis Cost-benefit analysis	Fishbone diagrams Process mapping and evaluation	Tracking

Measuring Customer Satisfaction

TEN STEPS TO CREATING AN ACTIONABLE CUSTOMER SATISFACTION STUDY

CONCEIVE	DEVELOP	INTERPRET & TRACK
1. Gather background data	**2.** Choose attributes to measure	**3.** Choose the right audience
4. Choose the basic CSM questions	**5.** Choose the right metric	**6.** Make analysis action-oriented
7. Consider segmenting the market	**8.** Interpret the measures correctly	**9.** Use results cautiously
	10. Create a tracking system	

How to Measure Service Quality & Customer Satisfaction

The Informal Field Guide for Tools and Techniques

How to Measure Service Quality & Customer Satisfaction

The Informal Field Guide for Tools and Techniques

Chuck Chakrapani, PhD
Standard Research Systems, Inc., Toronto

American Marketing Association
Chicago, Illinois

Library of Congress Cataloging-in-Publication Data

Chakrapani, Chuck.
    How to measure service quality & customer satisfaction : the
informal field guide for tools and techniques / Chuck Chakrapani.
        p.   cm.
    Includes bibliographical references (p. 290) and index.
    ISBN 0-87757-267-4 (hardcover)
        1. Customer services—Quality control.   2. Customer services—
Management. I. Title.
    HF5415.5.C445   1997   97-28835
    658.8'12—dc21   CIP

Published by American Marketing Association
250 S. Wacker Drive, Suite 200
Chicago, Illinois 60606 USA

Francesca Van Gorp, Editor
Anne Garry, Copy Editor

Cover design by Mary Kushmir

Manufactured in the United States of America.

For Brian Fine
&
for the memory of Ravi Gupta.

Contents

        Customer Satisfaction
            Quadrant Analysis   236
            Appendix: Modeling and Measuring Customer
                Satisfaction—An Example   247

Part V   Toward a Philosophy of Quality   251
21   A System of Profound Knowledge   253

22   Deming's 14 Points   257

Part VI   Putting It All Together   269
23   Choosing the Right Technique   271

        General References   275
        Index   277

Preface

WHAT THIS BOOK IS ABOUT

This book is an informal, user-friendly introduction to service quality and customer satisfaction measurement techniques. It brings together a wide variety of techniques of service quality measurement in one volume. The techniques described here are accessible to interested researchers from several sources, but they are scattered throughout different books and journal papers. My objective is to provide easy access to these techniques.

Even though the book covers a wide variety of techniques, I have kept it short and nonintimidating. Keeping the book short meant that I had to choose between providing an overview of a large number of techniques and providing in-depth coverage of a few. I have chosen breadth over depth deliberately. I have tried to increase the book's readability by keeping intrusive references to a minimum. This book is not intended to be a scholarly work but rather an informal guide. The purpose of this book is to let readers know what can be done in a given situation and, if they want to pursue that, where to go for further help.

WHAT THIS BOOK CAN DO FOR YOU

After reading this book, you should be able to
- identify a suitable technique for a given problem,
- understand what the technique does,
- understand the steps involved in implementing the technique,
- assess how the technique fits in the measurement environment, and
- know where to obtain more detailed information on a given technique.

It is important to know beforehand that though this book can be your entry point in measurement, you are likely to need more. Suppose you are interested in benchmarking. This book will tell you what it is, what it does, what the interpretation involves, and what you should be cautious about. But it does not go into details. If the description in this book makes you believe that a given technique is suitable for your purpose, you should explore the details elsewhere. To make your search easier, I have provided further references for each technique.

I have attempted to provide more information on lesser-known topics, such as common cause and special cause variations, and less information on better-known topics, such as focus groups and survey research.

More than a compendium of techniques

Although the book covers a number of techniques, it is not just a compendium. I believe that no service quality measurement is meaningful unless there is an underlying philosophy of quality. If we do not know why we are doing something or why we are measuring something, the numbers generated by the measurement procedures are of little value. Consequently, I have tried to place the measurement techniques in the broader context of the philosophy of quality. No one has influenced me more in this regard than the late Dr. W. Edwards Deming.

Immediate help for the harried

Because this book is an overview and not a critical review of the techniques discussed, I have adopted a user-friendly style. I have structured the book so that it can be read through in order to get the overall picture. Subsequently, it can be used as a reference to solve specific measurement problems. To make referencing easier, I have used marginal notes, summaries, and charts, which identify specific techniques for a given problem.

I hope this book will provide immediate help to the harried manager and researcher, or the academic, who must find a suitable technique for a given problem and understand what it does and how. In a hurry. On a late Friday afternoon.

ACKNOWLEDGMENTS

In various ways, several people were instrumental in projects leading up to this book. Rosemary Cliffe of Bank of Montreal, who critically read my earlier articles on measuring service quality; Brian Fine of AMR:Quantum Harris, who was instrumental in publishing a preliminary version of this book in Australia; Christine Mole of Standard Research Systems, who helps me in everything I do; and the hundreds of seminar participants around the world who challenged my exposition over the past several years deserve specific mention. For critically reading the final draft of the entire book in one weekend, Elaine Freedman deserves special thanks. My discussions with Suresh Chawla of S. Chawla and Associates provided me the inspiration I needed to finish this book. Dr. Barrie Wilson and David Lithwick deserve thanks for their willingness to share some of their published and unpublished materials.

The comments on the manuscript by Alicia Shems of the American Marketing Association were invaluable in improving the structure of the book. This book would not have come into being but for Francesca Van Gorp of the American Marketing Association. It is her interest in the book that eventually overcame my usual excuse—"I'm too busy now to write!" My special thanks to Francesca.

Chuck Chakrapani

A NOTE ON TERMINOLOGY

Wherever the term *customer* is used in this book, it refers to both customers and consumers. Although the term *customer* may be more appropriate in business-to-business research, it should be read *consumer* when dealing with mass-market goods and services.

Part I

Managing
Service Quality

What Is Quality?

W̶e live in the postindustrial age. Most products we use are standardized. Even no-name store brands far exceed the minimum standard, which makes them acceptable alternatives to nationally branded products. Companies such as IBM and Xerox still may command respect, but they do not evoke the awe they once did. Rapidly increasing global competition makes established companies even more vulnerable, especially from the point of view of pricing. The modern communications revolution is making it increasingly easy for customers to switch their loyalties.

- *The changing face of business*
- *Standardized products*
- *Global competition*
- *Ease of customer migration*

These trends point to two basic factors. First, the economy as a whole is becoming service oriented. Second, we need a point of differentiation that is not entirely dependent on product quality. Product quality is a necessary, but not a sufficient, condition for a thriving business in the years to come. But what is this point of differentiation? Dr. Edwards Deming, who is often cited as the driving force behind the Japanese economic miracle, contends that it is quality. Quality decreases the cost of doing business by increasing efficiency and by eliminating rework and waste. In that process, quality also increases customer and employee satisfaction. The purpose of this book is to provide a description of the tools and techniques used in measuring service quality (as opposed to product quality) and customer satisfaction.

SERVICE QUALITY AND CUSTOMER SATISFACTION

If we deliver service quality, we need to assess how well we are doing. Customer satisfaction provides this measure. In this sense, customer satisfaction measurement can be perceived as a subset of service quality measurement. Although customer satisfaction can be carried out irrespective of the quality of service provided, to measure something without context is of little value. In this book, we treat customer satisfaction in the context of service quality delivery.

We recognize "quality" when we experience it. Yet, it is hard to define. We can avoid getting into an academic definition of quality by accepting some operational definitions. For our purposes, *a product or service has quality if customers' enjoyment of it exceeds their perceived value of the money they paid for it.* For competitive markets, we can extend this definition: *In a competitive market, the product and/or service with the highest quality is the one that provides the greatest enjoyment.*

The definitions mentioned previously need further clarification. A product or service that enhances customer enjoyment is one that *consistently meets customer needs and expectations.* A product or service that is of higher quality exceeds customer expectations. A definition of quality, then, should not be restricted to aspects of the product or service but should be related to customer satisfaction. Both aspects—quality in fact (i.e., as per customer specifications) and quality in perception—are critical. For example,

- A computer manufacturer produces a sturdy portable computer that is too heavy to carry around. Although the sturdiness itself is a desirable attribute of the product, it does not generate enjoyment for consumers who find it inconvenient to carry. By our definition, the product lacks quality.

- A restaurant uses only fresh ingredients and has a highly competent chef, but it employs waiters who are curt, which interferes with customers' enjoyment of what is being offered. By our definition, this restaurant lacks quality.

Our definitions relate quality to the price of the product or service. Yet, a product or service can have quality even when it is offered at no cost or there is nothing with which to compare it. For such noncommercial contexts, the definition must be modified. Although this book deals with service quality in a commercial context, there is no reason why the philosophy and techniques could not be extended to noncommercial contexts.

As we define it, the main focus of service quality is the customer. When a firm that lacks customer focus attempts to deliver quality, it is likely to fall into the trap of delivering quantity (more product features) rather than quality (features that enhance customer enjoyment). Increased product features almost always result in increased cost; yet, they do not always guarantee increased customer enjoyment.

WHAT DO CUSTOMERS WANT?

Quality, from customers' perspective, can be viewed as features that fulfill their wants in three basic psychological domains: cognitive, conative, and affective. Customer enjoyment tends to be based on continuous improvement of these three dimensions. As Exhibit 1.1 shows, customers' enjoyment increases as a service gets faster (or slower under certain conditions), gets cheaper (or provides better value at the same price), and exceeds expectations.

Exhibit 1.1
Continuous Improvements in the Three Basic Psychological Domains

Domain	Deals with	Relevant Dimension	Relevant Consequence
Cognitive	Perceptual aspects	Time	Works faster
Conative	Behavioral aspects	Work	Works better
Affective	Feeling aspects	Delight	Exceeds expectations

When we deliver on these dimensions, we enhance customer enjoyment and thus provide high-quality service.

But how do we get there? What do we need to do to make sure that we do things that will enhance customer enjoyment? Delivering service quality is not a one-time task. It requires continuous improvement. Continuous improvement in what? Although a person should strive for continuous improvement in all areas of his or her business, three basic areas (Tenner and DeToro 1992) are particularly important:

Customer enjoyment tends to be based on continuous improvement on three basic psychological dimensions: cognitive, conative, and affective.

1. Customer focus,

2. Process improvement, and

3. Total involvement.

We need to shift our focus from product features to customer enjoyment, from employee-dependent service to process improvement, and from piecemeal implementation of quality initiatives to total involvement with customers and the processes. The measurement techniques we discuss in this book will affect these three areas.

2

How Does Quality Affect Profitability?

THE CASE AGAINST SELECTIVE DELIVERY

A widely held assumption about quality is that delivering it adds cost to the organization. This is one of the reasons why many organizations—if they are interested in delivering quality at all—are concerned about the cost. In fact, some organizations reserve the delivery of quality service to their more profitable clients. Delivering quality selectively is detrimental to the delivery of quality. It labels customers, teaches employees to discriminate against certain clients, and introduces variability in service quality.

The lifetime value of a customer. It is a mistake to believe that a customer is unimportant just because he or she is not highly profitable. Losing a customer who visits your restaurant twice a month and spends about $50 a visit may not seem to be a great loss. But if a customer visits his or her favorite restaurant for a long period of time (say ten years), the business worth of this customer is about $12,000. And if, during this period, the customer introduces the restaurant to just two other people who also frequent it for a similar length of time, the "small customer" could represent a substantial amount of business to the restaurant.

Small customers do not always remain small. Most service businesses have a substantial repeat business component. Consequently, the business worth of a small customer could be high if viewed from a cumulative perspective. In addition, a small customer also can grow into a large one.

- **The lifetime value of a customer must be considered.**
- **Small customers do not always remain small.**

A study commissioned by the American Business Conference (Clemmer 1990) reveals the following: 43 out of 45 high-performing, midsized companies owed their superior performance to the delivery of high value rather than low price. Customers will pay more if they are convinced they are getting a high-quality product or service. However, because delivery of quality should precede profits, quality programs increase the cost of doing business at the initial stages. Therefore, it is important for us to be convinced that quality will eventually decrease the cost of doing business.

WHY POOR QUALITY INCREASES THE COST

Just as higher quality delivers higher profits, lower quality delivers lower profits. Such costs are not always visible.

Visible costs of poor quality

Not delivering quality can be expensive. In the service sector, nondelivery of quality is accompanied by

- The cost of handling irate customers. This usually takes up the time of senior personnel in the organization.

- The cost of losing customers. A current customer automatically generates business. When a customer leaves an organization, he or she takes the business stream along. And it could be several years' worth of business, because a satisfied customer will stay with an organization for a long time.

- The cost of rework. When things are not done right, it costs more to fix them. For example, it might be cheaper to fix a computer program that produces billing errors than to deal with many unhappy customers.

Visible costs of poor quality
- **The cost of handling irate customers**
- **The cost of losing customers**
- **The cost of rework**

Invisible costs of poor quality
- **Costs likely to be out of control**
- **The cost of countering negative publicity**
- **The cost of replacing lost customers**
- **Higher marketing costs**

Invisible costs of poor quality

Lower quality often indicates that the production/delivery process is out of control. When a process is out of control, so are the costs associated with it.

- *The cost of countering negative publicity.* A dissatisfied customer talks about his or her dissatisfaction to other people. This makes the cost of attracting new customers even higher.

- *The cost of replacing lost customers.* When a company does not deliver quality, it tends to lose customers. According to the Technical Assistance Research Program (TARP), the cost of getting a new customer is five times higher than the cost of retaining a current customer. In other words, the company that does not deliver quality spends a lot more to stay where it is, compared with another company that delivers quality and retains its customers.

- *Higher marketing costs.* Unlike high-quality products, low-quality products will not get "free marketing" from such sources as word-of-mouth advertising generated by satisfied customers or free publicity generated in the media.

The downward spiral

If the increased costs encourage the company to cut corners or to reduce staff, the result is a downward spiral (Exhibit 2.1). The cycle can be broken only through offering higher quality.

Exhibit 2.1
The Downward Spiral

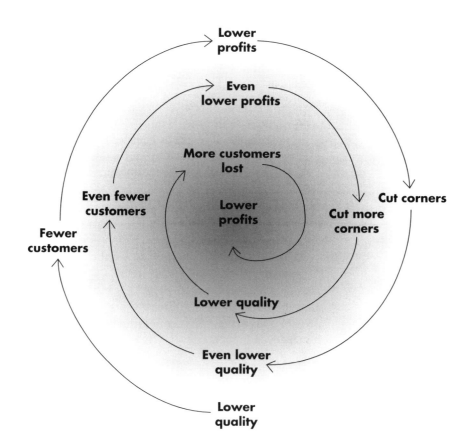

THINKING ABOUT QUALITY

Firms that are new to the service quality game tend to approach service quality from a purely cost/benefit point of view (*The Economist* 1992). Although high service quality results in higher profits (Deming 1986), profits

Poor quality begets even poorer quality.

are affected by a number of factors. Furthermore, service quality improvement may not result in increased profits in the short term. When quality programs do not result in immediate profits, the programs tend to be discarded.

When the fundamental commitment is to profits rather than to quality, quality programs are implemented mechanically, with employees simply going through the motions. The appearance of quality seems as critical as—if not more critical than—quality itself. Customers often can distinguish genuine currency from counterfeit notes. Phony smiles, the inability to understand a customer's complaint, reassurance with no meaningful remedial action, quality control bureaucracy, verbally polite conversation with hostile body language, and other such attempts are not substitutes for quality delivered with passion and commitment. All resources spent on such substitutes are not likely to result in higher profits.

One helpful way to think about quality is to view it as a nonoptional expense associated with your service. Just as an automobile manufacturer would not think of making a car with three wheels to save costs, a firm also should not think of providing service that lacks quality. One reason most companies fail to deliver quality is the lack of commitment to it, except insofar as it can be related directly to profitability. Thinking of quality as an option decreases the organization's commitment to it and therefore is detrimental to the delivery of quality.

As *The Economist* (1992) points out, quality programs should be measured against customer expectations and not against quarterly profits. The fundamental requirement for delivering service quality is commitment. Or, in Deming's words, constancy of purpose. And quality is quality when customers say so. Service quality programs that are geared to increasing profits rather than to fulfilling and exceeding customer expectations are not likely to deliver profits. Neither are they likely to deliver quality. Quality is not an add-on—an optional extra reserved for a company's more profitable customers. Quality is an integral part of any product or service. Higher quality results in higher profits, but not necessarily in the short term.

What is spent on programs relating to quality can be either an investment resulting in higher profitability or an expense resulting in lower profitability and frustration, as the following model shows:

a. Commitment $\longrightarrow$ Quality $\longrightarrow$ Profit $\longrightarrow$ Quality is an an investment

b. Lack of $\longrightarrow$ Appearance $\longrightarrow$ No profits $\longrightarrow$ Quality is an Commitment of quality expense

Commitment (or constancy of purpose) is the key. As mentioned previously, there may not always be a one-to-one relationship between service quality and profitability, which can be due to two reasons: First, there may be other intervening marketing variables; and second, there might be a considerable lag effect. To result in profits, quality should be viewed as an enduring way of doing business rather than as a shortcut to improving the quarterly balance sheet.

Commitment (or constancy of purpose, as Deming calls it) is the key.

THE COST OF QUALITY

A frequent argument against providing service quality is the cost associated with it. Researching service quality requires special expertise, which also adds to the cost. Costs are associated not only with delivering quality, but also with maintaining and monitoring it.

What is the cost of quality? Many world-class quality performers appear to believe that the cost is around 3% of their sales revenue (e.g., Band 1991); that can be a lot of money. If your sales volume is $100 million, maintaining service quality will have an average price tag of $3 million.

Companies that do not deliver quality as an integral part of the product can easily make service quality the first casualty of hard times, such as when the company starts losing money or when a recession hits the economy. If you run a $100 million company and it shows a net loss of $2 million, you can turn your company around just by eliminating expenditures associated with delivering service quality. It is a temptation that many companies give in to when times are tough.

How effective are such cost-cutting (quality-cutting) measures? They can indeed be effective in the short term. Then, as we illustrated previously, as quality goes down, the downward spiral begins. The quality versus cost dilemma is related to long-term versus short-term goals of the organization. Is the organization willing to pay the price in the short term to achieve long-term profitability? As we noted previously, when a service quality program is implemented, it initially increases the cost of doing business. The lag between the investment in quality initiatives and the generation of profits may not always be a short one. Therefore, the success of any service quality program depends on an organization's commitment to the goal, undeterred by short-term costs.

3

Why Is Management Always the Last to Know?

f an organization loses just 5% of its customers and fails to attract just that many new customers, the amount of resources it needs to spend will be several times higher than the amount it would have spent on service quality. There are several estimates of how expensive it is not to provide service quality. These figures vary depending on what exactly is included in "service quality." But all estimates point to one thing: Providing service quality is a lot less expensive than not providing it.

Many organizations are lulled into complacency because they receive very few customer complaints.

Many organizations are lulled into complacency because they receive few customer complaints. However, voluntary complaints are poor indicators of customer dissatisfaction. For example, a complaint level that would have affected 2.5 million potential customers may generate as few as 50 recorded complaints. The rest of this section explains how this can happen.

A THEORY OF PROPAGATION OF DISCONTENT

Stage 1—customers to management

1. Let us assume that a bank has 1,000,000 customers.

2. 10% of them (a fairly large proportion) are dissatisfied. This could potentially generate 100,000 complaints.

3. However, in most cases, only 4% of those (or 4,000 customers) will actually complain. This reduces the complaining customers to 4 out of every 1000.

4. Most of these complaints never reach even junior management. Only 4% of the 4000 will reach top management (see "The Iceberg of Ignorance" section later in this chapter). When we see that the first level of complaints is received by nonmanagement or "nonrecording" employees of the organization, the magnitude of

the problem becomes evident. For example, a dissatisfied bank customer might complain to the cashier. Normally, complaints are not recorded at this level.

> **Only 4% of dissatisfied customers will complain. Only 4% of the complaints actually launched will reach top management.**

5. If only 4% of the 100,000 dissatisfied customers complained, and if only 4% of these complaints reached top management, it works out to about 160 complaints, or three complaints per week spread over a year.

Although 10% of the customers are dissatisfied, management is exposed to a complaint level of just .16% of the dissatisfied customers—a trivial proportion by any standard.

Stage 2—customers to others

Although customers may be reticent about talking to management, they are not so reticent when it comes to talking to others about the institution.

1. When a customer has a minor service problem (transactions worth less than $100), he or she will tell 9 or 10 people about it. In our example, 100,000 dissatisfied customers will talk about their dissatisfaction to almost 1,000,000 others.

> **Although customers may be reticent about talking to management, they are not so reticent when it comes to talking to others about the institution.**

2. Now, a population that is as large as a financial institution's customer base (1 million people) knows about the poor service!

3. It gets worse if the transaction size is $100 or more. In this case, 100,000 dissatisfied customers will tell an estimated 1,600,000 people—much larger than the company's current customer base.

Stage 3—"critical mass" (common knowledge)

When the number of people who know about a certain thing reaches a certain level (the critical mass), it can become common knowledge. (The critical mass is an informal theory that holds that the more people who know about something, the more a disproportionately higher number of other people are exposed to it, presumably due to incidental exposure to that information.)

Therefore, the fact that few complaints are recorded is no guarantee that customers are happy. The actual level of discontent could be higher, and a large number of people who are not even customers could be aware of it.

Exhibit 3.1
How Discontent Spreads[1]

Suppose you have 1,000,000 customers and 10% of your customers are dissatisfied. You could lose 1.6 million potential customers

Your initial customers (1,000,000)

☺☺☺☺☺☺☺☺☺☺☺☺☺☺☺☺☺☺☺☺☺☺☺
☺☺☺☺☺☺☺☺☺☺☺☺☺☺☺☺☺☺☺☺☺☺☺
☺☺☺☺☺☺☺☺☺☺☺☺☺☺☺☺☺☺☺☺☺☺☺
☺☺☺☺☺☺☺☺☺☺☺☺☺☺☺☺☺☺☺☺☺☺☺

Your dissatisfied customers (100,000)

☹☹☹☹☹☹☹☹☹☹

tell this many people (1,000,000)

☹☹☹☹☹☹☹☹☹☹☹☹☹☹☹☹☹☹☹☹☹☹☹
☹☹☹☹☹☹☹☹☹☹☹☹☹☹☹☹☹☹☹☹☹☹☹
☹☹☹☹☹☹☹☹☹☹☹☹☹☹☹☹☹☹☹☹☹☹☹
☹☹☹☹☹☹☹☹☹☹☹☹☹☹☹☹☹☹☹☹☹☹☹

and do not act as your PR person for this many people (500,000)

☹☹☹☹☹☹☹☹☹☹

The figures presented above assume that customers are dissatisfied with a transaction that costs less than $100. If the cost of the transaction is $100 or more, then 10% of dissatisfied customers result in a loss of 2.5 million potential customer pool, as shown below.

Dissatisfied customers	100,000
They tell this many people	1,600,000
They do not act as your PR person for	800,000
For a total potential loss of customers	2,500,000

- Although the negative message has reached over 1.5 million potential customers, management would have received only 160 complaints. In fact, the recorded number of complaints could be as low as 50.

Getting 2.5 million customers is far more expensive than keeping your current customers happy. A happy customer will act as your PR person by telling 5 to 8 other potential customers about his or her satisfaction.

[1]This exhibit is loosely based on various research findings, such as the ones published by TARP. The exact numbers are less critical than the conceptual model presented.

SATISFIED CUSTOMERS: DO THEY COMPENSATE?

If a dissatisfied customer tells ten other people about his or her dissatisfaction, we might assume that when a customer is satisfied, he or she would tell others about it. The assumption is correct—except that satisfied customers tell only half as many people: on average, five other people. In other words, an organization needs two new satisfied customers for every dissatisfied customer just to retain its current status.

Keeping current customers happy is much more cost-

The fact that few complaints are recorded is no guarantee that customers are happy.

effective than trying to reach new customers to replace them. As we noted, every 100 dissatisfied customers could cost a company 1600 to 2500 potential customers. Conversely, every satisfied customer works as an unpaid and credible salesperson for an organization. Every 100 satisfied customers tell 500 to 800 potential customers. Consequently, dissatisfied customers are extremely costly to a service organization, and special efforts

Dissatisfied customers are extremely costly to a service organization.

should be made to keep customers happy and satisfied. Dissatisfied customers complain, and only a fraction of the complaints are ever recorded. The paradigm discussed so far explains how there could be a large gap between the perceptions of management and those of customers.

WHY CUSTOMERS DO NOT COMPLAIN

Why don't customers complain to the organization? After all, customers are not reticent. When they are dissatisfied, they tell many people. It would appear logical then, that if there are few complaints, customers are happy with the service. What most organizations are unaware of is that customers simply exclude the company management from the list of people to whom they complain. This sounds rather illogical. After all, if anyone could solve the problems, management can. Yet, customers avoid contacting management. Why?

Why don't customers complain?
- **Customers may not know to whom to complain.**
- **Customers are used to having their complaints handled poorly.**
- **Customers may believe that complaining is an exercise in futility.**

The reasons why customers do not complain are diverse and varied. Only one of those reasons is because they are satisfied. TARP identified other reasons, including the following:

Customers may not know to whom to complain. If a person is unhappy with the service he or she received in a bank, with whom should a complaint be lodged? The person at the counter? The person behind the desk? Someone at the head office? The public relations officer? The bank manager? If the bank manager, would the customer have to make an appointment?

Customers are used to having their complaints handled poorly. Some customers are given nonanswers, such as "That's company policy," as if that should take precedence over any logic or customer concerns. There is little motivation to complain when the response is a nonanswer.

Customers may believe that complaining is an exercise in futility. Customers may feel patronized or ignored when they make a generalized complaint. For example, they may complain about poor service that is the cumulative result of many minor things that are not done right. Unless the person receiving the complaint is sensitive and caring (not a common experience), many customers perceive the exercise as completely futile.

Consequently, they find walking out (forever) to be an easier and more pleasant alternative. Besides, they often believe that it is the job of management (not their job) to run the organization efficiently.

THE ICEBERG OF IGNORANCE

When discontent about an organization is spreading outside, management may know less about the problems than the frontline staff. Information tends to be suppressed at various levels within the organization, especially if it has negative implications. People who work in organizations do not tend to pass on "bad news" when they communicate with their superiors.

Researcher Sydney Yoshida asked a cross-section of workers in a large factory to note all significant problems of which they were aware. His results showed that top

Top management knows only 4% of the problems of which the rank-and-file have knowledge.

management knew only 4% of the problems of which the rank-and-file had knowledge. Even general supervisors knew only about one in ten problems. This phenomenon of management having little knowledge of problems is commonly referred to as the "iceberg of ignorance."

There are several reasons for the existence of this phenomenon. The most important of these is that any person who takes problems to his or her boss is not generally welcome. "Shooting the messenger" is a time-honored custom that exists in subtle forms in most organizations. An organization intent on improving service quality should institute procedures that will keep management informed about problems. Management should take specific steps to counter the iceberg phenomenon with a view to creating an effective information system.

The credibility and image of an organization erode over a period of time. However, the iceberg phenomenon makes it appear sudden and abrupt as far as management is concerned. This gives management little time to institute countermeasures. The best way to counter the iceberg phenome-

Exhibit 3.2

The Iceberg of Ignorance

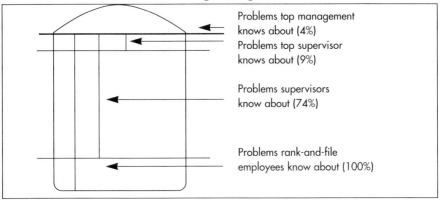

Problems top management
knows about (4%)
Problems top supervisor
knows about (9%)

Problems supervisors
know about (74%)

Problems rank-and-file
employees know about (100%)

non is to take specific steps that will encourage the expression of complaints by customers and continuous information flow from the rank-and-file to upper management. The biggest impediment to information flow is fear. Much as we would like to believe that the days of shooting the messenger are long gone, fear of subtle punishments for the bearer of bad news still exists and, in many cases, justifiably so. There are also other reasons why potential problems are not identified.

- Customers often state what is bothering them in a conversation, without appearing to be complaining. It is easy to miss the point that the customer is unhappy with the service received.

- If a complaint is being made about the quality of service, the person receiving the complaint may not pass it on to his or her superiors because this might make the employee look bad. We shall see later what techniques can be used to overcome the problems mentioned previously and elicit legitimate customer complaints.

So we have two potential problems: One, customers bring only a fraction of problems to the organization. Two, only a fraction of these ever reaches management. Therefore, any service quality measurement program should attempt to increase the flow of information from the customer to management.

Why Are Philosophers of Quality Relevant to Measurement?

In service quality and customer satisfaction research—perhaps more than in any other area of research—the philosophy behind measurement will determine research methods and analyses. For instance, if we question the use of performance-based measures as tools for improving quality, it does not matter how precisely we measure performance.

In service quality and customer satisfaction research, the philosophy behind measurement will determine research methods and analyses.

So far, we have discussed the need for creating and measuring a service quality program. Much of the discussion on quality has been inspired by the work of Dr. W. Edwards Deming, who is generally credited with fostering Japan's postwar economic miracle. Because research projects will be related inextricably to what one believes should be measured, it is time to review briefly the acknowledged gurus of quality.

DR. W. EDWARDS DEMING

Until his death in December 1993 at the age of 93, Deming continued to offer his four-day seminar on quality on a regular basis and was a university professor and consulting statistician to many companies. In the 1920s, Deming came under the influence of Walter Shewhart of Bell Laboratories, who applied statistical concepts that originated in agricultural research to manufacturing.

After World War II, Deming became an independent consultant. He addressed Japanese business leaders and pronounced that "the customer is the most important part of the production line." Japanese businesses quickly adopted this philosophy. In 1951, Japan created the Deming prize, Japan's most coveted industrial award. (Deming's philosophy of quality is discussed at length in Chapter 22.) Deming emphasized constancy of purpose. Although he used statistics, he insisted that the heart of his message be not in quantitative measurement or in visible numbers. The problem is invariably the same—management. Because the problem is management, the solution should start there. Top management should commit itself to quality. A clerical worker dealing with a customer cannot perform properly without management's prior and consistent commitment to quality. In fact, Deming was known to turn down invitations to consult unless invited by top management, because he strongly believed that such top management commitment is vital to quality improvement programs.

> **The customer is the most important part of the production line.**

Exhibit 4.1
How Quality Affects Market Share

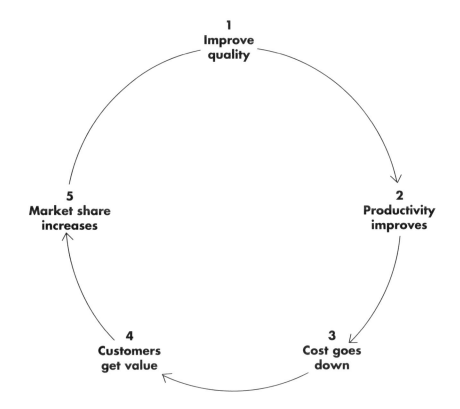

1
Improve
quality

5
Market share
increases

2
Productivity
improves

4
Customers
get value

3
Cost goes
down

According to Deming, reducing variability of output is at the heart of quality. Variability arises out of sources such as common causes (the system) and special causes (the individual). Most variability in performance can be attributed to the system within which an employee works. Because only management can change the system, the responsibility for reducing variability and improving quality rests with management.

When quality improves, costs come down, and consumers are happy and tell other people. This brings in more customers. As a result, profitability improves. The process of improving quality, according to Deming, is "so simple."

Implications for Research

If we accept Deming's view of quality, we need to refrain from customer satisfaction research with a view to rewarding or punishing the staff on the basis of results. As we discuss subsequently, rewarding and punishing employees, when the system is stable, results in lowering rather than enhancing quality. Measuring performance should have only one goal—to help employees perform better.

Evaluating the performance of one department against another and evaluating one employee against another has the effect of each department and individual working to maximize individual as opposed to collective well-being. A business should be run more like a symphony rather than a bowling team. In a symphony, all individual persons work toward a common goal rather than fight for individual superiority.

JOSEPH M. JURAN

Joseph M. Juran, a contemporary of Deming, has followed a similar path. Juran's career paralleled that of Deming. Like Deming, Juran worked for Western Electric and came under the influence of Walter Shewhart. After World War II, Juran, like Deming, became an independent consultant and propagated his philosophy in Japan. It is often said that "if Deming is the Socrates of the quality movement, Juran is its elder statesman."

Juran defines quality as *fitness to use*—reliability of the product or service to its customers. There are three aspects to this philosophy: quality planning, quality control, and quality improvement. Juran looks upon quality as a step-by-step process. Every step in a process affects the next step. Work on a project is passed from one employee to the next. When this happens, the employee who receives the work becomes the client (customer). The process becomes one of meeting the needs of the customer and one of *identifying your customer.* In practical terms, it could mean management listening to employees, who are "clients" of management.

Juran defines quality as fitness to use.

Juran urges management to examine the entire process to identify problems—from subcontractors to the ultimate consumer. Every employee should be trained to do the same. In practice, this means breaking up into small groups (quality circles), which should be trained in problem solving, group dynamics, and teamwork. Employees should be taught to identify cause-and-effect relationships in workplace problems.

There are two types of costs associated with quality: avoidable and unavoidable costs. The avoidable costs are waste, failure, and rework. The unavoidable costs are those associated with quality improvement measures. Juran's aim is to eliminate avoidable costs. They are eliminated when adequate quality improvement programs are instituted. Like Deming, Juran believes that most quality problems (80%, according to Juran; 85%, according to Deming) are the responsibility of management.

Implications for Research

Juran's approach concentrates on the process. Customers are not defined just as those who consume the product or service in the end, but as everyone who is connected with the process at any level. A research program should concentrate not just on the ultimate consumer but on everyone involved from the beginning to the end.

OTHER PROMINENT EXPERTS

Although Deming and Juran may be the two biggest names in quality consultancy, there are other prominent names such as Crosby, Feigenbaum, Ishikawa, and Taguchi.

Philip B. Crosby

Philip B. Crosby, who runs the Florida-based Philip Crosby Associates and is the author of *Quality Is Free* (1979), is another major figure in the area of quality. Crosby calls for zero defects in products. Although he uses statistical methods, he places less emphasis on them than do Deming or Juran. All three emphasize total commitment. However, their approaches differ. Deming begins from the top and works down. Juran concentrates on middle management—

one can work up or down the ranks. Crosby, on the other hand, emphasizes conformance requirements and consequently puts greater responsibility on employees.

Like Deming, Crosby has his own list of 14 points and then some. He believes in four quality absolutes: a definition of quality, prevention rather than appraisal, a performance standard of zero defects, and measurement of quality (or the cost of nonconformance). Crosby contends that if people do not believe in zero defects, it will be impossible for them to achieve that goal.

Crosby's four quality absolutes: a definition of quality, prevention rather than appraisal, a performance standard of zero defects, and measurement of quality.

Armand Feigenbaum

In 1956, Armand Feigenbaum published a book titled *Total Quality Control*, which summarizes his approach. Because quality is everyone's job, the purchasing department, for example, must check with the users of the materials it buys to determine their desirability and suitability. Feigenbaum believes that quality is a technology that can be systematized and taught.

Kaoru Ishikawa

Kaoru Ishikawa, a Japanese quality management expert, simplified the statistical methods of Deming and others into *seven basic tools*, which are charts that anyone can use. Such tools include Pareto charts, histograms, and scattergrams. Ishikawa set out to turn quality control into a mass movement. He believes that the seven tools can solve 95% of all problems. His book, *Guide to Quality Control* (1986), which was written originally in Japanese for workers, is the most popular text on statistical quality control. Many of Ishikawa's tools, such as Pareto charts and the fishbone diagram, are discussed in Part III, "Tools and Techniques of Measurement."

Genichi Taguchi

A four-time winner of the Deming prize, Genichi Taguchi contends that quality must be built into the product, because defective products result in "losses" to the society from the time they are shipped. Taguchi calls his methods *quality engineering*. He places emphasis on the design stage with the objectives of product and process robustness, inherent capacity to withstand environmental variations, and maintaining optimal performance.

MAKING SENSE OF CONFLICTING APPROACHES

A newcomer to the field of quality measurement can be baffled easily by the conflicting views held by the top experts.

Crosby has such slogans as "Zero defects!" and "Quality is free!" but Deming says to eliminate slogans. Juran argues that fear can bring out the best in people, whereas Deming insists that fear should be banished. There are many other differences. So who is right?

Many people believe that the differences among quality experts are not that critical and that the differences have more to do with style than with substance. For example, each of the top three experts—Deming, Juran, and Crosby—believe that

- the entire organization should be committed to quality improvement;

- quality improvement is basically the responsibility of management;

- you should identify your internal and external customers and satisfy their needs;

- you should eliminate waste;

- the organization should instill pride in workers; and

- the organization should create an environment of constant quality improvement.

Such agreement on basic principles makes disagreements trivial by comparison. *BusinessWeek* (1991), in its special issue "Quality Imperative," alluded to the rivalry between the two giants of the quality movement: Juran and Deming. Juran replied, "My 'dueling' with W. Edwards Deming consists mainly of editorial effervescence. We have followed different paths, but they have intersected in the field of managing for quality. Our area of agreement is much greater than our area of difference" (*BusinessWeek* 1991).

Agreements on basic principles make disagreements of quality experts seem trival by comparison.

The differences among quality experts are not always trivial. But when we look at all the areas of agreement, it appears that one can hardly go wrong adopting the philosophy of any one expert consistently. All the same, one should be cautious and, as *BusinessWeek* put it, "distinguish the high priests from the hucksters."

Similarly, we should be concerned about whether most of what passes for service quality research or customer satisfaction studies is of any value. Such measurements, with no theoretical basis, may do more harm than good.

Part II

How Standard Measurement Techniques Can Mislead

The Nature of Service Quality

If a manufacturer sells a product and if a service organization markets a service, should not the principles of research apply equally to both? Why do we need a different set of techniques to research service quality? To answer these questions, we need to explore the differences between products and services. Although the research principles are the same in both contexts, there are some critical differences that dictate we not use research procedures interchangeably. These differences are explored in the sections that follow.

THE NEED TO UNDERSTAND MOMENTS OF TRUTH

Any contact between an employee of an organization and a customer constitutes a moment of truth. Any of these encounters, however brief, gives a customer the opportunity to make up his or her mind about the organization (Carlzon 1987). An important feature of service quality is the presence of pervasive moments of truth—the points at which a customer is likely to feel pleased or irritated. When a customer enters a firm's premises to do business, should the firm care whether

- the customer can park his or her car nearby;
- the customer has a comfortable place to wait; and
- an employee makes the customer feel welcome?

Where does an organization's responsibility start? Where does it end? We can view that every aspect connected with a person's doing business with an organization is its responsibility. For example, if a customer calls us, he or she should not be put on hold unnecessarily. That is our responsibility. When the customer visits us, he or she should be able to park conveniently. That is our responsibility. When the customer is inside the office, he or she should have a comfortable place

27

to wait. That is our responsibility. When the customer meets any employee, the employee should make the customer welcome. That is our responsibility.

Each moment of truth in itself is trivial. A customer is not likely to walk out just because parking was not convenient, chairs were not comfortable, or an employee did not bother to smile. The effect is cumulative. A customer is more likely to walk out because parking was inconvenient *and* he or she was not comfortably seated *and* an employee was not polite *and*. . . .

Moments of truth are a pervasive reality whether we deal with products or services. However, because services involve much more contact with customers, moments of truth are critical for delivering service quality, even more so than for product quality.

> *Any contact between an employee of an organization and a customer constitutes a moment of truth. Because services involve more contacts with customers, moments of truth are critical for delivering service quality, even more so than for product quality.*

THE NEED TO UNDERSTAND TRANSFERENCE

When customers are dissatisfied with an employee, sometimes they transfer this dissatisfaction to the organization as a whole. Suppose a customer decides to buy a Mercedes-Benz. If the salesperson was offensive to the customer, the customer still might buy a Mercedes, but perhaps from another dealer. In other words, the product often can be separated from the service. The dissatisfaction with the Mercedes salesperson is not transferred to the product itself. Consider, however, an instance in which a bank officer treats a customer discourteously. In this instance, it is much more likely that the customer will transfer his or her account to a different bank altogether rather than to another branch of the same bank. Where service is the product, organizations are less likely to be differentiated from the outlet.

THE NEED FOR AN UNDERLYING MODEL

We cannot satisfactorily measure different aspects of service quality without an underlying model. In product research, we mostly measure tangibles (e.g., the speed, acceleration, and legroom of an automobile), whereas in service quality, we need to measure intangibles (e.g., courtesy, efficiency). These intangibles are abstractions. For example, courtesy is an abstraction—it is an interpretation of a person's behavior and is influenced subjectively. The model must state explicitly what needs to be measured and why. At the very least, the model should be a framework for measuring the core dimensions.

THE NEED TO MEASURE LATENT ATTRIBUTES

Latent attributes are abstractions. Courtesy is an abstraction inferred from other behaviors such as attentiveness and smiling. In measuring service quality, we have a constant need to measure latent variables. Although latent variables can be relevant to product quality as well, product quality attributes (e.g., color, gas mileage, and legroom of an automobile) tend to be tangible in nature.

Conceptually, service quality aspects can be grouped into two categories: functional service and personal service (see Exhibit 5.1). *Functional service* refers to attributes of service that are akin to attributes of a product. Attributes of functional service can be improved individually and without direct reference to customers. Waiting time in the emergency ward of a hospital, brokerage statements that are clear to the customer, and so on are examples of functional service. *Personal service*, on the other hand, refers to attributes of service that are difficult, if not impossible, to improve without reference to customers. As shown in Exhibit 5.1, functional service is a

Exhibit 5.1
Aspects of Quality

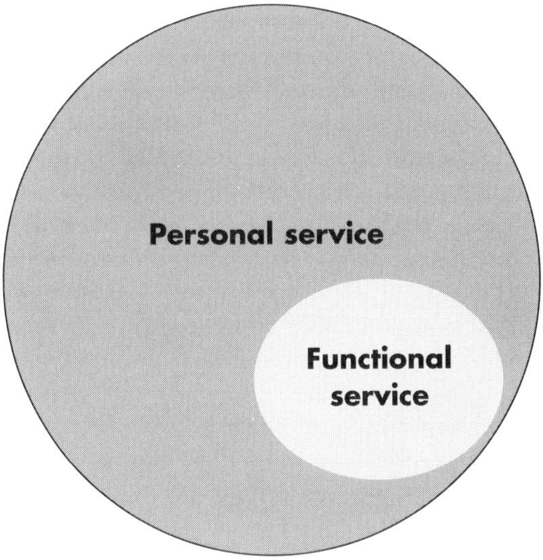

Personal service

Functional service

small part of personal service quality. Concern for customers, flexibility in dealing with customers, and taking customer complaints seriously are all examples of personal service.

Personal service is strongly associated with service quality

In most people's minds, the term *service quality* evokes aspects of personal rather than functional service. For example, Jim Clemmer (1990) was given the following list when he asked a group of executives what service quality meant to them:

- Prompt attention to complaints or problems,
- Availability,
- Good customer communications,
- Showing respect and common courtesy,
- Keeping appointments and commitments,
- Educating maintenance people,
- Quality workmanship,
- Recommending future products,
- Appearance and neatness,
- Technical knowledge and ability, and
- A high-quality job.

Note how closely personal service is associated with service quality in general.

Personal service is more difficult to measure

Personal service aspects of quality are intrinsically more complex and more difficult to deliver consistently, and consequently, they pose greater methodological challenges than do functional service aspects of quality. Personal service attributes, such as competence and concern for the customer, are abstractions (latent variables). Measurement of functional service quality attributes tends to be much less complex (being manifest variables, very similar to product attributes) and straightforward compared with measurement of personal service quality attributes.

Routine and nonroutine aspects of personal service

Personal service can include routine and nonroutine aspects. Routine aspects of service are those that arise in the normal course of doing business. Examples of routine aspects include having efficient procedures for withdrawals and deposits or having a short waiting period in an emergency ward of a hospital. Such needs can be anticipated and streamlined. Nonroutine aspects, on the other hand, are less frequent events and cannot be anticipated with any degree of certainty. Again, nonroutine aspects are more closely associated with service quality than are routine aspects. Nonroutine aspects, by definition, are more difficult to measure because they cannot be formulated precisely for the purpose of measurement.

Personal service cannot be developed overnight

Another important difference between functional and personal service is the speed with which each can be implemented. Aspects of functional service can be implemented quickly. For example, an organization can extend its working hours or install faster computer terminals to help customers. These things can be done immediately. Personal service, on the other hand, is more difficult to develop quickly. It requires more than the availability of resources; it requires the commitment of management, resource allocation to support the commitment, cooperation of employees, and change of attitudes—all these have to happen, at least to a certain extent, before personal service can be improved. It is "about as difficult a job as a company can undertake, because it means reforming attitudes and practices in nearly every department" (*Fortune* 1987).

Aspects of personal service are recognized more slowly

The need to measure latent attributes

- Personal service is strongly associated with service quality.
- Personal service is more difficult to measure.
- Personal service cannot be developed overnight.
- Aspects of personal service are recognized more slowly.

Aspects of functional service, such as longer business hours and more readable statements, are not solely subjective experiences and, hence, are easily recognized by customers as soon as they are offered. Aspects of personal service, on the other hand, are based on subjective evaluation. When an organization changes its course and attempts to offer personal aspects of quality service, customers may not recognize them immediately. This means that research undertaken to measure the impact of newly instituted personal service measures may initially show that customers have hardly noticed the improvement. It is important, then, to recognize that there will be a lag before customers realize that the improvement in service quality is genuine.

Personal service as a soft dimension of quality

Another way to look at the distinction between functional and personal service is to view them as soft and hard dimensions. The hard dimension includes the functional aspects of service quality, whereas the soft dimension includes the personal aspects of service quality. The distinction between hard and soft dimensions is conceptual. An even more useful distinction can be made if we view service quality as three-dimensional.

SERVICE QUALITY: A THREE-DIMENSIONAL MODEL

We begin with the assumption that there are some underlying dimensions that are common to all service quality measurements. If we collect all attributes that we believe are related to quality, then we can identify the underlying dimensions, either by logically grouping those attributes or by using statistical techniques such as factor analysis. Not all researchers agree on the same logical grouping of variables. Although statistical techniques, such as factor analysis, provide somewhat objective groupings, they can operate only on the basis of a researcher's assumptions as to what attributes constitute quality. Consequently, different researchers may not come up with the same set of underlying dimensions or factors.

For example, Garvin (1987) identifies the following eight items as dimensions of service quality: Performance, Feature, Reliability, Conformance, Durability, Serviceability, Aesthetics, and Personal Quality. In their SERVQUAL model, Berry, Zeithaml, and Parasuraman (1985) identify ten determinants of service quality—Reliability, Responsiveness, Competence, Access, Courtesy, Communication, Credibility, Security, Understanding the Customer, and Tangibles, and they distill them into five—Reliability, Assurance, Tangibles, Empathy, and Responsiveness (Zeithaml, Berry, and Parasuraman 1990).

There is (or can be) no agreement as to how many factors underlie service quality. However, a larger number of factors implies a highly specified model. Such models are more constrained than less highly specified ones. From a conceptual viewpoint, less highly specified models have wider applicability. A model that I have developed using several factor analytic and multiple regression analysis studies consists of three underlying dimensions: functional service, personal service, and exceeding expectations (see Exhibit 5.2). This model is not necessarily better or superior to the other schemes discussed; however, it is simpler and more generalized. More important, each of the three dimensions calls for different research techniques, which is the central focus of this book.

Exhibit 5.2
The Three-Dimensional Model of Service Quality

Dimension	Corresponds to	Nature of Attributes	Examples
Service/product	Functional service	Hard (manifest)	Itemized statements
Dependability/support	Functional/Personal service	Hard/Soft	Courtesy, efficiency
Exceeding expectations	Personal service	Soft (latent)	After-hours service

Implications of the model

The model proposed here has implications for visualizing a strategy and for developing a research design. We first consider how the model can be used conceptually:

- Conceive a service/product and develop its features.

- Have a mechanism in place that continues to recognize customers—whether or not they generate revenue for the organization—and rewards them for dealing with you (or for having dealt with you).

- Identify ways you can exceed customer expectations.

The first dimension is absolutely critical to anyone in business. The second dimension is where customer loyalty begins. Unfortunately, this is often where the customer is treated inconsistently. The third dimension is where customer loyalty is consolidated, which is the most neglected and least understood of the three dimensions.

PRODUCT RESEARCH VERSUS SERVICE QUALITY RESEARCH

We are now in a better position to answer the question, "What is different about service quality research?

Product research

Product research evaluates products from two perspectives: objective and subjective. The first aspect—the product's quality—can be answered by objective tests. It is easy to decide whether a product is delivering what it is supposed to deliver. For example, a car's fuel efficiency can be tested as well as the cleaning power of a detergent. The second aspect—consumers' perception of the product—also can be tested fairly easily through marketing research. However, the emotional benefits of some products can be difficult to assess through survey methods. For example, a person may be reluctant to admit to driving a BMW to impress others, but such benefits are relatively easy to identify through other methods, such as qualitative research.

Service quality research

We may have difficulty assessing service quality by similar means. Measuring service quality attributes involves measuring *soft attributes* such as courtesy and politeness, which are inferred generalizations with no agreed-upon definitions. How does one measure whether "x" amount of courtesy and "y" amount of flexibility were delivered to the customer? The objective qualities of a product, however, can be independently tested (e.g., miles per gallon) and improved without reference *to* customers. A product can be improved in a laboratory. A service, on the other hand, cannot be enhanced meaningfully without reference to customers. Furthermore, judgment of service quality also depends on the handling of nonroutine problems that, by definition, cannot be identified easily. Exhibit 5.3 shows the differences between product and service quality aspects.

Exhibit 5.3
Product Versus Service Quality

	Product	Service
Moments of truth	Fewer	Pervasive
Soft attributes	Fewer	Many
Transference	Low	High
Attributes	Mostly manifest	Mostly latent
✓ Need for a model	Low	High
✓ Customer involvement	Can be low	High

IMPLICATIONS OF SERVICE QUALITY RESEARCH

The inherent differences between product and service quality research lead to some major errors when we attempt to apply standard research techniques to service quality. Such errors can be in the

- use of quantitative techniques,
- use of qualitative techniques,
- use of metrics, or
- interpretation of results.

These are discussed in greater detail in the next few chapters. Although standard measurement techniques are applicable to service quality research, we must use special techniques and analyses as well. Some of these techniques are modifications of those already known to most researchers, whereas other are less well-known.

6

How Standard Quantitative Research Can Mislead

Standard quantitative research can be useful in service quality research. However, two areas are problematic. The first problem relates to measuring several attributes pertaining to a service. This atomic measurement approach may work well for products but can present problems when used with services. The second problem relates to the rating scales used in service quality research.

PROBLEMS RELATING TO ATOMIC MEASUREMENT

Atomic measurement is the measurement of different service attributes as stand-alone attributes. When we ask customers to rate different attributes of a computer, such as its RAM, clock speed, and modem capabilities, we are using an atomic approach. It is possible to produce a computer with features that are most important to customers and leave out the ones that are not as important.

When we measure service quality, this approach can mislead. With a product, we can distinguish clearly the presence or absence of each attribute, because most of them (e.g., size and color) are tangible and can be specified clearly. If a computer does not have an internal modem, it is not likely to affect our judgment of its other related features. However, in service quality measurement, this is not so, especially if we are dealing with the second (dependability) or the third (exceeding expectations) dimension of service quality, because they deal with intangibles and abstractions. Consider a soft attribute, such as courtesy. Because this is an abstraction (unlike, for example, an internal modem), several attributes must be present to create this abstraction. A customer service representative who smiles, greets the customer, and is otherwise pleasant may not be considered courteous if he or she looks away from the customer when speaking to her. That the representative fulfilled many attributes that constitute courtesy may not matter. If the customer perceives the representative to be discourteous, the representative's fulfillment of courtesy-related attributes might even be perceived as insincere.

Atomic approaches to measurement tend to fail whenever what is being judged is an intangible abstraction. Because there is evidence to support service quality being heavily dependent on intangibles and abstractions in addition to tangibles, standard measurement procedures can mislead. We may need to apply special techniques, such as factor analysis, to understand which intangible attributes are related, so that we can treat them as one single dimension.

PROBLEMS RELATING TO INFLATED SCORES FROM RATING SCALES

There is empirical evidence to show (Devlin, Dong, and Brown 1993) that traditional scales tend to inflate the evaluative ratings in service quality research. From a theoretical perspective, we note that there are at least three factors at work that create these inflated ratings.

Regression toward the scale midpoint

Rating scales do not have intrinsic meaning. They are ways of evaluating the relative standing of different alternatives. For example, a computer that received a rating of 8 on a 10-point scale five years ago may get a rating of only 3 now. The rating of 8 or 3 reflects an evaluation in the context of available or known alternatives. Generally, customers tend to accept what is available as the standard. Judgment of inferiority or superiority is relative. If all available alternatives for a product or service are of poor quality, then this is the standard for this product. Customer ratings will be inflated as a result.

If, for example, customers receive poor service from all financial institutions, then poor service becomes the norm for the industry. Scores will regress to the midpoint of the scale. Consider a situation in which customers have a choice of several institutions ranging from mediocre to excellent. On a 10-point scale, mediocre institutions may score an average of about 2 or 3. Excellent institutions may score an average of about 7 or 8. But when all institutions offer mediocre service, the scores will cluster around the midpoint of the scale. Institutions that are marginally better may get a score of 7 or 8. This commonly observed regression-toward-the-midpoint[1] phenomenon can result in inflated scores of satisfaction.

Artifact of satisfied customers

Services that reach a large number of people will include a number of customers whose service needs are low. (They generally follow the Pareto pattern or the negative binomial distribution, meaning that a large proportion of customers will use only a small proportion of services offered.) Those who have low service needs are unlikely to have many grievances against the organization. For example, most people do not have any significant dealings with their utility companies, except on the rare occasions when things go wrong; many bank customers use only one or two of the many services offered by the bank. Most customers of large service organizations require no more than minimal routine service and are unlikely to have serious concerns about the quality of service they receive. As a result, any service industry will automatically generate a large segment of satisfied customers, which has the effect of inflating the average satisfaction score even further. (Dissatisfied customers may be small in number, but they may have more dealings with the organization and, hence, may have a greater impact on its profitability.)

Perception is limited by current framework

Three factors—regression toward the midpoint, the artifact of satisfied customers, and perception limited by current framework—may interact to inflate customer satisfaction scores.

Customers do not normally think outside the current framework when asked what they would ideally like. Innovations do not come from customers. It is not customers who demanded automated teller machines or cellular phones. Therefore, it is difficult to determine from customers what constitutes service quality. It is not that customers do not want to tell the researcher but simply that they do not know.

DYNAMICS OF SPURIOUS CUSTOMER SATISFACTION SCORES

The three factors described in the previous section—regression toward the midpoint, the artifact of satisfied customers, and perception limited by current framework—may interact to inflate customer satisfaction scores. We illustrate this with a hypothetical example.

---

[1]The term *regression toward the midpoint* here means that customers tend to gravitate to the midpoint of the scale when all rated objects are similar.

Exhibit 6.1
From Mediocrity to Excellence

Dynamics of spurious customer satisfaction ratings
(In poorly serviced, static markets, it is possible to get high customer satisfaction scores, even when customers are not particularly happy with the service received.)

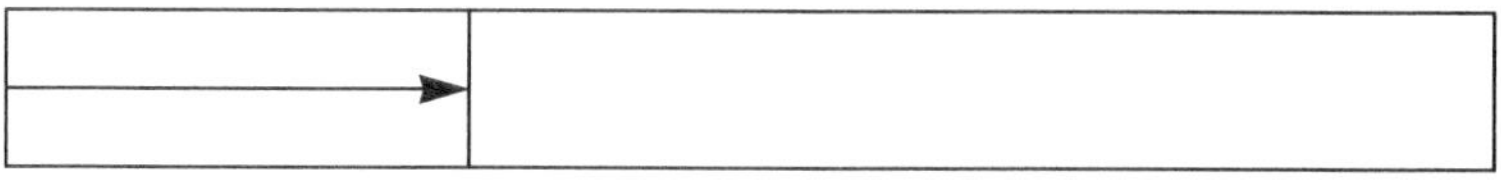

The "true" satisfaction rating is 3.

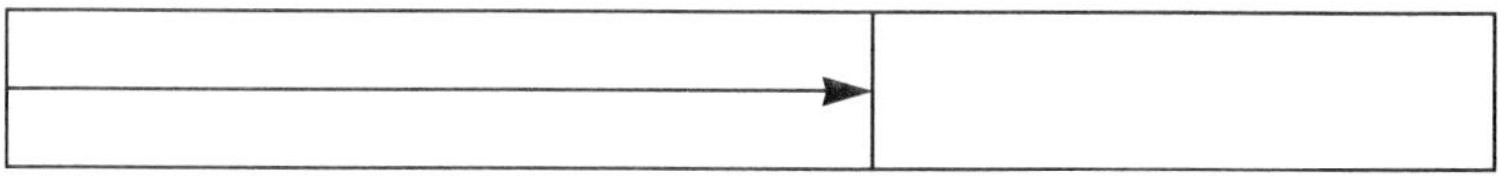

Regression toward the midpoint increases the rating to 5.

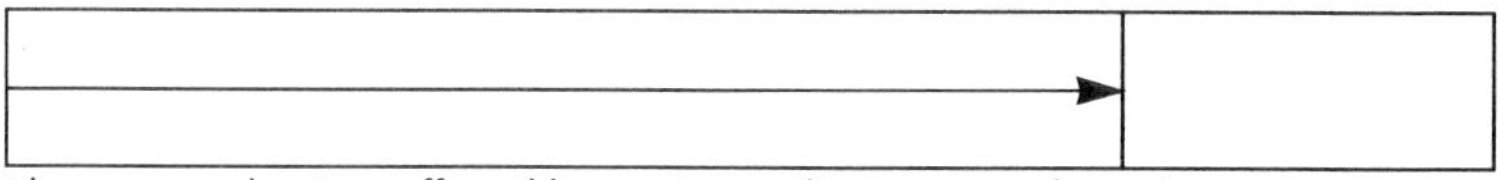

The segment that is unaffected by service quality increases the rating to 6 or 7.

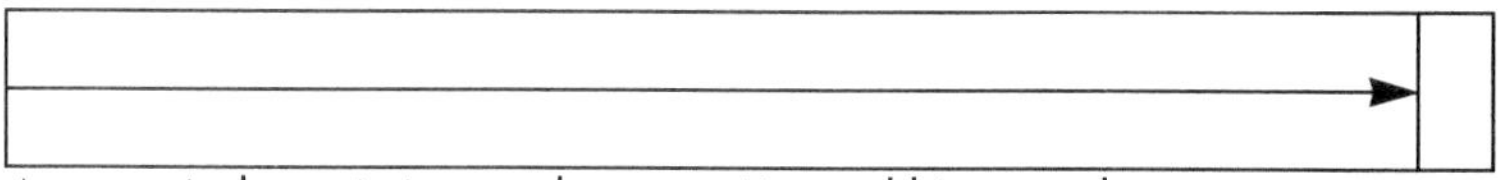

Any marginal superiority over the competition could increase the average score to 7, 8, or even higher.

Suppose that an organization's "true" rating on service quality is 3 on a 10-point scale where 10 is high and 1 is low (see Exhibit 6.1). Because all institutions in the category offer poor-quality service, the actual ratings regress toward the midpoint; that is, the average moves up to 5. If we assume that such ratings follow the normal curve, a certain proportion of customers will be very dissatisfied and a certain proportion very satisfied for no specific and identifiable reason. Let us say that approximately 5% of the customers are very satisfied. If we conservatively estimate that only one-third of customers do not need or expect high-quality service, we can add them to the ranks of very satisfied customers. Because these two groups of customers are happy with the institution, they might give it an average rating of 8. Because almost 40% of the respondents gave a rating of 8, the overall average moves up to between 6 and 7. If the organization is marginally better than average, 1 or 2 rating points will be added, resulting in an average rating of 7 or 8 or even higher. An average score of 7 or 8 might seem high and lead us to believe that customers are very satisfied with the institution. Yet, as we saw previously, all it means is that the institution is mediocre, perhaps marginally better than the competition in certain attributes.

Similar problems also can occur in product rating scales. However, the problems described previously do not arise in product testing to the same extent. The reason for this could be that product specifications and standards are explicit and are exceeded often by manufacturers.

HOW STANDARD QUANTITATIVE TECHNIQUES CAN MISLEAD

Atomic measurements and inflated ratings are two ways by which standard quantitative research can mislead. The problem of atomic measurement can be solved partly by the use of special techniques, such as factor analysis, whereas the problem of inflated ratings can be solved partly by a careful selection of rating scales and by testing for their adequacy in the specific measurement context.

7

How Standard Interpretations Can Mislead

Quality has two facets: consistency and level. A person who flies in first class receives a higher level of service compared with another who travels economy. The first-class passenger is provided with many amenities such as free drinks, more flight attendants per passenger, and wider seats. The difference between higher and lower levels of service is by and large quantitative. Although most of us tend to concentrate on the level of service, quality experts such as Deming and Juran maintain that consistency is the cornerstone of quality. Because consistency is considered central to quality delivery, we consider it in greater detail here.

CONSISTENCY

Human performance shows variation from time to time. When the underlying causes of variability are not understood, the use of measurements to improve quality is likely to result in poorer quality and lower morale. Ongoing measurement of a process is not meaningful if the cause behind the observed variability is not understood. Can we really have a satisfactory system of customer satisfaction measurement if we genuinely cannot attribute the increase or decrease in scores to our efforts?

A company cannot solve its service quality problems by simply making employees responsible for their actions. The problem manifested by an employee could be the result of a number of factors that are not under the direct control of the employee—such as policies, procedures, people, and equipment already in place—and may have little to do with factors under his or her control. It is not uncommon for management with a nascent commitment to quality to declare that

- employees who are "well below average in performance measures" will be warned or punished;

- management will not tolerate more than 10% deviation from specified standards;

- to ensure quality service, management will "get to the bottom" of the problem in every instance in which an employee performs below specifications;

- management will monitor deviations from specifications and constantly change its procedures with a view to "fine-tuning" the firm's service; and

- management will assess the performance of different employees (e.g., branches, departments) with a view to rewarding those who perform best on service quality criteria.

Human performance shows variation from time to time. When the underlying causes of variability are not understood, the use of measurements to improve quality is likely to result in poorer quality and lower morale.

Although such assertions may be well-meaning, they lack a basic understanding of how quality is created and maintained. Some of these noted procedures, if implemented, can have the exact opposite effect of what is intended. To determine why this is so, we need to understand how variability in performance comes about.

TWO COMPONENTS OF VARIABILITY

All measurements are subject to variability, even when the measurement is of a physical object. When competent human beings measure the same physical dimension, such as the length of an object, we cannot assume that their measurements will be identical. It is likely that there will be differences due to parallax errors. Even if we believe that we arrive to work at the same time every day, precise recording of time will show that it is never *exactly* the same time (though the deviation may not be large enough to make any material difference). Because variability affects all human performance, we must pay more attention to this aspect.

Consistency is the key to delivering quality. A high-quality product or service is one on which a firm can rely. Therefore, we need to understand what works against consistency. In other words, we must understand the sources of variability. Statisticians and quality experts have done extensive work in this area and find that variability has two sources: common causes and special causes (see Exhibit 7.1). *Common cause* variations are produced by the system within which a person operates. They are random variations and

Exhibit 7.1
Common and Special Causes

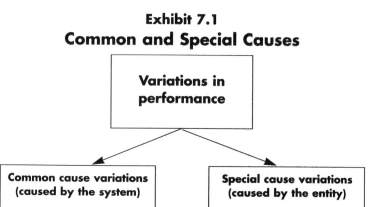

will repeat themselves unless the system itself is changed. *Special cause* variations cannot be attributed to the system but to specific and assignable causes such as a poorly trained employee. Special causes will not repeat themselves when the cause is identified and the problem is rectified.

Common cause variations

Any variation produced by an employee that is not under his or her direct control can be construed as having been produced by the system within which the employee operates. As an example, consider an online help system for a computer software program. If it took Mary 45 minutes to serve a customer, can we directly use this as a measure of her efficiency? If Jim took only 15 minutes to serve a customer with a similar problem, does it mean that he is more efficient? The simple answer to this question is that we do not know. We need additional information to assess how much of the difference in service time between the two representatives can be attributed to them personally.

Mary's higher service time could have resulted from many factors that may have nothing to do with her efficiency. For example, the customer could have been less knowledgeable and might have required many detailed instructions. He or she might not have had the required information such as the model number handy. Another employee who might have needed Mary's expertise urgently could have interrupted her. All such factors are created by the system and are not under the direct control of the employee.

Any variation produced by an employee that is not under his or her direct control can be construed as having been produced by the system within which the employee operates. These are common cause variations.

One of the points repeatedly made by Deming and Juran is that management rushes to reward and punish its employees as the sole means of improving quality, and then wonders why quality has not improved or has even gone down. Deming contends that, in a large number of cases, employees are already doing their best and it is management's responsibility to understand the system. Many organizations do not achieve their ideal of better quality because they are manipulating the wrong variables—employees rather than the system that constrains them. In a majority of cases, Deming believes that rewards and punishments have deleterious effects on quality enhancement.

Special cause variations

Not all variations are caused by the system or the process under consideration. For example, an employee who provides inconsistent service may be a temporary employee not properly trained. Or a computer an employee has to use may have developed an unexpected problem. These factors produce variations that cannot be attributed directly to the system or the process itself. Such variations can be called *special cause variations*, which means that the variations are due to irregular and assignable causes. We cannot get rid of special cause variations simply by improving the system.

Special cause variations cannot be attributed to the system.

COMMON CAUSE VARIATIONS AND QUALITY

Many organizations concerned with service quality tend not to distinguish between these two types of variations and attribute all variations to the employee. Generally, an employee is "fully responsible" for the results he or she produces and is evaluated on that basis. If the customer satisfaction score is 6.5 for one retail outlet and 7.5 for another, it is assumed that the outlet with a higher satisfaction score is the better performing one—hence, the tendency to fine-tune service quality, punish employees who perform below average, and attempt to get to the bottom of every problem. Yet, these can be misguided measures. One of the most destructive ways of using service quality measurement is to treat all variations as being due to special causes.

In any situation over which an employee has no control—such as the number of phone calls he or she must handle, the complexity of customer queries, the lunch hour rush, or the availability of shared computer terminals—there will be common cause variations, which are generated by the system currently in place. These variations, though purely random, may appear to have identifiable patterns.

When common cause variations are larger than special cause variations (which is often the case in stable systems), rewarding or punishing an employee on the basis of raw measurement numbers is no better than consulting a table of random numbers to measure performance. In fact, it is worse because both management and employees believe it to be a meaningful measure and, as a result, take actions that will have no positive effect on the system. For example, Mary, who took longer to serve a customer than did Jim, might be persuaded to believe that she is not efficient enough to serve customers quickly. She then may try to serve customers more quickly. However, because the variation (i.e., the longer time) was not caused by her but by the system, she is more likely to *increase* the variability of the system. This is because the system that caused the variability remains unchanged, while Mary has increased the variability in her service to compensate for a deficient system.

Many organizations concerned with service quality tend not to distinguish between these two types of variations and attribute all variations to the employee.

When we interpret customer satisfaction scores as the true representation of the performance of an outlet and a performance measure as the true representation of an employee's performance, we are ignoring common cause variations. This leads us to interpret customer satisfaction and employee performance measures in an erroneous way. As we saw previously, they are not simply wrong; they actually can be destructive. If Mary has been the most competent employee and, consequently, the most difficult problems are passed to her, her longer service time would reflect this reality. If time needed to serve a client is used as a performance measure (in which "shorter" means more efficient), then Mary would do poorly on this measure even if she is competent. When changes in performance can be attributed to common causes, rewarding or punishing employees on the basis of performance measures amounts to random rewards and punishments. An employee or an outlet rewarded or punished at random is unlikely to maintain high morale. Hence, it is important that we go beyond standard interpretation of the data and actually distinguish the two types of variations.

8

How Standard Focus Groups Can Mislead

WHEN FOCUS GROUPS ARE USEFUL

Qualitative research is an extremely useful tool in understanding service quality. However, run-of-the-mill qualitative research, such as focus groups, can be as misleading as run-of-the-mill quantitative research.

To understand why this is so, the contexts in which qualitative research is particularly useful are as follows:

1. when follow-up questions cannot be decided in advance, as in a questionnaire;

2. when the motives for a purchase are too complex, too sensitive, or too latent to be elicited through standard quantitative research; and

3. when not enough is known about a field of inquiry to construct a standard questionnaire.

WHEN FOCUS GROUPS ARE NOT USEFUL

When none of these criteria are met, qualitative research is more likely to mislead than enlighten. Consider a situation in which the motives of customers are straightforward and clear-cut. In such cases, the focus group, in a sense, becomes a small-scale quantitative study.

When we have the basic information and have conducted a few focus groups, no new insights usually emerge. When this happens, the interpretation centers on how frequently and forcefully an idea was expressed. It is easy to slip into thinking that the strength of an attribute is determined by the frequency with which it is mentioned. Yet, the frequency is a function of the group itself.

A sizable proportion of service quality focus groups fall

into this category—there is nothing mysterious about what customers want. It is the same thing they told us in other focus groups six months ago (in some cases, six years ago). It is the same thing that they have been telling us in every piece of quantitative research as well. This is not to suggest that we should not do any qualitative research. On the contrary. The point is that standard qualitative research will help us understand service quality needs of customers only in a limited way. We need qualitative research, but with modifications.

WHEN TO USE DIFFERENT APPROACHES

There are many instances in which focus groups are routinely used, such as to answer the following questions. The main rationale for this is that standard quantitative techniques cannot be used to obtain answers to these questions:

1. Poor service quality is a fundamental offense to the values held dear by the customer. What do we know about these situations? Do we know how a service organization can offend a customer, even though the institution is "right" and the customer has signed a contract accepting the institution's terms?

2. Service quality means offering unexpected benefits. Many institutions define *service quality* as a process that offers customers benefits they are not expecting. How do we find out what customers are not expecting?

3. When customers are unable to express what they want but can tell us what is bothering them, how do we figure out what they want?

Service quality is seen as the process of eliminating the obstacles to delivering what the customer wants. Systems and procedures already in place can inhibit service quality, but they are there for a reason. Yet, what if the underlying reasons for these systems and procedures no longer are valid? How do we identify opportunities and eliminate these obstacles?

The use of standard focus groups in these contexts may appear reasonable, but we can do much better. The use of alternative techniques—such as laddering, wish lists, problem detection systems, and dimensionality reduction—are likely to provide much better insights. In spite of the availability of better alternative techniques, focus groups are frequently being carried out in all of the previous situations, which can lead to inappropriate marketing conclusions.

As discussed previously, standard focus groups can mislead when nothing new can be learned. There are many contexts in which standard focus groups can be used without modification. However, there are also instances when we must use related techniques such as brainstorming, nominal group techniques, or laddering.

Part III

Tools and Techniques of Measurement

9

The P3D3 Matrix

Service quality measurement involves some special issues, and therefore, we simply cannot apply the standard research techniques of measurement and interpretation. We first address several problems, such as

- measurement of latent attributes,
- rating scales that yield inflated scores,
- focus groups that provide little insight, and
- measurement of common and special causes.

We saw how traditional research techniques—both quantitative and qualitative—can mislead. We need to modify and extend current approaches, as well as consider others.

Not all methods to be discussed are new. Some have been used in product research in different ways. The only difference is that these methods are chosen and used with specific purposes and in specific ways to overcome the limitations of run-of-the-mill service quality research. Other methods come from industrial quality control procedures. Although such techniques are limited only by the imagination of the researcher, a few of them are discussed here to demonstrate how researchers can overcome the limitations of traditional research techniques.

For each stage of implementation of the service quality program, we potentially need appropriate research techniques for

- diagnosing problems,
- understanding problems in a detailed way, and
- implementing the solutions.

THE P3D3 MATRIX

To provide a framework for these techniques, we view service quality as the result of three interacting forces:

- *Producers*: the people whose responsibility it is to deliver quality. In broad terms, this would mean the company and its employees.
- *Processes:* the means or systems through which the producers deliver service quality.
- *People:* the customers to whom these efforts are directed.

We need techniques to measure these three P's of quality delivery—producers, processes, and people.

Producers	Processes	People

We also must consider that we may need different techniques of measurement depending on how far ahead we are in our quality development program. We can be in any one of the following three stages:

- *Diagnosing:* The initial stage of the implementation of a quality program that calls for exploratory techniques.
- *Detailing:* The middle stage of the implementation process that requires detailed measurement techniques.
- *Delivering:* The final stage, leading to and continuing after the implementation that calls for decision and tracking techniques.

Combining the three interacting forces—producers, processes, and people (3 P's)—with three developmental stages—diagnosing, detailing, and delivering (3 D's)—we arrive at the P3D3 matrix of nine different cells, as shown here.

	Producers	Processes	People
Diagnosing			
Detailing			
Delivering			

Each cell in the matrix calls for a different set of measurement techniques. Exhibit 9.1 shows the expanded P3D3 matrix, which includes the suitable techniques for each cell. The exposition of techniques follows this matrix in sequence.

Each technique is placed in a cell for exposition purposes. However, many techniques have multiple applications. For example, focus groups can be used during any phase of service quality delivery; force field analysis can be used not only in connection with producers, but also in connection with people. Techniques that appear in a cell are illustrative of those that can be used for the purpose at hand. One should neither exclude nor overlook other suitable techniques discussed outside the immediate context.

Exhibit 9.1
Measuring Service Quality
The P3D3 Matrix

	PRODUCERS	PROCESSES	PEOPLE
DIAGNOSING	Structural analysis Check sheets Mystery shopping Internal focus groups	Graphic techniques Run charts Stratification Flow charts	Complaint elicitation Content tracking Belief system analysis Pareto charts

DETAILING	Nominal group
	  technique
	Benchmarking
	Deleting
	  dimensionality
	The as-if frame
	The video camera
		Control charts	External focus groups
			Survey research
			Laddering
			Factor analysis
			Gap analysis
			Wish lists

DELIVERING	Brainstorming Force field analysis Cost-benefit analysis	Fishbone diagrams Process mapping and evaluation	Tracking

USING THE RIGHT TECHNIQUE FOR THE RIGHT PROBLEM

When one is exposed to so many techniques, the question always is one of selecting the right tool for the right job. As a general guide, I present the following:

CONTEXT	TECHNIQUE
How to elicit and analyze customer problems	Structural analysis
How to understand what customers really mean by poor-quality service	Laddering
How to deliver the unexpected	Wish lists
How to eliminate prior expectations in observing service procedures	The video camera The as-if frame

How to track the interconnectedness of different activities with a view to improving the process	Process mapping and evaluation
How to find out where the breakdown occurs in a system	Run chart
How to find out how the customer really feels	Mystery shopping
How to understand the interconnectedness of service quality attributes	Factor analysis
How to understand overall customer expectations regarding service quality	Focus groups Depth interviews
How to elicit and analyze customer complaints	Content tracking Run charts Pareto charts Belief system analysis
How to measure variations in performance	Control charts
How to understand overall customer expectations regarding service quality	Focus groups Depth interviews
How to generate ideas to improve service quality	Brainstorming
How to understand barriers to change How to understand driving forces	Force field analysis
How to convert customer information into preliminary performance target measures	Nominal group technique
How to close the gap between you and the best in your category	Gap analysis Benchmarking

These techniques are a fair representation of specialized techniques used in service quality research; however, they are by no means exhaustive. They are a reasonable (and extensive) sampling of techniques that show how to overcome the problems posed by service research. The list includes several traditional techniques that still can be extremely useful as long as we take into account the ways in which they can mislead. Subsequent chapters describe the research and measurement contexts and techniques that are useful in each context. For the sake of completeness, both traditional and nontraditional techniques are covered.

10

Diagnostic Techniques: Producers

P1D1: Producers and Diagnosing

	PRODUCERS	PROCESSES	PEOPLE
DIAGNOSING	Structural analysis Check sheets Mystery shopping Internal focus groups	Graphic techniques Run charts Stratification Flow charts	Complaint elicitation Content tracking Belief system analysis Pareto charts

DETAILING	Nominal group
	  technique
	Benchmarking
	Deleting
	  dimensionality
	The as-if frame
	The video camera
		Control charts	External focus groups
			Survey research
			Laddering
			Factor analysis
			Gap analysis
			Wish lists

DELIVERING	Brainstorming Force field analysis Cost-benefit analysis	Fishbone diagrams Process mapping and evaluation	Tracking

When we begin setting up a service quality program, the best place to begin is with ourselves. Where do we stand? What is our internal structure? Who are our suppliers? Who are the internal customers? Is our current setup helping or hindering the delivery of quality? To answer these questions, we start with a structural analysis of the organization, supported by other measurement techniques such as check sheets, mystery shopping, and internal focus groups.

55

STRUCTURAL ANALYSIS

WHAT IS STRUCTURAL ANALYSIS?

Structural analysis is a formal look at the way an organization functions. It is concerned with the internal structure of the orgnization. In addition, it involves taking into account two frequently overlooked links in the chain of service quality—*suppliers* and *internal customers.*

> **Structural analysis *answers* such questions as**
> - **What is our internal structure?**
> - **Who are our suppliers?**
> - **Who are our internal customers?**

Suppliers

Modern businesses are heavily dependent on other businesses. Not all components of an automobile are manufactured by the automaker. Not all components of a computer are manufactured by the computer maker. Every major organization uses the services of external suppliers. Therefore, it is difficult for an organization to deliver quality unless that organization manages its suppliers, including its subcontractors, so that quality is maintained at every level. This aspect is often overlooked. For example, suppose you are an automobile manufacturer and you subcontract roadside assistance to another company. If the subcontractor does a poor job, it will reflect poorly on your company rather than on the subcontractor. If you manufacture computers with defective chips, it is your computer, not the chip manufacturer, that is visible to customers. Therefore, even if an organization is committed to service quality, unless such commitment extends to its suppliers, it is quite possible that the organization's efforts will fail.

> **Modern businesses are heavily dependent on other businesses. So, an organization that is committed to service quality should extend its philosophy to its suppliers. Otherwise, it is likely that the organization's efforts will fail.**

If a supplier is directly responsible for a service area, it might appear straightforward to simply change the supplier in favor of another one when things do not work out. But, in practice, it is not that simple. For example, a supplier may not be responsible for any given process as a whole, but only for providing input into the process. If the process is the joint responsibility of an organization and its suppliers, it is difficult to identify the source of the problem. Consider a process in which a supplier is responsible for setting up a computer system and the organization is responsible for the use of that system. Both these aspects have to work together for the customer to receive quality service. If the supplier sets up a system that requires greater skills than can be reasonably expected from most of its users, it will result in less-than-optimal use of the system and may lead to customer dissatisfaction. Who is responsible for this—the supplier or the user?

Single suppliers: Taking a second look

Many organizations have a policy of requesting quotes from multiple suppliers. This can make it difficult to control the quality of the product/service delivered by the supplier. A solution to this problem may be to have a single supplier that understands your goals and works with you. The term *single supplier* does not necessarily mean having only one supplier; rather, it is having one or more suppliers with whom you do business consistently. The single supplier concept refers to the practice of dealing with the same set of suppliers unless there are compelling business reasons for not doing so. This solution is strongly recommended by many quality experts, including Deming.

There is considerable resistance among Western business organizations to the concept of the single supplier. This appears to be caused by the fear that the use of a single supplier will result in the supplier taking the business for granted, thus becoming uncompetitive and complacent. Yet, this need not be the case. A well-chosen supplier can be well monitored to ensure quality and competitive pricing. Those who tend to reject the concept of a single supplier system also tend to overlook its advantages, which are as follows:

- Security accorded to the supplier, which makes it worthwhile for the supplier to go the extra mile;

- The supplier always being aware of the standards expected; and

- The enormous savings effected in terms of organizational time spent on tendering and supplier selection processes.

Intelligent utilization of a single supplier requires the careful selection of a suitable supplier. It also requires monitoring the supplier continually for price and quality. The single supplier system does not mean mindlessly choosing a supplier and accepting sloppy work and outrageous prices. It does mean not changing suppliers unless the work becomes sloppy or the prices become unreasonable. As noted previously, a *single supplier* seldom refers to just one supplier. It is usually a small set of suppliers with whom you work on a consistent and predictable basis. The single supplier system provides many advantages. It means lower variability, which leads to higher quality. A single supplier also can be trained to the organization's quality specifications. For these reasons, anyone concerned with quality should seriously consider this option.

Internal customers and employees

Another important link in the chain is the internal customer. Internal customers are those to whom an employee delivers his or her services. There are basically three types of relationships: between employees and external customers, employees and internal customers (also employees), and employees and other employees only.

In the first type of relationship, both the employee and the internal customer jointly provide customer service (external). In addition, the employee provides input to the internal customer. In the second type of relationship, the employee provides input to another employee (the internal customer), who, in turn, uses that input to provide customer service. In the third type of relationship, the employee simply provides input to the internal customer. Although the internal customer can use this input to provide customer service (external), the employee does not know how the internal customer is using the input. This third type of internal structure hinders employees in two ways. First, they cannot provide intelligent alternatives to internal customers, because the employees do not know how the information is being used. Second, they may find it difficult to serve external customers when called on to do so because they were not made aware of the way in which the information was expected to be used.

1. Employee ⟷ Internal customers → External customers

2. Employee → Internal customers → External customers

3. Employee → Internal customers ⇸ External customers

Internal versus external customers

In general, an internal customer should be treated exactly the same way as an external customer in terms of service quality. However, there are some critical differences. The differences arise when the needs of internal and external customers are in conflict. Should an employee concentrate on external customers, who are the basis of the business, or on the internal customer, who may have a say on the future of the employee within that organization?

Structural analysis of employees should center around questions such as, How is the organization structured in terms of internal customers? Is an employee faced with contradictory or unreasonable demands from his or her internal customers? Why do such problems arise? How can the processes be structured so that an employee and an internal customer do not work at cross-purposes?

The not-so-apparent influence of suppliers and internal customers can be considerable and can support or sabotage the efforts of an organization. An individual employee has little say regarding the selection of suppliers or internal clients. Therefore, the initiative for the structural analysis of internal customers and suppliers rests solely with management. Structural analysis involves collecting information to understand how suppliers and internal customers fit in the process of delivering quality.

WHY CARRY OUT STRUCTURAL ANALYSIS?

Any improvement in service quality is dependent on the system that is expected to deliver quality. Structural analysis shows how the system is structured, so that we can identify the possible hindrances to delivering service quality.

Structural analysis provides us with the first glimpse of how things actually work within the organization. Any improvement in service quality is dependent on the system that is expected to deliver quality. Factors such as unreliable suppliers and ineffective internal customer relationships can impede service quality delivery. Structural analysis alerts us to the problem by providing a general map of the territory. It shows the interconnectedness of the organizational structure and the effective delivery of quality to customers.

HOW TO CARRY OUT STRUCTURAL ANALYSIS

Carrying out structural analysis at this stage is akin to having a bird's-eye view of the territory in which we are interested. As we progress, internal customers, external suppliers, our requirements, and the organizational structures change. New questions arise. The best that can be done at this early stage is to gain some understanding of the organizational structure. Our understanding can be sharpened by other techniques, which are discussed subsequently.

Although carrying out the structural analysis is not a rigidly defined procedure, I suggest the following seven steps:

Step 1. Draw an organizational chart, as it is functionally structured. Draw detailed organizational charts for each unit (or department). These charts should reflect the actual, not the ideal or intended, state of affairs. Although almost all organizations tend to be hierarchically organized, not all of them are structured rigidly. How rigid is the structure? Are contacts between departments highly formalized?

Step 2. Define internal customers at each level. What type of internal customers are they? Do internal customers in the organization use external resources, even though internal resources are presumably available? For example, does the accounting department use outside programmers, even though computer programmers are available within the organization? If so, why?

Step 3. *Identify the internal line of communication that leads to customer service.* Each department may be an internal client for several other departments in carrying out a single function. For example, the complaints department might be dependent on the switchboard for receiving calls, the systems department for retrieving stored information needed to handle and adequately understand the complaint information, and the technical department to provide a satisfactory solution to the problem at hand. Thus, the complaints department can be an internal customer for many other departments. The relationships can be different with different departments.

Step 4. *Identify the potential conflict between serving internal and external customers.* There is often conflict within the organization between serving internal and external customers. For example, do the demands placed on employees' time leave them enough time to handle customer complaints in a responsive and timely manner? Some of these aspects may not be immediately apparent. Our aim at this stage is to understand the organizational structure to the greatest extent possible. Our initial understanding can be revised as further information becomes available.

Step 5. *Consider whether the organizational structure should be changed to minimize possible friction among employees.* We are still at a preliminary stage. No changes actually should be made yet at the structural level until more data are gathered and the benefits of change become obvious.

Step 6. *Consider the list of external suppliers.* Who are they? How long have they been with the organization? Can we develop long-term relationships with some of them? How is quality maintained and monitored? What is the real cost of asking for tenders each year? Can we convert some of our high-quality suppliers into single suppliers?

Step 7. *Consider the implications.* Is the organizational structure conducive to delivering service quality? Are there conflicts between external and internal customers? If the organizational structure has to be changed, how should it be changed? Overall, is there anything in the internal structure that will hinder the delivery of quality and, if so, what items?

When management understands the dynamics and structure of these relationships, it can devise methods such that

Steps in preliminary structural analysis

1. Draw detailed functional organizational charts.
2. Define internal customers at each level.
3. Identify internal lines of communication.
4. Identify potential conflicts.
5. Consider whether the organizational structure should be changed.
6. Consider the list of external suppliers.
7. Consider the implications. What items hinder delivery of quality?

suppliers and internal customers aid, rather than hinder, the processes that result in high-quality service.

HOW TO INTERPRET STRUCTURAL ANALYSIS

Structural analysis can be as broad or as detailed, as quantitative or as qualitative, as is necessary. Because of this, no standard analysis procedure can be applied to the information collected at this stage. The analysis consists of looking at the structure of the organization with the objective of answering such questions as "Is the structure helping or hindering service delivery?" "What is our relationship to our external supplier?" "What impact does it have on service quality?" "How do internal and external customers interact?" and "Is there conflict between internal and external customers?" We are unlikely to find definitive answers to these questions at this stage, but the analysis is likely to point to potential strengths and weaknesses of the organization with regard to the delivery of service quality.

While carrying out structural analysis, it is important to remember that the purpose of the exercise is to understand how the organization actually functions. What we are looking for is not another organizational chart. Rather, we are trying to understand how the organization works from a functional point of view. In some cases, it may be worthwhile to have more than one person do the structural analysis, independently of one another, and then reconcile the analyses later to get a complete picture of the functional structure of the organization.

The findings can be used to generate hypotheses that need further exploration.

To know more

Structural analysis of an organization is not a defined technique but an exploratory approach. To understand its significance, readers may refer to an excellent book that deals with quality delivery: Deming, W. E. (1986), *Out of the Crisis*. Cambridge, MA: MIT CAES.

CHECK SHEETS

Knowing where an organization stands is the first step in implementing a service quality program. Structural analysis is a good start. But we need to know more. We must know where we stand now and how the processes in place in the organization function. We need to go beyond structural analysis and understand the *functional aspects* of the organization. We need to check our hunches. We need to get an idea of the nature and extent of the problems we face. A good place to start is with check sheets.

Conventional wisdom permeates many organizations. Management may have some opinions as to the nature and frequency of a problem. For example, management of a utility company may believe that the majority of customers complain about mistakes in billing rather than the waiting period for service. This perception may or may not correspond to reality. To the extent that it does not, precious resources and efforts can be diverted to less productive areas. Therefore, the first priority in implementing a quality program is confirming our hypotheses, so that we can deal with facts rather than preconceived ideas of unknown validity. Check sheets help us translate opinions into facts.

WHAT ARE CHECK SHEETS?

Check sheets are formalized and objective records of the frequency of occurrence of specific events. An event could be (and often is) a problem, such as a billing error. The purpose of a check sheet is to keep an unbiased tally of problems that occur within an organization. A typical check sheet consists of a series of events and space to record the occurrence of that event. Every time an event occurs, it is recorded on the check sheet in the appropriate place. In summary form, a check sheet will show how frequent the events are and when they occurred.

In practice, we might encounter many problems when we attempt to construct check sheets. Many of these problems relate to the objective recording of events. Because the check sheet exercise may be carried out by more than one person in an organization, there should be an agreement on the definition of each problem. If the purpose of the check sheet is to

Check sheets are formalized and objective records of the frequency of occurrence of specific problems.

identify cause for late arrival of employees, at what stage do we record a person as being late? If we do not define this, one observer might record someone as being late even if that person is only one minute late. Another observer may not consider someone late unless that person is at least five minutes late. Thus, the check sheets might reflect the inter-observer variations and not the true state of affairs.

WHY CONSTRUCT CHECK SHEETS?

Check sheets create data that are easy to understand and can be applied to any key area of performance. They differentiate facts from conventional wisdom. They force everyone connected with the exercise to agree on precise definitions of what is being measured. This, in turn, can be used to arrive at focused solutions. For example, when a term such as billing problem is used in a generalized set-ting, different people may interpret it differ-ently—billing errors, late billing, delays in cred-iting the customer's account, and so on—and offer different solutions, some of which are not relevant to the problem at hand. Properly designed check sheets avoid this by clearly focusing on the specific problem. Their simple format also makes them self-explanatory.

> **Check sheets can be used whenever we need to objectively test our subjective assessments of events.**

HOW TO CONSTRUCT A CHECK SHEET

> **How to construct a check list**
> 1. **Agree on a precise definition of the event to be observed.**
> 2. **Define the time period (both length and frequency) that is represented and adequate for the measurement of the occurrence of events being observed.**
> 3. **Design easy-to-use check sheets.**
> 4. **Make sure that the data are collected honestly and accurately.**

Step 1. Define precisely the event to be noted. This means that everyone involved in noting the observation will have the same definition of the event. For example, if "unduly long waiting time" is the event that must be noted, it must be objectively and precisely defined. A definition for "unduly long waiting time" could be *a delay of more than 15 minutes during peak hours or more than 8 minutes during nonpeak hours from the time a customer joins a lineup and the time he or she gets to the counter to be served.* Again, peak and nonpeak periods must be precisely defined.

Step 2. Define the time period during which data are to be collected. This time period should be long enough to be representative of the event occurrence. For example, if we observe a waiting line at our service counter during the first three days of the week for four weeks, we are likely to miss the lineup that is usually formed on Fridays, especially when it happens to be payday.

Step 3. Develop a check sheet that is clear. Check sheets should be self-explanatory and easy to use. For an example, see the Appendix at the end of this chapter.

Step 4. Make sure that the data are collected honestly and accurately. Beware of possible biases from collecting the data through people who may have a vested interest in the results obtained.

HOW TO INTERPRET A CHECK SHEET

When interpreting check sheets, we mainly are looking for answers to two questions: Which problems are more frequent? What is the pattern of occurrence of these problems? For example, Faster Delivery Company's rates traditionally have been high. The company receives a number of complaints over its toll-free line. Management believes that most such complaints pertain to cost. However, the new marketing manager wants to confirm this perception before implementing corrective measures. To understand the nature of the complaints better, the manager develops a check sheet. On the basis of his past experience, the manager assigns problems to major categories. In Exhibit 10.1, we show how the check sheet looks. In Exhibit 10.2, we show how the check sheet may look after completion.

Exhibit 10.1
An Example of a Blank Check Sheet

Problem	Mon.	Tues.	Wed.	Thurs.	Fri.	Total
Late delivery						
Incorrect delivery						
Rude employee						
High cost						
Billing problems						
Other problems						
Total						

It is clear from the check sheet that nearly one-third of all problems have to do with billing rather than the cost of the service. If this is confirmed by additional checklists, it would mean that there could be a major problem that relates to billing. For a better insight into this, the marketing manager might want to break down billing problems into finer categories such as

- incorrect billing,
- unclear billing,
- delay in crediting payments, and
- not allowing enough time for payment.

Exhibit 10.2
An Example of a Completed Check Sheet

Problem	Mon.	Tues.	Wed.	Thurs.	Fri.	Total
Late delivery	III	II	I	III	III	12
Incorrect delivery	II	I	I	I	III	8
Rude employee	II	II	II	III	IIII	13
High cost	I	I	II	II	III	9
Billing problems	IIIII	IIIII II	IIIII II	IIII	IIIII III	31
Other problems	IIIII	IIIII I	IIIII I	IIIII	IIIII II	29
Total	18	19	19	18	28	102

Check sheets are analyzed with a view to understanding the frequency of the event and the pattern of its occurrence.

The check sheet also shows that complaints are distributed evenly across all days, except Fridays, when the company receives more complaints.

Although constructing a check sheet appears to be a simple task, many pitfalls await the unwary. Some common ones are referred to as follows:

- *Flawed sample.* If you decide to use check sheets, make sure you sample time periods properly and that the number of time periods chosen for observation is adequate for the purpose of quantification. If you are not sure, consult a statistician.

- *Perceptual bias.* If there are marked differences among observers in the pattern of occurrence of an event, check to make sure they are observing the same event and no specific biases are inherent in their observations. Check sheets are particularly useful in situations in which we tend to generalize on the basis of anecdotal evidence.

- *Problems of execution.* This involves not following the procedures precisely. For example, if a delayed response to a phone call is defined as not picking up the phone until after it has rung for the sixth time, it is conceivable that the person collecting the data

could estimate the sixth ring without actually count-
ing, thereby introducing an unreliable element to the
measurement process.

- *Problems of missing or incomplete data.* Sometimes
  the data are not collected the way they were originally
  intended. For example, if it was agreed initially to
  collect the data three days a week for eight
  weeks, and if on two of those eight weeks the
  data were not collected, are they still meaningful? The answer to this question depends on a
  number of factors: Is a six-week sample adequate to cover the process being tracked? Do
  the missing two weeks have any specific pattern—for example, are they both the first week of the
  month? If so, does this distort the results?

What to watch for:
- **Flawed sample**
- **Perceptual bias**
- **Problems of execution**
- **Problems of missing or incomplete data**

To know more

Almost any book dealing with product or service quality
measurements contains references to check sheet analysis.
Some such books include the following:

Chang, R.Y. and M.E. Niedzwiecki (1993), *Continuous
Improvement Tools*, Vol. 1. Irvine, CA: Richard Chang Associates.

Mears, P. (1995), *Quality Improvement Tools & Techniques.*
New York: McGraw-Hill.

MYSTERY SHOPPING

How do our customers see us? Are we as good as we think we
are? How would we judge ourselves, if we were on the receiving end? How would we feel if we put ourselves in a customer's shoes? Mystery shopping is a way of answering these
questions. In doing so, we must look into two types of problems that customers face: routine and nonroutine problems. A
problem is routine when many customers face similar problems. Suppose you call a computer company for technical
support because your hard drive is not functioning properly.
This is a routine problem, because many other customers who
call this company also may have problems with their hard dri-
ves. On the other hand, if your problem is unique to your
requirements and not normally faced by other computer users
(such as converting a file created by a less widely used operating system), then the problem is nonroutine. Nonroutine
problems contribute heavily to the perception of quality
(Parasuraman 1987). Although it is easy enough to assess the

nature of routine problems, it is not so easy to assess nonroutine problems. By definition, nonroutine problems are less frequent and undefined, so standard research procedures are of limited help. Mystery shopping provides a method by which we can assess both routine and nonroutine problems.

WHAT IS MYSTERY SHOPPING?

Mystery shopping refers to a person who is not a genuine customer, posing as a customer in order to understand how genuine customers are handled. People who carry out mystery shopping could be senior executives of the organization or consultants with special expertise in this field. In a typical mystery shopping exercise, a senior executive of the firm poses as a customer and does everything that a customer does to be served. The mystery shopper can present problems—large and small—to an employee in order to understand how a customer with a problem is handled.

Mystery shopping may provide direct understanding of the problems customers face.

To make it really work, however, the mystery shopper should be more interested in finding out about the service process rather than evaluating the person providing the service. The mystery shopping process has to be repeated several times to avoid forming impressions on the basis of superficial observations or of situations that may be exceptional rather than typical.

Making it realistic

It also helps if the mystery shopper places constraints on himself or herself similar to those a customer would face. For example, if you do not have any constraint on your time, it does not matter whether you are served in 5 or 10 minutes. However, if you are a harried customer who has to fit lunch and banking into 45 minutes, the difference between 5 and 10 minutes would be important. Because nonroutine, rather than routine, tasks have greater impact on service quality perception, mystery shopping can be used to create nonroutine problems and present them to employees. The way such problems are handled might provide additional insights into the way in which an organization operates.

Mystery shopping should simulate the actual constraints faced by customers.

Quite often, management is unaware of the problems faced by customers; mystery shopping may provide direct understanding of these problems. As pointed out previously, the problem is that mystery shopping, when carried out by management not properly trained, often degenerates into an evaluation of a specific employee, which may be unfair to the person involved, as it may not be a proper sampling of the employee's work. Again, the inefficiency exhibited by the employee may be a function of the processes he or she has to work with rather than the employee's own shortcomings. (Later in this book, we return to the topic of the importance of processes and systems in influencing a person's performance.) If used properly, mystery shopping can be an effective tool for quality improvement. It will have no bearing on quality, however, if it is used for the purpose of spying on employees.

As noted previously, it is important to know how employees handle nonroutine requests. Mystery shopping provides an excellent way of presenting nonroutine problems to employees in order to understand how they handle such problems. For example, how does an employee handle a customer who has a complicated request when there is a large lineup of customers waiting to be served? How is a customer who asks that the service charge be waived dealt with?

Mystery shopping can provide insights into customers not normally available through other channels.

Why carry out mystery shopping?

Mystery shopping provides management with a glimpse of what it is like to be a customer. This insight is not readily available through larger-scale studies or even through focus groups. Because most customers tend not to complain and take substandard service for granted, some sources of customer dissatisfaction may never become available to management through normal channels. Mystery shopping may close this gap in management information. It also can be used to track customer satisfaction, even after a service quality program has been instituted.

HOW TO CARRY OUT MYSTERY SHOPPING

Step 1. *Define clearly what you want to understand about your service.* This could include the time needed to serve customers during peak and nonpeak hours, an employee's knowledge about the specific products and services you offer, the courteousness with which an employee deals with customers, and the skill with which an employee deals with nonstandard problems.

Step 2. *Define the time period during which data are to be collected.* This time period should be long enough to represent the way in which the organization functions as it deals with its customers. For example, if the problem is determining the flow of customers during different times, such as different days of the week, different weeks of the month, and so on, you need an observation period long enough, such as three months, to provide the details you require. However, this is not a strict requirement. If the information is collected even for a month, it can prove to be valuable. A shortcoming would be, if our sample is too small, we may end up with unreliable information. For example, suppose we collect customer flow information for just one week, but this week happens to be atypical (for example, during a school break). Consequently, the information could be misleading.

How to carry out mystery shopping

1. **Define clearly what you want to understand about your service.**
2. **Define the time periods and number of observations required.**
3. **Identify the people most qualified to carry out this project.**
4. **Prepare a mystery shopper checklist for data collection.**
5. **Make sure that the information is collected and used for its intended purpose.**

Step 3. *Identify the people most qualified to carry out this project.* This could include senior management and trained professionals.

Step 4. *Prepare a questionnaire or checklist for the mystery shoppers, so that they can observe and record consistently.*

Step 5. *Make sure that the information is collected and used for its intended purpose.* This step is critical, because misuse of information at this stage can result in lower employee morale if employees suspect they are being spied on. It also can result in hostility toward management, a situation not conducive to delivering quality.

For a sample mystery shopping data collection form, see the Appendix at the end of this chapter.

HOW TO ANALYZE THE RESULTS

Mystery shopping results can be analyzed both qualitatively and quantitatively. If you want the data to be analyzed quantitatively, you must ensure that the amount of data you collect and the way you collect them conform to proper sampling procedures; the data must be representative of the processes being investigated. If the data are essentially qualitative (as is likely the case when you investigate nonroutine problems), then the purpose of the analysis is to understand the causes of such problems (e.g., employees not empowered, untrained employees) rather than to estimate the frequency of their occurrence.

From a service quality perspective, qualitative analysis is likely to provide greater insights than quantitative analysis, especially during the initial stages.

There are some shortcomings to this technique that should be considered:

- *Cost.* It may not always be feasible for the senior executive to carry out the mystery shopping. If outside professionals are used, they can be expensive on a per-shopping incidence basis.

- *Identification of the mystery shopper.* If the mystery shopper is not careful, he or she may be spotted by employees. They then may behave differently, thus spoiling the objective of the exercise.

- *Employee resentment.* If employees come to know about the project, they may resent it and consider it an invasion of their privacy. They may perceive it as unfair spying by management.

- *Biased professionals.* The mystery shopping professionals may not be objective themselves. They may have their own perceptions of how they were treated, which may distort their findings.

To know more

The published exposition of this technique is sparse. The following book contains a brief description:

Whiteley, R. (1991), *The Customer Driven Company.* Reading, MA: Addison-Wesley.

INTERNAL FOCUS GROUPS

When we have no knowledge of where we stand and do not know where to begin, we may want to start with loosely structured discussions. The focus group is a good technique for this purpose. When we are fuzzy about our problems, focus groups provide an unstructured environment for clarifying our own thoughts on problems and possible solutions. As we discussed in Chapter 8, focus groups do not necessarily lead to answers. Sometimes they can even mislead. However, focus groups can be an excellent exploratory technique.

WHAT ARE FOCUS GROUPS?

Focus groups are discussions of a specific topic among small groups of people, with a moderator leading and guiding the discussion. A typical focus group consists of 8 to 12 respondents and may last between 1 and 3 hours.

A focus group is a small, informal group of people (usually between 8 and 12) brought together for the specific purpose of discussing a specific topic. A moderator, who is a trained professional in the art of group dynamics, leads and guides the discussion. It is the moderator's responsibility to ensure that everyone has an opportunity to contribute to the discussion and that no one person dominates the group. Focus groups generally last between 1 and 3 hours. Although the discussion is essentially unstructured, the moderator is charged with the responsibility of ensuring that topics of interest are covered.

Focus groups can be used both internally (within the organization) and externally (with customers). Here, we are interested in internal focus groups. Internal focus groups may be used with employees as well as with management.

Internal focus groups with employees can be used to find out

- how employees feel about the system they are in,

- how employees feel about the organization and its relationship to customers,

- what ideas employees have for improving the quality of service, and

- what factors employees believe are helping or hindering it in the delivery of high-quality service.

Internal focus groups with management can be used to find out

- how well managers believe the current system is working,

- how managers feel about the organization and its relationship to customers,

- what ideas managers have for improving the quality of service, and

- what factors managers believe are helping or hindering it in the delivery of high-quality service.

In such focus groups, it is important that the participants be assured total confidentiality. It is vital that employees feel free to speak out without fear of retribution.

Focus groups may be used as a starting point for understanding the organization's mission, as perceived by employees, and for understanding the organization's shortcomings and strengths, as perceived by customers. Focus groups are useful for understanding the breadth and depth of opinions held by the target groups. They are less useful and can be misleading, however, when used as tools of measurement.

Types of internal focus groups

Internal focus groups typically fall into three major types:

1. *Management focus groups*, in which all participants are managers and executives;

2. *Employee focus groups*, in which all participants are employees, excluding management; and

3. *Mixed focus groups*, in which both management and nonmanagement employees are present.

The first two types of focus groups enable management and nonmanagement employees to discuss freely among themselves the issues they consider important, whereas the third type creates a dialogue between management and nonmanagement employees.

Suppose we carry out focus groups among all three groups to assess what we should do to provide high-quality service to our customers. The management focus group could provide several ideas as to what nonmanagement employees should do to provide high-quality service to customers, whereas employee focus groups could provide an equally large number of reasons that would show management what is hindering employees from doing so. A management–nonmanagement discussion could identify the constraints within which each group is operating. As an example, management might believe that employees should provide faster service to customers, whereas the employees might point out that this would require quicker access to computers and better training, both of which only management can provide. In a common focus group, each of these issues can be discussed further to arrive at a common understanding of the problem, taking into account the resources available.

Three types of internal focus groups:
Management focus groups
Employee focus groups
Mixed focus groups

Who should carry out internal focus groups?

In many cases, senior managers within the organization lead internal focus groups. However, there are several reasons why this may not always be a good idea. Unless all participants are approximately equal in organizational status and feel generally unafraid to offer their opinions, an internal moderator may have the effect of inhibiting the free flow of ideas. For these reasons, it is better to have an outside moderator who can elicit opinions from participants in an indirect and skillful manner.

How many groups?

Typically, several focus groups will be used to explore a given topic. As an example, if our objective is to explore the sources of customer dissatisfaction, as perceived by employees, we may plan to hold seven focus groups:

PARTICIPANTS	NUMBER OF GROUPS
• Top management	1
• Middle management	1

- Junior management   1
- Nonmanagement employees   2
- Mixed group (management and
  nonmanagement)   7

> **Keep the number of focus groups to a minimum. Do not increase the number, unless there are specific reasons for doing so.**

There are no hard and fast rules as to how many focus groups should be carried out in any given context, though there are several informal criteria: Are we likely to generate more useful ideas if we increase the number of groups? Are members of a group likely to be less inhibited if they interact only with their peers? The number of focus groups, however, should not be increased unless there are specific reasons for doing so.

WHY INTERNAL FOCUS GROUPS?

> **Why focus groups? Focus groups enable us to explore areas that we know little about, as well as areas that are sensitive in nature.**

Unlike such highly structured techniques as check sheets, focus groups are nonstructured, which makes it possible for the moderator to explore a topic without the constraints of highly standardized procedures. As such, it is highly useful when there is not sufficient knowledge to structure our investigation, or when we want to explore an area that is sensitive and will not lend itself to a highly structured probe.

HOW TO CARRY OUT INTERNAL FOCUS GROUPS

Step 1. Define the objectives of the focus groups. The initial objectives of the study can be clarified by answering the question, What information would you like to have when the exercise is completed?

Step 2. Define the type of respondents needed for each group. This step defines the scope of the investigation (see Step 4). The type of respondents to be included in each group will be determined by the study objectives (Will these respondents be important to the achievement of the objectives?) and by the expected cohesiveness of the group members (Will the respondents interact freely with one another?).

Step 3. Define how the respondents are going to be selected for each group. For example, if you would like a group of employees who deal with customers on a day-to-day basis, what procedure should you use to select them? Do you want to select only those employees who have significant contact with customers, or do you want to assemble a cross-section of all employees who deal with customers? Once again, the objectives of the study are the key to the selection process.

Step 4. *Identify the moderators.* If they are internal moderators, make sure that this will not inhibit the participants. Consider whether an untrained internal moderator will do the job as well as a trained outside moderator. Take into account other advantages and disadvantages of internal and external moderators (e.g., knowledge of the problem, cost, bias). Choose an appropriate moderator.

Step 5. *Develop a discussion guide.* Focus groups do not usually use questionnaires. Rather, the moderator is given a list of areas to explore. The moderator can cover these areas in any sequence, as long as it is done in a meaningful way and does not result in biased results. (For a sample discussion guide, see the Appendix in Chapter 15.)

Step 6. *Carry out the focus group discussions at a suitable location.* Internal focus groups can be held within the office or elsewhere. Often it is a good idea to hold these discussions outside the office setting. Conducting them outside decreases the possibility of a participant being contacted while the discussion is in progress. It also may provide a more relaxed atmosphere and make the discussions less inhibited.

Step 7. *Obtain debriefing from the moderator.* After the discussion is completed, the moderator usually will submit a report outlining his or her interpretation of the main ideas generated during the discussion, along with supporting arguments and quotes from participants. If the discussion is taped, the moderator's interpretation provides additional help in putting the discussion into perspective.

How to carry out internal focus groups

1. Define the objectives of the focus group.
2. Define the type of respondents needed for each group.
3. Define how the respondents are going to be selected for each group.
4. Identify the moderators.
5. Develop a discussion guide.
6. Carry out the focus group discussions at a suitable location.
7. Obtain debriefing from the moderator.

HOW TO INTERPRET THE FINDINGS

The moderator who conducts the focus group generally interprets its findings. This means that the quality of a focus group discussion, as well as the interpretation of its findings, is largely dependent on the skill of one individual. There is no easy way of overcoming this limitation, though many standard ways of analyzing focus group data have been suggested (for example, see Dey 1993). One way to overcome individual biases might be to ask one other participant to act as an observer and independently interpret the discussion. The two interpretations then can be compared and recon-ciled. This procedure can be useful especially in instances when the moderator is not trained in car-rying out and interpreting focus groups, as is the case in many internal focus groups.

Most focus group findings are generally interpreted subjectively by the moderator. It also is possible to use objective techniques to analyze these findings.

Many pitfalls are associated with carrying out focus groups. Some of the more common ones include the following:

- **Biased selection of participants.** Focus groups are not quantitative studies. For this reason, we do not assume that views of the participants are a true reflection of the views held by nonparticipants. This, however, does not mean we can choose respondents in a way that can potentially introduce bias. If the participants are biased, their opinions may distort the true state of affairs.

- **Moderator bias.** If the moderator has definite views on how things are or should be, he or she likely will dis-tort the results. This may be particularly true of inter-nal moderators. Even when an outside moderator is used, the way in which the moderator is briefed can result in biased results.

- **Incompetent moderators.** In a focus group, the partici-pants often take cues from the moderator and other participants. If a moderator is unfamiliar with group dynamics or with the subject under discussion, the results arising out of focus group discussions could be biased and misleading.

To know more

Most sources concentrate on focus groups in general rather than on internal focus groups specifically. Some recent books on focus groups include the following:

Schwarz, R.M. (1994), *The Skilled Facilitator.* San Fran-cisco: Jossey-Bass.

Templeton, J.F. (1994), *The Focus Group.* Chicago, IL: Probus Publishing.

APPENDIX:
AN EXAMPLE OF A MYSTERY SHOPPING CHECKLIST

Battery Mystery Shop

Name of representative:	John Smith
Store:	Ridgeway Auto
Date:	January 9, 1997

Customer Service			**Comments**
Were you greeted?	<u>Yes</u>	No	_____
Did you have to wait longer than 15 minutes?	Yes	<u>No</u>	_____
Was the service friendly?	Yes	<u>No</u>	*But not rude*
Did the representative answer technical questions well?	Yes	<u>No</u>	*But tried to be helpful*
Did the representative inform you about the features?	Yes	<u>No</u>	_____
Did the representative inform you about the price?	<u>Yes</u>	No	_____
Did the representative inform you about the terms?	<u>Yes</u>	No	*Only after being asked*
Was the representative concerned about your needs?	<u>Yes</u>	No	*Only marginally*
Was the service courteous?	<u>Yes</u>	No	_____

1. How would you rate the service provided overall?

Excellent _____   Good __X__   Poor _____

2. Why?

> *The representative lacked knowledge to answer our questions adequately (provide example).*
> *He was courteous but was in a hurry to get rid of us so he could attend other customers.*

3. What suggestion, if any, do you have to rectify the situation?

> *Enroll the representative in a technical course.*
> *Make sure there are enough representatives to serve customers.*

4. Did you observe anything that could affect the performance of the representative?

> *The establishment appeared to be understaffed. Several customers appeared to be irritated with the wait. This could partly explain the poor service. The computer system was down, which made the situation even more difficult for the representative.*

(Adapted from Lithwick 1995.)

11

Diagnostic Techniques: Processes

P2D1: Processes and Diagnosing

	PRODUCERS	PROCESSES	PEOPLE
DIAGNOSING	Structural analysis Check sheets Mystery shopping Internal focus groups	**Graphic techniques** **Run charts** **Stratification** **Flow charts**	Complaint elicitation Content tracking Belief system analysis Pareto charts

DETAILING	Nominal group
	  technique
	Benchmarking
	Deleting
	  dimensionality
	The as-if frame
	The video camera
		Control charts	External focus groups
			Survey research
			Laddering
			Factor analysis
			Gap analysis
			Wish lists

DELIVERING	Brainstorming Force field analysis Cost-benefit analysis	Fishbone diagrams Process mapping and evaluation	Tracking

When we have a preliminary understanding of how our organization is structured and how it functions, our concern shifts to the processes in place within the organization. At this stage, we can use a number of visual techniques such as charts and graphs. Some of these charts—such as bar charts—are simple and can be done by anyone. Others—such as flow charts and stratification—may demand greater skills.

GRAPHIC TECHNIQUES

When we start gathering data about the processes, we can use charts and graphs to organize, summarize, and display data. These charts are fairly easy to construct and use, and most of us already possess this knowledge. As information is readily available from several sources, charts can be drawn easily using any spreadsheet program. Because graphs look deceptively simple, many researchers tend to overlook their usefulness as an analytic tool and mainly use them for decorative and presentation purposes. The purpose of this chapter is to demonstrate how even simple charts, such as bar and scatter charts, can provide useful insights. Because information on graphs is widely available, I have chosen only a few graphical techniques to illustrate their effectiveness.

Simple charts and graphs usually deal with two attributes at a time. They can be used to answer such questions as the following:

• What is the relationship between the day of the week and the number of complaints received?

• What is the relationship between the number of customers served and the number of mistakes made?

Sometimes we may be interested in understanding a single variable, such as the flow of customers during the day. At other times, we may focus on the relationship between two variables, such as training and service quality. At yet other times, we may be interested in several variables (for example, knowing the aspects of customer service in which we lag behind the rest of the industry). Graphic techniques can be used in all these instances. Here, we provide three examples of graphic techniques, which represent each one of the data types listed in Exhibit 11.1 (univariate, bivariate, and multivariate).

Exhibit 11.1
Data Types and Charts

Data type	Representative chart
Univariate data	Bar charts
Bivariate data	Scatter charts
Multivariate data	Radar charts

BAR CHARTS

What are bar charts?

What are bar charts?
Bar charts represent different quantities with the use of rectangles. In its simplest form, each bar has the same width. The height of each bar visually depicts the differences among the different items.

Bar charts are used to compare different quantities, such as the number of complaints received by different departments within an organization. The standard bar chart consists of a series of rectangles whose width is the same. The height of each bar shows how the quantities differ. A vertical bar chart shows the items being compared under consideration on the horizontal axis and the quantity being compared on the vertical axis.

Vertical bar charts are sometimes referred to as column charts. (Bar charts also can be displayed horizontally. In horizontal bar charts, the y-axis depicts the items and the x-axis the quantities. The width of the bars is held constant, and the length of the bars is used to provide comparisons.)

Why use bar charts?

Bar charts can be useful aids to understanding patterns. They can show the patterns that underlie the event of interest and provide insights into the process under observation.

How to construct a bar chart

Creating bar charts is fairly straightforward. The following steps show how to create vertical bar charts:

Step 1. *Decide which categories you want to observe.* For example, this could be the number of customers handled at different periods during the day.

Step 2. *Make sure the categories chosen are neither too broad nor too narrow.* Inappropriate categories will obscure the underlying patterns. For example, if we define periods as broadly as mornings and afternoons, we might miss some important patterns, such as a slow midmorning or frantic end-of-day flow of customers. Similarly, defining periods narrowly at 15-minute intervals could provide details that are unnecessary and confusing. An hourly flow of customers might be more appropriate. Exhibits 11.2 and 11.3 depict such intervals.

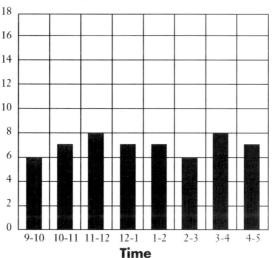

Exhibit 11.2
Flow of Customers (Dept. A)
Average number of calls = 56

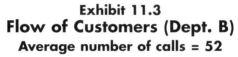

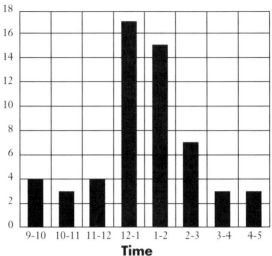

Step 3. *Create bars such that the height is proportional to the number of observations for each category.* Ensure that all bars are of equal width. In our example, each bar will represent an hour, and the height of each will correspond to the number of customers for each hour.

In practice, you can use any good spreadsheet or graphic program to create a bar chart.

How to interpret bar charts

By identifying the patterns that underlie events, bar charts can help us arrive at important conclusions. Consider two departments of a retail outlet. Both departments serve about the same number of customers and are short staffed. We use bar charts to keep track of customer flow, as shown in Exhibits 11.2 and 11.3.

An analysis of the charts shows that the same staffing solution will not work in both departments. Although, on average, both departments receive an equal number of calls, Department B receives the bulk of its customer calls between 12 P.M. and 2 P.M. This finding suggests that additional staffing during lunch hours would be of help to Department B but would be of little relevance to Department A. Adding staff members indiscriminately to Department B might result in underutilization during off-peak hours, while not fully solving the problem of having to handle too many calls during peak hours. The bar charts also suggest that the staffing problem faced by Department A could be solved by adding more staff members.

Because bar charts are used when the items considered are discrete or can be divided into discrete units, we can rearrange the order. For example, we can arrange the bars in a descending order. If our chart refers to complaints received by different departments, a descending bar chart will call attention visually to departments that receive the highest and lowest number of complaints.

One enhancement you may want to avoid is the decorative (pseudo) three-dimensional bar chart. Such charts tend to distort size comparisons. When charts are used to understand patterns in the underlying processes, it is best to keep them simple.

SCATTER DIAGRAMS

What are scatter diagrams?

Scatter diagrams are graphic plots that depict the simultaneous relationship between two variables. We can use scatter diagrams to understand the relationship between two measured variables. For example, we can use these diagrams to understand the relationship between the number of overtime hours worked and the number of billing errors made by an employee.

Why a scatter diagram?

Understanding the relationship between two attributes is one of the basic tools of quality improvement. Such questions as, "What is the relationship between time spent on training and productivity?" or "What is the relationship between number of hours worked and errors made?" are the basic building blocks of any service quality program. Scatter diagrams provide answers to these questions in a visual format, and they are easy to understand and explain.

How to draw a scatter diagram

Step 1. *Define the relationship in which you are interested.* For example, you may be interested in the relationship between the number of days of on-the-job training received and the number of mistakes made per day.

Step 2. *Collect information on several data points.* For example, you could use the following:

Day	Number of hours worked	Number of mistakes made
1		
2		
3		
...		
n		

Step 3. *Draw the horizontal (x) and the vertical (y) axes on a graph sheet.* Identify and calibrate the scales of both axes. (In the previously noted example, the x-axis is the number of hours worked, and the y-axis is the number of mistakes made per day. The range of the axes is based on the actual range obtained in the data.)

How to draw a scatter diagram
1. **Define the relationship of interest.**
2. **Collect information on data points.**
3. **Draw x- and y-axes. Identify and calibrate the scales of both axes.**
4. **For each observation, identify the intersection of x- and y-axes.**

What should go on the x-axis, and what should go on the y-axis? If you believe one variable is the cause of another variable, the causal variable should be on the x-axis. For example, if you believe that long working hours cause more errors, working hours should be on the x-axis and the number of errors made should be on the y-axis.

Step 4. *For each observation, identify the intersection of x- and y-axes.* (For example, if the average number of mistakes made by those who worked ten hours is six, then a symbol is placed at the intersection of 10 on the x-axis and 6 on the y-axis.)

How to interpret it

Consider Exhibits 11.4 and 11.5, where the x-axis shows the number of hours worked and the y-axis shows the average number of errors made. Exhibit 11.4 shows that the average number of mistakes is a direct function of the number of hours worked. Exhibit 11.5 shows the opposite.

Scatter diagrams also reveal other types of relationships. An example is shown in Exhibit 11.6. This scatter diagram shows no specific pattern. In other words, the average number of errors made is *unrelated* to the number of hours worked. Although such relationships can be assessed more precisely using correlational techniques, scatter plots visually and readily show the nature of the relationship.

Scatter diagrams can be produced easily using standard spreadsheet programs. If the relationship is unclear, spreadsheets also can calculate the correlation coefficient that

Exhibit 11.4
Hours Worked and Accuracy (1)

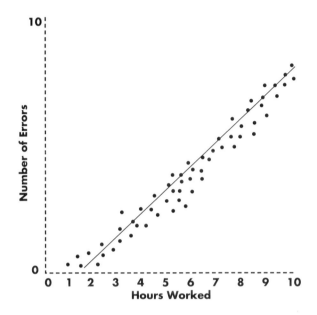

Exhibit 11.5
Hours Worked and Accuracy (2)

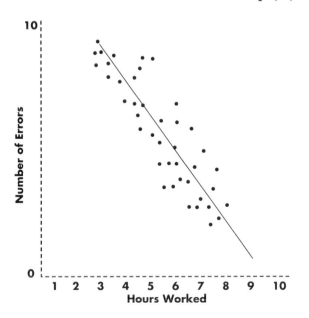

Exhibit 11.6
Hours Worked and Accuracy (3)

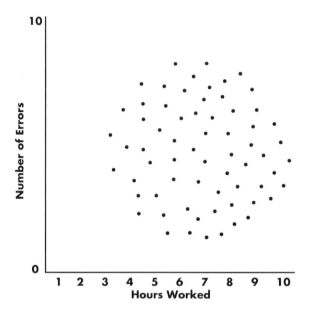

would indicate the direction and strength of the relationship between the two variables in question.

Scatter diagrams simply depict relationships. We cannot assume automatically the existence of a cause-and-effect relationship. For example, a scatter diagram may show a relationship between the number of years worked in a position and the proportion of customers satisfactorily handled. However, it also may be true that those who have been with the company for a longer period of time received more training in handling customers. Consequently, satisfactory handling of customers might be related causally to training received rather than to number of years as an employee.

The relationship depicted in a scatter diagram does not necessarily imply causality.

Like other charts, unless scatter diagrams are drawn properly, they can mislead. Scatter diagrams can be distorted easily (intentionally or unintentionally) by simply changing the scales distances on the x- and y-axes.

RADAR CHARTS

What are radar charts?

Radar charts are used to depict a number of variables on a single chart. Such depiction enables us to compare our performance in these dimensions with that of a competitor or of consumer expectations. It also can show where we are strong and where we are not.

Why use radar charts?

Radar charts are used to depict a number of variables on a single chart.

Radar charts show our strengths and weaknesses at a glance and highlight the gap between our current and desired positioning on different attributes. It shows where we may need remedial action and where we are ahead of the ideal or the competition.

How to construct radar charts

Step 1. Assemble a team consisting of those who are knowledgeable about the service. For example, if the service relates to the emergency ward of a hospital, assemble a team that consists of the person in charge of receiving patients, the person in charge of doing the paperwork, and the doctors who treat emergency patients.

Step 2. Determine the most salient rating categories. These could be the adequacy of staff at the admission desk, the length of the normal waiting period, the workload, the availability of doctors, and so on. Although a large number of attributes can be used, radar charts are effective when a limited number of categories (no more than eight) are used.

Step 3. Ask the participants to rate different aspects of the services provided by the organization. If there are wide discrepancies in the ratings, they should be resolved through discussion to ensure that the ratings are reliable and focused. Common definitions should be agreed on. For example, "long waiting periods" may be redefined as waiting for more than one hour to be admitted. Average each rating across all participants.

Step 4. To construct the radar chart, draw a circle, the radius of which will represent the rating scale used. If a ten-point scale is used to rate the emergency service, then the radius of the circle is ten units.

Step 5. Identify the center of the circle and draw as many spokes as there are attributes. Write in the attribute that corresponds to each spoke at the end of the circle.

Step 6. On each spoke, mark the position of the average ratings and connect the points. (See Exhibit 11.7 for an example.)

Variations

A variation of this chart consists of plotting two points on each spoke—one corresponding to the "ideal" rating and the other to the actual. The ideal points are connected (this con-

How to construct a radar chart

1. **Assemble a team consisting of those who are knowledgeable about the service.**
2. **Determine the most salient rating categories.**
3. **Ask the participants to rate different aspects of the services provided by the organization.**
4. **Draw a circle, the radius representing the rating scale used.**
5. **Identify the center of the circle and draw as many spokes as there are attributes.**
6. **On each spoke, mark the position of the average ratings and connect the points.**

ceptually becomes the end points), as are the actual ratings. (Another variation of this technique is to replace ideal ratings with the ratings of the nearest competitor.) Steps 1 through 3 also can be replaced by research data, in which consumers can be asked to provide the ratings, which can then be used as described.

How to interpret radar charts

The difference between the desired rating and the actual rating on each spoke is the gap between the ideal and the actual. This is because we have assumed that the end points are ideal. In a more realistic version, both ideal and actual points will be rated. In either case, the attribute with the largest gap usually needs immediate attention. However, if the attribute that has the largest gap is less critical, the decision maker may choose a more salient attribute to attend to first, even though it may not have the largest gap.

OTHER GRAPHIC TOOLS

We have discussed three graphic tools, just to show how even simple graphs can be utilized as effective tools in service quality measurement. Other commonly used charts, such as pie charts, area charts, and line charts, also can be used to understand and visually communicate the relationships among the variables that affect quality. There are two other types of charts that are particularly useful in service quality measurement: run charts and Pareto charts. Because of their special importance, they are discussed separately.

AVOIDING FANCY FEATURES

While using any form of graphs, avoid features that can potentially distort visual perception. Simple graphs are the best. As mentioned previously, avoid graphs that use a pseudo three-dimensional perspective (i.e., adding depth). Such graphs may be visually pleasing, but, unfortunately, they can hide significant patterns inherent in the data.

Simple graphs are the best.

To know more

Any standard book on statistical charts or quality improvement will provide information on graphical techniques. (Many basic

Exhibit 11.7
Radar Charts (Restaurant Satisfaction)

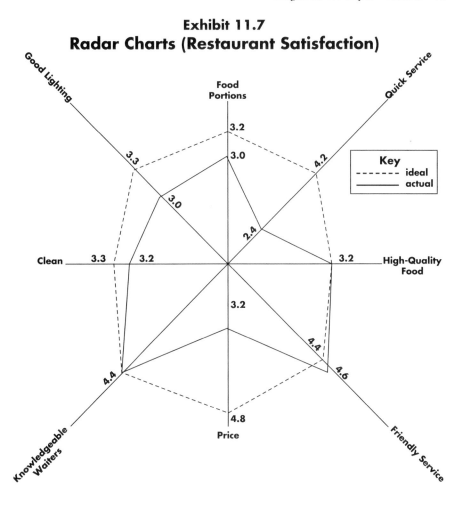

books on statistics also may contain information on creating graphs and charts.) Some texts include the following:

Cleveland, W.S. (1994), *The Elements of Graphing Data.* Summit, NJ: Hobart Press.

The Economist (1993), *Guide to Business Numeracy.* New York: John Wiley & Sons.

Ishikawa, Kaoru (1982), *Guide to Quality Control.* Tokyo: Asian Productivity Organization (this is especially good if you are interested in scatter diagrams).

Kosslyn, S.M. (1994), *Elements of Graph Design.* New York: Freeman.

Mears, P. (1995), *Quality Improvement Tools & Techniques.* New York: McGraw-Hill.

RUN CHARTS

One of the most crucial aspects of service quality is maintaining the standards. No matter how good our programs are, as time goes by and as the circumstances change, we cannot assume that the processes once responsible for delivering service quality still do so with the same efficiency and effectiveness. In any quality implementation program, it is necessary to assess the processes continuously. A basic tool that is associated with this task is known as the run chart. Run charts are one of the basic tools of quality management, and we shall encounter them again in other contexts subsequently.

What are run charts?

Run charts are plots of measurements over a period of time, such as the number of phone calls answered by salespeople on each day of the week. The purpose of these charts is to identify significant shifts in trends. For example, you may want to plot the time it takes for a new employee to do a specific job. (In this instance, you would probably expect a downward trend as the new employee becomes more experienced.) Because of its visual impact, run charts often are considered to be a quality indicator.

Why use run charts?

Run charts have several uses. They can be used to monitor performance of many service quality indicators (such as accuracy or time to complete a transaction), with a view to detecting trends and exceptions. They also can be used to gauge the effect of management efforts, such as training programs and changes in the work environment. They enable management to detect any potential problems, as opposed to day-to-day fluctuations in performance. (This is explained in the subsequent section on control charts.)

> **Run charts identify trends and exceptions, the effect of management efforts, and potential problems.**

How to construct run charts

Step 1. *Create a graph with x- (horizontal) and y- (vertical) axes.* For example, an insurance company may want to create a run chart of complaints received each day.

Step 2. *Assign the x-axis to a time sequence.* In our example, the x-axis will be assigned to days (day 1, day 2, day 3, and so on).

Step 3. *Assign the y-axis to the attribute being measured (for example, number of phone calls received).* In our example, the y-axis will be assigned to the number of complaints received daily.

Step 4. *Collect the data.* Data collection is not always straightforward. In some cases, we may have to define the variable being observed. For example, if we are plotting the number of times a customer was not served promptly (as shown in Exhibit 11.8), we must operationalize the concept "promptly," so it means the same thing no matter who collects the data. When you use a operationalized definition (e.g., that the phone was not picked up before it rang for the fifth time), make sure the definition is explicitly stated in the chart.

Step 5. *Plot data on a sequential basis.* Connect each data point. This line now will show the trend in complaints. Is the number of complaints on the rise? Are there cyclical patterns? Are there any unusual patterns in the flow of complaints?

Step 6. *When you have enough points, compute the mean.* Draw a line representing the mean. The mean line makes it easier to identify the patterns, exceptions, and trends in the data.

How to create a run chart

1. Create a graph with x- and y-axes.
2. Assign the x-axis to the time sequence.
3. Assign the y-axis to the attribute being measured.
4. Collect the data.
5. Plot data on a sequential basis.
6. Plot the average.

How to interpret run charts

When interpreting run charts, our objective is to look for stability and change. Does the process under observation continue to be stable, or does it show an upward or down-

Exhibit 11.8
Run Chart

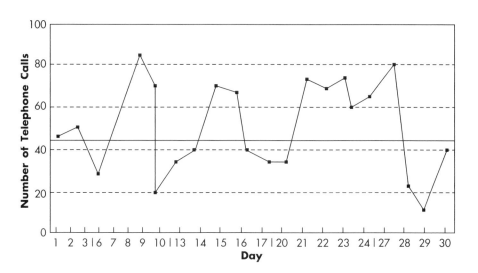

ward trend? Are there any notable exceptions? What we are interested in charting is what happens to a variable (e.g., number of phone calls received) over a period of time. Sequence is important in run charts.

Run charts also can be used to evaluate whether things are under control and whether any specific event **Plot one variable at a time.** (e.g., attending a training program) has any identifiable influence on the variable being measured. Such run charts can provide a warning about a gradually deteriorating situation. Although the interpretation of run charts is quite simple, their value is increased considerably when they are used to create control charts that can track the quality process quantitatively. We return to the interpretation of run charts when we discuss control charts in Chapter 14.

We should be careful not to use the same run chart to plot several variables. Plotting more than one variable on a run chart is justified only when you want to compare the relationship between two variables. Even here, a simple scatter chart will provide better information than a multilayered run chart.

To know more

The run chart is a basic quality maintenance tool. Therefore, any book that deals with quality improvement will contain information on creating run charts.

Brassard, M. and D. Ritter 1994), *The Memory Jogger II.* Metheun, MA: Goal/QPC.

Mears, P. (1995), *Quality Improvement Tools & Techniques.* New York: McGraw-Hill.

QIP, Inc./PQ Systems Inc. (1995), *Total Quality Tools.* Miamisberg, OH: Productivity-Quality Systems Inc.

STRATIFICATION

The data we collect may have hidden patterns that can reveal significant relationships. Graphs and charts, useful as they may be, still can hide certain internal relationships. One reason for this is that the data we collect often comes from a heterogeneous group of people. For example, suppose we collect information on employee performance. If we pool all employees, we may inadvertently pool both trained and untrained employees. These two groups may perform a task differently. If we knowingly or unwittingly ignore this reality, we would be dealing with a heterogeneous group and would miss some of the very patterns that the data might reveal. To elaborate, suppose trained employees take three to six minutes to deal with a customer, whereas untrained employees take eight to twelve minutes. If we simply plot the average amount of time it takes for a group of employees to deal with customers, it could range all the way from three to twelve minutes, with the average time being around seven minutes. The range and the average obscure several facts:

- Once we take training into account, average time to complete a task has a much narrower range than is indicated.

- The average can be misleading, because the two groups of workers will have distinctly different averages.

- Both the range and the average tell us nothing about the effect of training on performance. An employee who takes longer may be more suited for the job but just may lack training.

The effect of ignoring subgroup differences can lead to misleading conclusions. Stratification can help identify this pitfall.

WHAT IS STRATIFICATION?

Stratification is the process of dividing the data into categories or subgroups. The main reason for stratification is that it enables us to eliminate the confounding effects of other categories present in the system. The subgroups are chosen to be homogeneous with regard to the variable under observation. It is the process of grouping "apples with apples" and "oranges with oranges," so that they can be properly compared. Consider the scatter diagram in Exhibit 11.9, which shows the relationship between hours of supervision and quality of service rendered. The chart implies that supervision is not related to service quality, because there is no apparent pattern in the scatter diagram.

> **Stratification is the process of dividing the data into categories or subgroups. The subgroups are chosen in such a way as to be homogeneous with regard to the process under observation.**

But what if supervision improves performance in some areas but not in others? For example, it is conceivable that, for simple tasks, supervision has a negative effect, while for more complex tasks, it has a positive effect. If this were indeed the case, putting both types of tasks on the same scatter chart would only obscure the pattern. In such cases, stratification helps us eliminate the influence of unwanted variables. When we separate simple and complex tasks, we find the relationships shown in Exhibits 11.10a and 11.10b. For

Exhibit 11.9
Scatter Chart (Supervision and Accuracy)

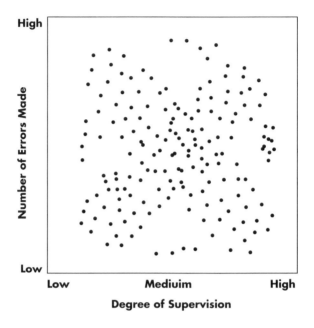

Degree of Supervision

Exhibit 11.10a
Supervision and Accuracy–Easy Tasks

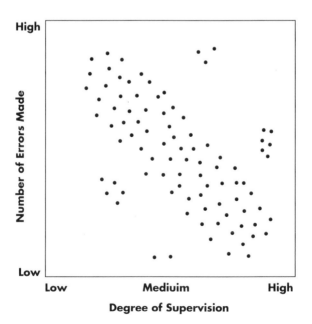

Degree of Supervision

Exhibit 11.10b
Supervision and Accuracy–Difficult Tasks

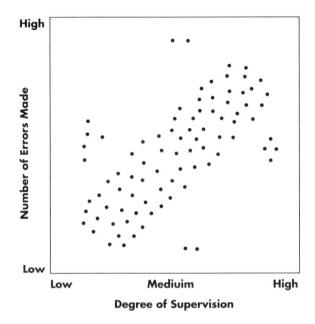

complex tasks, the level of supervision improves performance, and for simple tasks, the level of supervision has a
detrimental effect on performance. Although the initial chart
led us to believe that there is no relationship between supervision and performance, stratification showed quite the
opposite. It also identified the differential effect supervision
had, depending on the type of task involved.

Stratification should be considered in the following
instances:

1. We do not see any patterns where we might logically
   expect to find one.

2. There are reasons to believe that the group being considered is likely to be heterogeneous with regard to
   the task at hand.

3. There are obvious ways of dividing the group to make
   it more homogenous.

How to carry out stratification

Step 1. Select the variables to be stratified. For stratification
to work, the variable under consideration should be related

to the stratification variable. For example, when we consider the average time to serve a customer, we can hypothesize that it might be related to whether the employee had received any training. Accordingly, we can use stratification and create two separate strata: trained and untrained employees.

Step 2. Establish categories. For example, the categories in which we are interested could be related to the level of training received by an employee—highly trained, moderately trained, or untrained. Such categories can be discrete (e.g., male or female) or continuous (e.g., different levels of experience).

Step 3. Establish the minimum number of observations required in each category. Make sure you have an adequate number of observations. For example, if 30 employees are assigned to the task of handling customer service and only 2 of them had any training, stratification will be of dubious value. We must ensure that both the overall sample and the sample within each stratum are adequate to represent the process under consideration.

How to carry out stratification
1. Select the variables to be stratified.
2. Establish categories.
3. Establish the minimum number of observations required in each category.
4. Use graphic techniques to display results.

Step 4. Use graphic techniques to display results. Although the process of stratification does not dictate that we use graphic techniques, the effect of stratification can be illustrated very effectively with their use.

HOW TO INTERPRET STRATIFICATION

To interpret stratified information, we compare stratified data with unstratified data. If there are no significant differences between the two, then we can conclude that stratification does not add any new information and continue to work with unstratified data. If stratified data show patterns that are dissimilar to the global data, then we can conclude that global analysis is perhaps inappropriate, because they average out the subgroup differences. In this case, we concentrate on stratified, rather than unstratified, data. We compare the different strata directly to note how and to what extent they differ. If the stratification variable is continuous, we also look for changes in relationships as we move from the lower level to the higher level of the variable. For example, if we stratify employees by the training they received and study their level of efficiency, we will be interested in noting the change in their level of efficiency as we move from the lowest to the highest level of training. Is there a linear relationship between training and efficiency? Does efficiency level off after a certain amount of training?

The process of stratification should follow some logical hypothesis. There must be some reason for stratification. Because it is possible to stratify the data in any number of ways, it is important that we carefully examine the reasoning behind the proposed stratification.

Although stratification, as described here, is fairly basic, more sophisticated stratification can be carried out when we attempt to understand customer needs. For example, some customers might prefer faster service, whereas others may prefer more leisurely service. Customers can be stratified, according to their needs, by using more complex statistical techniques such as cluster analysis.

To know more

Books that deal with product or service quality measurements usually contain references on stratification. Some examples follow:

Chang, R.Y. and M.E. Niedzwiecki (1993), *Continuous Improvement Tools, Vol. 2*. Irvine, CA: Richard Chang Associates.

Mears, P. (1995), *Quality Improvement Tools & Techniques.* New York: McGraw-Hill.

Whitely, R.C. (1991), *The Customer Driven Company.* Reading, MA: Addison-Wesley.

FLOW CHARTS

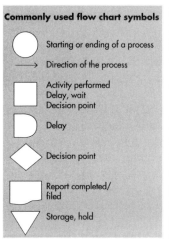

Commonly used flow chart symbols

○ Starting or ending of a process

⟶ Direction of the process

▢ Activity performed
Delay, wait
Decision point

▷ Delay

◇ Decision point

▭ Report completed/ filed

▽ Storage, hold

Graphs and charts show how specific parts of the system operate. Our concern here is to identify how any specific system or process works as a whole. Flow charts can be used for this purpose.

WHAT ARE FLOW CHARTS?

Flow charts are pictorial representations that trace the sequence of steps from the beginning to the end of a process. For example, what sequence of events takes place when a customer calls for a pizza home delivery? What sequence of events takes place when a customer complains about a product he or she bought recently? Flow charts are useful when we need to identify a current sequence of actions and compare it with an ideal sequence. The charts can be used to explore how the various components of a process work together and how the process can be made more efficient.

WHY USE FLOW CHARTS?

Every process involves a series of steps. When a person is entrusted to carry out a process (such as admitting incoming patients to the hospital), that person tends to follow what he or she is taught or what worked for that person in the past. However, what one was taught or what worked in the past may not be the best way to carry out the task. Although, overall, the process may work well, it still could be improved. Flow charts force us to pay attention to steps involved in carrying out the process under consideration. This, in turn, helps us identify redundancies and inefficiencies.

> **Flow charts force us to pay attention to steps involved in carrying out the process under consideration. This, in turn, helps us to identify redundancies and inefficiencies.**

HOW TO CREATE A FLOW CHART

The following paragraphs illustrate the steps involved in the creation of flow charts, with a hotel check-in procedure as an example. A flow chart diagram is created by actually observing the process being flow charted. This is supplemented by a discussion with the people involved in the process to ensure that what is being mapped accurately reflects what actually happens. (Alternatively, people involved in the process can discuss its necessary steps and create a flow chart. This can be confirmed later by actual observation of the process.)

Step 1. *Define the process to be flow charted.* For example, we would like to flow chart the process that starts from the time the customer arrives at the hotel reception desk until he or she is given a key to the room.

Step 2. *Define the major process tasks.* Observe the process in order to understand what actually happens. For example, after observing a number of transactions, the process can be defined as consisting of the following sequence of actions:

a. The customer is asked if he or she has a reservation.

If yes, go to b; if no, go to e.

b. The customer is asked for his or her name.

c. The receptionist checks for the name in the computer.

If the name appears on the computer, go to d; if not, follow the procedures laid out in flow chart B.

d. Check to see if the computer shows the customer's preferences.

If yes go to g; if no, go to f.

e. Check to see if rooms are available.

If no, go to k; if yes, go to f.

How to create a flow chart
1. Define the process to be flow charted.
2. Define the major process tasks.
3. Draw a flow chart using the conventional symbols indicated earlier.

f. Check to see if the customer would like a no-smoking room, a suite, or other options available.

g. Check to see if the customer would like help with his or her luggage.

If no, go to I; if yes, go to h.

h. Arrange to have the luggage carried to the room.

i. Hand the key to the customer.

j. Thank the customer.

k. Explain that no rooms are available. Thank the customer. Suggest alternative accommodations.

Step 3. *Draw a flow chart using the conventional symbols indicated earlier.* See Exhibit 11.11.

HOW TO INTERPRET AND USE FLOW CHARTS

When the flow chart is drawn, it can be studied to improve the efficiency of the process by

- eliminating redundant procedures;
- identifying tasks that need to be done, but are not done now;
- making the system more efficient, if possible;
- eliminating potential bottlenecks; and
- considering alternative ways of handling the process.

One way of achieving improvement in the system is to commission an expert (or experts) with special knowledge of the process and ask them to draw a flow chart that reflects the most efficient way of executing the process. This ideal flow chart then is compared with the actual process flow chart described previously. The differences between the two can be

Exhibit 11.11
Hotel Check-in Flow Chart

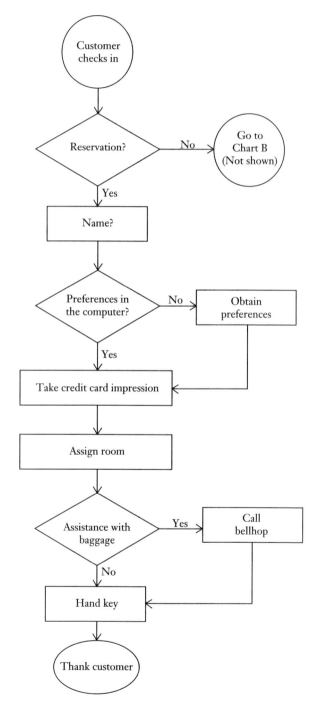

studied to understand the areas in which improvements can be effected.

When comparing a flow chart of a process as it actually happens with a chart created by an expert, work systematically, considering the following points:

Do the two charts follow similar sequences? If not, do the differences have any significance? If they have significance, what can be learned from them? (Note that all differences do not have to be significant. Some actions can be performed in any sequence equally efficiently.) For example, customers may be asked to sign a form either at the start or at the end of their visits.

Consider the decision points. If a decision symbol is missing from the expert's flow chart, consider whether your decision symbol is a superfluous one. For example, obtaining the supervisor's approval for every service call (which may appear in your process chart) may be missing from the expert's chart. This may mean that that operation is unnecessary and, except under special conditions, seeking approval simply delays the process. Conversely, if a decision symbol is missing from your flow chart, consider whether you are missing something important for maintaining quality. Your process chart, for example, may not show checking with the customer to make sure his or her complaint was handled satisfactorily, which the expert may consider crucial.

Consult the expert before making the changes. Differentiate between changes that are critical and those that are not. Concentrate on the critical changes. To ensure that nothing important is missed, discuss the pros and cons of contemplated changes with the expert.

Be careful about the degree of detail required. Flow charts should be detailed enough to map the process faithfully, so that its inefficiencies can be spotted and remedied. A chart that is too detailed will draw attention to irrelevant details, whereas a sketchy chart will miss important opportunities for improvement. If different flow charts contain different degrees of detail, comparing them also will be difficult.

To know more

References to flow charting can be found in many books dealing with quality improvement, such as the ones mentioned here:

McLaughlin, C.P. and A.D. Kaluzny (1994), *Continuous*

Quality Improvement in Healthcare. Gaithersberg, MD: Aspen.

Mears, P. (1995), *Quality Improvement Tools & Techniques.* New York: McGraw-Hill.

Miller, G.L. and L.L. Krumm (1992), *The Whats, Whys and Hows of Quality.* Milwaukee, WI: ASQC Quality Press.

12

Diagnostic Techniques: People

P3D1: People and Diagnosing

	PRODUCERS	PROCESSES	PEOPLE
DIAGNOSING	Structural analysis Check sheets Mystery shopping Internal focus groups	Graphic techniques Run charts Stratification Flow charts	**Complaint elicitation** **Content tracking** **Belief system analysis** **Pareto charts**

DETAILING	Nominal group
	  technique
	Benchmarking
	Deleting
	  dimensionality
	The as-if frame
	The video camera
		Control charts	External focus groups
			Survey research
			Laddering
			Factor analysis
			Gap analysis
			Wish lists

DELIVERING	Brainstorming Force field analysis Cost-benefit analysis	Fishbone diagrams Process mapping and evaluation	Tracking

At the core of the business is the customer toward whom all business activities are targeted, either directly or indirectly. Without an understanding of the customer, neither service quality nor customer satisfaction is attainable. Customers often give us feedback in the form of complaints. They tell us what we should do to achieve service quality and customer satisfaction and what it would take to retain them as customers. Therefore, complaints are gifts (Barlow and Moller 1996), and we discuss how to elicit and analyze them here.

COMPLAINT ELICITATION TECHNIQUES

THE IMPORTANCE OF COMPLAINTS

Complaints are a valuable source of information. Every complaint is an inside look into a customer's mind, provided at no cost to us. Complaints tell us why customers are dissatisfied and what we can do about it. It is a mistake to treat complaints either as a nuisance or simply as something to be dealt with in the course of doing business. Complaints are low-cost opportunities to learn. Information provided through focus groups and surveys describes past events and, hence, is subject to distortion. On the other hand, complaints are current, real, and not subjected to memory distortions. When complaints are in reference to nonroutine problems, they provide an opportunity for us to institute service quality procedures ahead of the competition and move toward exceeding customer expectations. What we learn through customer complaints can be invaluable.

Just because the number of complaints received by management is small, we cannot assume that customers are happy. Let us consider a company that has 1 million customers and one complaint a day reaches management. It may be tempting to dismiss the complaint as an exception, because only one out of 1 million customers complains on any given day. Yet, we know that most complaints never reach management (in Chapter 3, see "The Iceberg of Ignorance"). If we work backward, using Yoshida's estimates cited previously, we have the following:

Number of complaints that reach management
during the year   365
Known to top supervisors   821
Known to supervisors   6,753
Known to rank-and-file employees
(assuming only 4% complain[1])   9,125
Total potential complaints   228,125

Although management may be under the impression that customers by and large are satisfied, in actuality, more than 22% of its customers may have complaints and be unhappy with the company. Because a dissatisfied customer tells eight

---

[1]The estimates actually range from 4% to 80%, depending on the industry and the seriousness of the problem. For low-priced mass-market products, the proportion of complainers is likely to be low, and thus the level of dissatisfaction could be higher than is indicated here.

to ten other people about the problem, more than 1 million people (who may be potential customers) also may be exposed to the complaints against the company. Hence, it becomes all the more important to elicit complaints and solve problems. TARP estimates that 70% to 90% of complaining customers will stay with a company if their complaints are handled satisfactorily.

A two-tiered problem

Customer complaints are subject to two filters. The first filter is the customer. Customers convey only a fraction of the total number of complaints to the company. The second filter is the employees within an organization. Employees will let management know only a fraction of the total number of complaints received.

Customer complaints are subject to two filters: customers and employees.

So, if we are to be successful in eliciting complaints, we need to encourage more customers with problems to complain to us. We also need to ensure that more complaints received by employees actually reach management.

Why customers do not complain

As we discussed in the first part of this book, most unhappy customers tend not to complain to the organization. The main reasons for this are the following:

Customers do not know to whom they should complain. To whom should customers complain? To the employee who is providing them with unsatisfactory service? To his or her supervisor? To the manager? To the head office? To the president?

Customers believe it is futile to complain. Many customers may have experienced the futility of complaining. The customers either were made to look unreasonable (e.g., "You are the first person to complain about this!") or were patronized, or their complaints were completely or partially ignored.

Why customers do not complain:
- **Uncertainty about to whom to complain,**
- **A sense of futility,**
- **Complicated procedures, and**
- **Possible repercussions.**

Customers may believe that the procedure is too complicated. Responses such as "If you would like to complain, you have to fill out this form and take it to our complaints department on the seventh floor, which is open from 10 A.M. to 3 P.M., Monday through Friday" indicate to customers that complaining is hard work.

Complaining can worsen the problem. Customers also can fear that if they complain, the second-rate service they receive now may get even worse as far as they are concerned. Customers may believe that even the poor level of service they currently are experiencing will not be maintained if they complain.

HOW TO ELICIT LEGITIMATE COMPLAINTS

By eliminating the factors that contribute to customers not complaining, we encourage them to complain when they are not satisfied with our service. Such measures can include the following:

- *Designating a person as being responsible for receiving all complaints.* This will eliminate the problem of a customer not knowing to whom to complain.

- *Making a complaint box available to customers.* This will achieve two purposes: First, the customer does not have to face a possibly unsympathetic listener; and second, it enables the customer to retain anonymity (if he or she so chooses) and thus not be concerned with any possible repercussions about employee hostility in the future.

- *Providing a toll-free number to customers for registering complaints.* This is similar to having a complaints box, except, in this case, the customer simply calls a toll-free number to voice his or her complaints. A toll-free number is probably better than a complaint box, because some people may not take the time to put their complaints in writing. However, this option is likely to be more expensive to install than a complaints box. A more advanced version of the toll-free number is the installation of a video booth. If a customer has a complaint, he or she simply goes into the booth and voices it. Such video booths can be installed on a temporary or permanent basis.

> **Countering customer reluctance to complain:**
> - A designated person to handle complaints,
> - A customer complaint box,
> - A toll-free customer complaint number and video booth, and
> - Official management response to complaints.

- Making it a policy of management to acknowledge all complaints and state what actions it proposes to take. This will eliminate the sense of futility that many customers may feel when they take the time to complain yet find that no corrective action is taken by the organization.

Why employees do not pass on complaints

We need to tackle the problem of employees not passing on the received complaints to management. As before, we must identify the causes of the problem and the means of solving it.

Complaints are self-incriminating and, hence, not passed on. Employees do not pass on complaints to management for two basic reasons. First, complaints can be self-incriminating. If a customer's complaint to an employee pertains to his or her rudeness or incompetence, it is unlikely that the employee will pass this on to his or her superiors. Second, employees often are afraid of the "shoot the messenger" syndrome. For example, if a customer complains about the long wait in a line, the employee may not pass on this message to management. There is a widespread belief—justified or not—that the messenger is somehow responsible for the message. Many employees do not want to be the bearer of bad messages—those they believe management would rather not hear.

Why employees do not pass on complaints:
- **Self incrimination**
- **Nonrecognition**

Complaints are not recognized as complaints when received. Some customers may find it unpleasant to complain. They may prefer to complain in a roundabout way, so as not to offend the employee. Comments such as "If I had known that the wait would be this long, I might have come some other day" actually can be a serious complaint regarding the inability of an organization to handle customers efficiently, except under ideal conditions. However, such comments by customers easily can be taken to mean that the customer miscalculated and should be better organized in the future.

Increasing management knowledge of complaints

We can encourage employees to pass on complaints to management by eliminating the factors that lead to it.

An anonymous mechanism, such as a suggestion box, can be provided to employees. This will enable employees to pass on customer comments to management without the fear of self-incrimination or without having to snitch on a fellow employee. This also will eliminate an employee from being the bearer of bad news.

Training programs to sensitize employees to customer complaints can be put into place. It is important for employees to recognize customer complaints, even if they are made in an indirect and nonoffensive manner; therefore, management might consider training employees in the art of identifying customer dissatisfaction. An outside communications expert can be called in for this purpose. Employees can be trained to record the complaints (if necessary, by eliciting them) and pass them on to management on an ongoing basis. Such training could involve video clips of complaints by customers (either real or simulated), in which customers talk about their concerns about the service or offer suggestions for improvement without actually complaining or criticizing.

Proactive procedures. Another approach to eliciting complaints is to approach customers before they come to us. For example, every senior officer of the company might make it a part of his or her job to talk to a certain number of customers on a regular basis. Doing so may result in identifying and solving a problem before it happens.

> **Countering employee reluctance to complain**
> • Anonymous procedures
> • Training procedures
> • Proactive procedures

What makes a complaint elicitation system good?

A good complaint elicitation system should be proactive. As mentioned previously, an unhappy customer does not necessarily complain. It is important that we remove all barriers to customers' complaints and encourage them to let us know when they are dissatisfied.

A good complaint elicitation system should be uncomplicated. A complaint system that asks for extensive documentation or directs the customer to a different department creates unnecessary work for the customer. Obviously, it is not a good idea to further inconvenience an already dissatisfied customer; yet, this is what most organizations end up doing.

> **A good complaint system**
> • is proactive,
> • is uncomplicated,
> • entails a quick response, and
> • has management commitment behind it.

Another feature of a good complaint elicitation system is a quick response. When a response is far removed from the initial complaint, it is natural for customers to assume that nothing has been done about the complaint. This, in turn, reinforces the initial dissatisfaction with the organization. Many organizations empower their employees so that customer grievances can be dealt with immediately.

Underlying a good complaint elicitation system are management commitment and employee training. Without these, complaints will not reach management and, if they do, are not likely to be acted on.

HOW TO INTERPRET COMPLAINTS

Interpretation of complaints can be carried out through a variety of techniques such as content analysis, content tracking, belief system analysis, and Pareto charts. These techniques are described in subsequent sections of this chapter.

To know more

Barlow, J. and C. Moller (1996), *A Complaint Is a Gift*. San Francisco: Berrett Kohler.

Naumann, E. and K. Giel (1995), *Customer Satisfaction Measurement*. Cincinnati: Thomson Executive Press.

COMPLAINT ANALYSIS TECHNIQUES

It is important to understand and interpret the complaints we elicit. A formal analysis of complaints can provide us with an objective view of where we stand, as perceived by our customers. Three techniques for analyzing complaints—belief system analysis, Pareto charts, and content analysis and tracking—are described here.

BELIEF SYSTEM ANALYSIS

Handling complaints to the satisfaction of customers is always worthwhile. When complaints are resolved quickly, more than 80% of customers continue to do business with an organization, even if the complaint happens to be a major one.[2] Yet, resolving complaints is a reactive strategy, an act of setting right something that has gone wrong. Complaints also can be used proactively to enhance overall service quality. They can be used as input to long-term service quality enhancement. Our objective in doing this is to lower the number of complaints and increase customer enjoyment of the service provided. Once we set up a system to capture customer complaints, the next step is to analyze these complaints. There are several methods available, three of which are discussed here: belief system analysis (BSA), Pareto charts, and content analysis and tracking.

BSA establishes the significance of service lapses from the point of view of customers.

When customers complain, talking about what upsets them, they essentially are telling us about their belief systems. They indicate how things should work in order for them to be satisfied customers. Although each customer may be different, this analysis usually shows a commonality of belief systems within a culture, which indicates how we can retain customers. Here are a few examples:

"Even though I am a long-term customer, you have rejected my check."

(Belief system: My loyalty deserves flexibility.)

"Although I am a customer with a large account, my check has to be countersigned by someone else before payment can be made."

(Belief system: A sizable customer should not be kept waiting.)

Belief system analysis is a way of identifying the psycho-

[2]Based on a cross-industry study carried out by the Service Impact Group, as reported by E. Naumann and K. Giel (1995).

logical equivalence of service lapses. It establishes the significance of such lapses from the point of view of customers and shows how service lapses are interpreted by them.

HOW TO IDENTIFY BELIEF SYSTEMS

Belief systems can be identified through statements that imply a causal relationship and are presented usually as a violation of that relationship. For example, a statement, such as "It is inexcusable for a large organization like yours to make so many mistakes," is a violation of an assumed causal relationship—mistakes are not excusable if made by large organizations. Such statements often can be found in oral or written customer complaints. We also can use special techniques, such as focus groups and laddering, to identify belief systems.

HOW TO INTERPRET AND USE BSA

Once the basic patterns are understood, customer service can be structured in such a way that, for the most part, customers' belief systems are not challenged by the organization. For example, if the dominant belief system among customers is that they should not have to wait for approval for small refunds on billing errors, individual employees can be authorized to provide on-the-spot refunds without authorization, provided they are within a certain amount. To carry out BSA, we can use techniques such as focus groups, individual depth interviews, or laddering. Laddering (the means-end model) is well-suited particularly to this purpose. The way we use BSA depends on the nature of our clients. If we have a few clients who have large accounts, and if we know them, then BSA can be used effectively in understanding their needs. Our service can be structured to conform to customer expectations. If, on the other hand, our clients are numerous, small, and relatively unknown, we can use BSA to communicate with them better and provide service that exceeds customer expectations.

> BSA provides insight into customers' assumptions and expectations. The results are interpreted with a view to providing the type of service with which customers will be satisfied.

Belief system analysis is a particularly useful technique when a firm depends on a small group of customers (such as aircraft buyers) who account for a significant proportion of the company's sales.

To know more

There is very little written about this type of analysis in service quality literature. However, any standard textbook on psychology that deals with belief systems can be of help.

PARETO CHARTS

The Pareto principle states that the relationship between cause and effect is not symmetrical. Thus, for example, we may observe that 20% of the employees in an organization may be responsible for 80% of the productivity. Or, you can gain a working knowledge of a computer program in a relatively short period, but mastering the program may take a long time. This asymmetry between independent and dependent variables is called the Pareto principle. Service variables tend to follow the Pareto pattern.

The underlying assumption of the Pareto principle is that a small category of seemingly trivial problems could be generating the most customer complaints. If we can identify these frequently occurring problems, they will enable us to focus our limited resources on areas that are significant to customers. Even when our resources are unlimited (an unlikely scenario), identifying problems that generate the most customer complaints will enable us to prioritize our action plan. A Pareto chart is a way of identifying a small number of recurring problems.

WHAT IS A PARETO CHART?

A Pareto chart is a pictorial depiction of events, such as customer complaints. It separates the "vital few" from the "trivial many" and shows the areas in which our actions are likely to produce the highest impact.

HOW TO CREATE A PARETO CHART

Step 1. Classify complaints into categories on the basis of how similar they are to one another. Suppose the problem is identifying the complaints received by the technical support hotline. We may want to group problems into categories, such as problems with regard to the inability to get through, fees charged for the help provided, unsatisfactory solutions provided, confusing instructions given, incompetent technical person, discourteous technical person, and so on.

Nature of complaint	No. received
Difficult to reach	12
Fees too high	88
Incompetent service	42
Unsatisfactory solutions	15
Instructions confusing	16
Employee discourteous	6

Step 2. Rank complaints from the most to the least frequent. The first step here is to convert the number of problems in each category to percentages. Then the categories can be sorted in the order of their frequency.

Nature of complaint	No. received	%
Fees too high	88	49
Incompetent service	42	23
Instructions confusing	16	9
Unsatisfactory solutions	15	8
Difficult to reach	12	7
Employee discourteous	6	3

Step 3. Cumulate the categories, starting with the most frequent to the least frequent. For example, if high fees are mentioned by 49% and incompetent service by 23%, then these two sets of problems account for 72% of all complaints received. Add the next most frequent problem set to this and continue the process until all problem sets are accounted for.

Nature of complaint	No. received	%	Cumulative %
Fees too high	88	49	49
Incompetent service	42	23	72
Instructions confusing	16	9	81
Unsatisfactory solutions	15	8	89
Difficult to reach	12	7	96
Employee discourteous	6	3	99

Step 4. Plot a line chart with the problem group on the x-axis and cumulative percentage of occurrence on the y-axis. (See Exhibit 12.1.)

HOW TO INTERPRET THE PARETO CHART

How to create a Pareto chart

1. **Group events in categories on the basis of how similar they are to one another.**
2. **Rank them from the most to the least frequent.**
3. **Cumulate the categories, starting with the most frequent to the least frequent.**

When interpreting the Pareto chart, we look for break points or where the events become less frequent. We would expect the first few complaint categories to account for most of the complaints received. Let us say that the first three categories of complaints account for some 78% of all complaints received. After this, each complaint group accounts for less than 5% of the complaints. So we identify these three categories as the most important in contributing to customer complaints.

By using a Pareto chart, we can identify the variables that are responsible for the largest number of problems. An organization can channel its resources very effec-

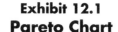

Exhibit 12.1
Pareto Chart

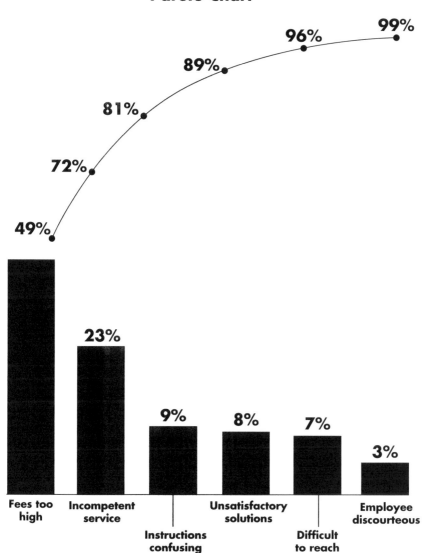

tively by concentrating on those variables closest to the y-axis, provided the chart exhibits a Pareto pattern. In general, Pareto charts deal with the frequency of problems and not with their importance. For example, although most complaints may relate to telephone waiting time, it may be much more important to customers that their queries are handled satis-

When interpreting Pareto charts, look for break points.

factorily once they reach the technical support person. So although we can achieve the highest leverage in reducing the number of problems through the use of Pareto charts, we should not assume that we are necessarily tackling the most critical problems—only the most frequent ones.

As noted previously, it does not follow that the most frequent problems are necessarily the most critical from the customer's point of view. Although Pareto charts often are said to distinguish the vital few from the trivial many, this is only true in a quantitative sense. It is quite possible that, from the customer's perspective, the trivial many may well be the useful many, as quality expert Juran notes. Although it is logical to concentrate on the most frequently encountered problems, we also may want to know the importance customers attach to different problems. For this reason, Pareto charts often are used in conjunction with other techniques such as quadrant analysis or cost–benefit analysis (both discussed subsequently). A Pareto chart can be used by itself or as a preliminary tool for a more sophisticated analysis.

> • **The most frequent problems are not necessarily the most important.**
> • **Make sure not to combine dissimilar "events."**

The Pareto technique also can be used to understand other events such as problems encountered in serving customers or the types of errors made in billing. Although the Pareto chart can be used in any context in which a "Pareto phenomenon" is expected, we should be careful not to plot dissimilar events on the same chart. For example, it is counterproductive to plot customer complaints that relate to product quality along with complaints that deal with service quality. Although both are complaint categories, they may not be comparable either qualitatively or quantitatively. Combining noncomparable categories of events is likely to distort the nature of the phenomenon being analyzed.

To know more

Pareto charts are a common tool of quality improvement. Most books that deal with quality improvement techniques contain details on constructing Pareto charts, including the following:

Chang, R.Y. and M. E. Niedzwiecki (1993), *Continuous Improvement Tools*, Vol. 2. Irvine, CA: Richard Chang Associates.

Mears, P. (1995), *Quality Improvement Tools & Techniques*. New York: McGraw-Hill.

Tague, N.R. (1995), *The Quality Toolbox*. Milwaukee: ASQC Quality Press.

CONTENT ANALYSIS AND CONTENT TRACKING

WHAT IS CONTENT ANALYSIS?

Most customer complaints contain two types of elements: affective and cognitive. The affective component tells us how a customer feels about the service he or she received, whereas the cognitive component tells us about the underlying structure or how the customer perceives the situation. In addition, some complaints can contain a third element, known as the *conative element*, that states what the customer wants us to do.

Several specific research techniques are available to describe and systematically analyze customer complaints. The complexity of the analysis depends on the purpose for which it is being used. There are many ways in which a content analysis can be carried out. For example, we can analyze the frequency with which certain words are used in describing a given problem; and we can analyze the frequency with which an idea, thought, or observation occurs with regard to a given problem. Computer programs are available to carry out content analysis, especially as it pertains to word counts.

Content analysis is a way of identifying the components of any message (e.g., customer complaints).

HOW TO CARRY OUT A CONTENT ANALYSIS

Content analysis covers a wide range of analyses. What follows is an outline of steps that can be used in analyzing customer complaints:

Step 1. Identify the following components of the complaint.
- What happened?
- What was the nature of the complaint?
- How did the customer perceive it?
- How did the customer feel?
- What were the customer's expectations?
- What were the customer's suggestions for improvement?

As an example, consider the following complaint:

"It is obvious to me that your company is more interested in making a big profit than serving its customers properly. I find it hard to believe that a company of your size does not have the resources to produce correct bills. If you really care for your customers, you would not deliberately overcharge them. Furthermore, your service people are

*rude and ignorant. Last Wednesday when I told one of your represen-
tatives that your company had overcharged me, he replied that I was
wrong, because your systems are not capable of making such mistakes.
He did not even have the courtesy to look through my bill to understand
the nature of my complaint. Some willingness on his part to understand
the problem would have made all the difference. It would be simple
enough for you to have someone in the organization trained to understand and deal with billing errors."*

- What happened?   *Billing error.*
- What was the nature
  of the complaint?   *Service.*
- How did the customer
  perceive it?   *Mistake not accidental.*
- How did the customer feel?   *Company does not care.*
- What were the customer's
  expectations?   *Service people should
  pay attention.*
- What the were customer's
  suggestions for
  improvement?   *Have a special person to
  handle billing complaints.*

Step 2. *After carrying out such an analysis for a period of time,
group complaints into categories* (as we did while using Pareto
charts). The length of time could be anywhere from one to
three months or longer, depending on the number of complaints received.

For example, billing complaints could include overbilling,
inconsistent billing, and charging interest on an "overdue
account," even when the bills are sent out late.

Step 3. *Create a separate table for each group of complaints.* By
doing so, we can find out how different customers felt about
the same complaint, as well as what their expectations and suggestions for improvement were for each problem. As an example, the following four customers complained about incorrect
billing. But all of them did not perceive it in the same way.

Problem	Customer ID	*How did the customer perceive it?*
Incorrect billing	1	Deliberate overcharging
	2	Obsolete systems
	3	Incompetent employees
	4	No procedures for checking

How to carry out content analysis
1. **Identify the components of the complaints.**
2. **Group complaints into categories.**
3. **Create a separate table for each group of complaints.**

There also are highly formalized versions of content analysis (Dey 1993). Highly sophisticated techniques such as the neural network analysis (Catpac by Terra 1995) also can be carried out on complaints data. Data thus derived can be used to understand customer dissatisfaction and its source. Data also can be used to track complaints over a period of time or to identify the most frequent complaints (see the section on Pareto charts, discussed previously).

CONTENT TRACKING

Once we isolate complaints, we may want to plot each one on a chart over a period of time, by using the run charts explained previously. Significant events can be noted on the chart to see how such events have affected the flow of complaints. For example, the average number of complaints with regard to billing may have stayed the same over a period of several months, even though we might have introduced a new computer system to make billing more efficient. However, if we properly track complaints, we may find a sharp drop in late billing when the new computer system was introduced. At the same time, we also may find an increase in some types of billing errors. Such tracking can pinpoint areas in which we need to take specific action. Furthermore, we can use content tracking to identify emerging trends. For example, complaints with regard to certain issues (e.g., smoking in public areas in a hotel) may show a growing trend. This may provide us with additional insights that we can use to provide added value to our customers.

When we isolate complaints, we can plot each one on a chart over a period time, by using run charts.

APPENDIX: CONTENT ANALYSIS—AN EXAMPLE

Customer complaints can be systematically recorded on code sheets such as the one shown in Exhibit 12.2.

Basic content tracking—an example

We may choose to track any information contained in any column of Exhibit 12.2 over a period of time. Usually this is done in the form of a run chart, as shown in Exhibit 12.3. For example, we can choose to create run charts of different types of service complaints. This will serve two purposes: One, we will know if there is a change in the nature of customer complaints over a period of time. Two, we will be able to identify

Exhibit 12.2
Content Analysis

What happened?	Nature of Complaint	Customer's perception	Customer's feeling	Customer's expectation	Customer's suggestion
Waiting too long for service	Service (waiting)	Shouldn't have to	Frustrated	Should be served fast (5 mins.)	Have more employees
Billing error	Service (billing)	Unacceptable	Organization does not care	No errors are acceptable	Have checking procedures

Exhibit 12.3
Content Tracking
(Number of complaints with regard to fees)

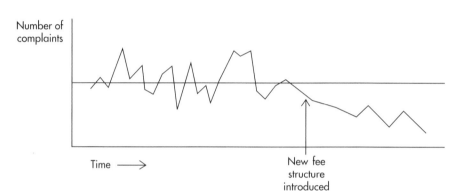

whether the changes introduced by the organization had any substantial effect on customer satisfaction.

To know more

If you intend to use complaint elicitation techniques, read the following texts:

Dey, I. (1993), *Qualitative Data Analysis*. London: Routledge.

Terra (1995) *Catpac 4 for Windows* (software). Birmingham, MA: Terra.

13

Detailing Techniques: Producers

P1D2: Producers and Detailing

	PRODUCERS	PROCESSES	PEOPLE
DIAGNOSING	Structural analysis Check sheets Mystery shopping Internal focus groups	Graphic techniques Run charts Stratification Flow charts	Complaint elicitation Content tracking Belief system analysis Pareto charts
DETAILING	**Nominal group technique Benchmarking Deleting dimensionality The as-if frame The video camera**	Control charts	External focus groups Survey research Laddering Factor analysis Gap analysis Wish lists
DELIVERING	Brainstorming Force field analysis Cost-benefit analysis	Fishbone diagrams Process mapping and evaluation	Tracking

Having completed the preliminary diagnostic work, we should have a reasonable idea as to where we stand. What we need now is a detailed understanding of what we can do further. As with the diagnostic stage, we start with the organization itself.

NOMINAL GROUP TECHNIQUE

As we move into the detailing stage of service quality measurement, we need to generate ideas. We can use internal focus groups for this purpose. However, ideas can be not only facilitated but also inhibited by focus groups. This can be a problem in rigidly structured, hierarchical organizations.

117

Even when the organization is not so structured, some participants may not feel confident enough to produce ideas if others in the group are more aggressive. Under these conditions, we can use a technique known as the *nominal group technique*.

WHAT IS THE NOMINAL GROUP TECHNIQUE?

The nominal group technique is a group discussion process, similar to a focus group. Nominal groups can be used at any stage of the service quality measurement program. The main advantage of this technique is that it can be less threatening than focus groups. In addition, it is especially well-suited to mixed groups. Nominal groups can avoid the problem of one or two participants dominating the group, as can happen in standard focus groups. It is particularly suitable when sensitive policy issues are being discussed, because it provides the participants with a nonacrimonious atmosphere in which to raise emotionally charged issues. It also provides anonymity to participants, which encourages frank discussion of issues without the fear of ridicule or retribution. When issues are sensitive, participants are encouraged to express their ideas individually. In some cases, the ideas also may be generated anonymously. Under these conditions, the term *group* is applied only in a nominal sense, hence the name *nominal* group technique.

The nominal group technique is a special type of focus group in which the participants work both as individuals and as a team.

HOW DOES IT WORK?

As with internal focus groups, the moderator assembles a group of executives (or other employees).

Step 1. *The moderator outlines the objective.* For example, our research might have shown us that we lag behind other organizations in face-to-face customer service. The objective of the nominal group is to find ways to improve our organization in this regard.

Step 2. *The moderator asks the participants to write all the relevant ideas that come to mind.* In doing so, each participant works independently. This encourages participants to put forth their views without fear of immediate rejection of an idea. At this stage, because each individual in the group works without reference to others, the group exists only nominally.

Step 3. *The moderator asks each participant to present one idea at each round.* The moderator then writes the ideas on a flip chart (or a similar medium). In our example, ideas generated may range all the way from "provide incentives to employees" to "make management provide leadership."

Step 4. *The moderator starts the discussion and helps participants eliminate illegal and redundant ideas.* At this stage, the moderator may eliminate duplicate and illegal solutions on the basis of the discussion. For example, "reward employees for excellent customer service" might be eliminated because "compensation should be linked to customer service" is already listed.

Step 5. *The moderator helps participants clarify and evaluate ideas.* Solutions that are thus clarified and evaluated are presented to the group.

Step 6. *Participants vote anonymously on the ideas.* Each member is asked to rank solutions. This is done anonymously. Again, participants work without reference to other participants. If there is great disparity in the ranking of solutions, further discussion is carried out to understand the discrepancy and, if possible, eliminate it. These discrepancies often may highlight different assumptions made by the participants. The rankings then are averaged to arrive at the overall priorities This is now the group decision.

In instances in which the issues are highly sensitive, participants may be asked to submit their solutions anonymously. The group members will not know which participant submitted the solution under discussion.

Steps in carrying out the nominal group technique
1. Moderator briefs participants on the issue.
2. Participants write down possible solutions.
3. Participants present their ideas one at a time.
4. Illegal and redundant ideas are eliminated.
5. Ideas are evaluated and clarified.
6. Participants vote anonymously on the ideas.

HOW TO INTERPRET THE FINDINGS

When interpreting the findings, we may want to consider how diverse the solutions and ideas are, who generated them, and how divergent the rankings are. Diverse solutions give us many options, at least some of which can be tested later. The source of each idea provides some clue as to how the problem is viewed by different strata within the organization. Are the ideas generated by management different from those generated by employees? The divergence of ranks tells us the fundamental differences in perspective and/or assumptions. If what we obtain at this stage is clearcut, we can use the findings directly. If the ideas and solutions are alternatives, then they must be tested further using other methods.

To know more

Delbecq, A.L., A.H. Van de Ven, and D.H. Gustafson (1986), *Group Techniques for Program Planning.* Middleton, WI: Green Briar Press.

QIP, Inc./PQ Systems Inc. (1995), *Total Quality Tools.* Miamisberg, OH: Productivity-Quality Systems Inc.

BENCHMARKING

Learning from others is a cost-effective way to achieve our goals. Benchmarking is the process of modeling excellence, in which we study a successful organization, understand why it is successful, and copy its procedures in order to produce similar results. It is a method of learning from other organizations' experience and is a structured way of imitating and implementing excellence in our own organization. For example, if your organization employs 3000 people to serve customers, and another comparable organization does the job as effectively with 2000 people, we can benchmark that organization. Or, as another example, say your organization is a utility company whose billing procedures create considerable customer dissatisfaction. You may be aware of another organization, perhaps in a different industry sector, that has similar billing patterns but uses procedures that are appreciated by customers. You can benchmark that organization and try to understand the steps it takes in billing its customers, which then leads to customer satisfaction.

Five types of benchmarking

There are five types of benchmarking (Mears 1995):

1. Internal benchmarking
2. Competitive benchmarking
3. Shadow benchmarking
4. Industrial benchmarking
5. Universal benchmarking

Internal benchmarking involves modeling the excellence achieved by one department within the company. If Department A always responds to information requests faster than other departments, then we may want to study the procedures used by Department A. If we find their procedures more efficient, then we may want to implement similar procedures in other departments as well.

Competitive benchmarking involves isolating the key competitive features of your product or service and then comparing yourself with your competitors on those features. For example, as a restaurant owner, you may isolate quality of food, price, and table service as your competitive features. You then may want to compare yourself with the restaurants that excel in each of these features.

Shadow benchmarking involves continuous monitoring and matching of the service quality features of a highly successful competitor. For example, if a highly successful hotel offers to check in customers within five minutes of arrival, the hotel that is shadow benchmarking can offer the same (or similar) feature. Shadow benchmarking is quite common in highly competitive markets.

Industrial benchmarking (also called functional benchmarking) involves observing the industry standard. For example, if the ratio of support staff to customer support personnel is much lower than the average for your industry, then you may want to consider whether the quality of service being offered by your firm is affected by this.

Universal benchmarking (also known as world-class benchmarking) involves comparing your service features with those of others, irrespective of the industry. Your organization may be a bank attempting to provide quick service to customers in a lineup. There is a similarity between this situation and that of a hamburger chain. Both involve similar features, such as line-ups, peak and nonpeak hours, limited time at the disposal of customers, and processing time that might vary, depending on the needs of the customer. So, quite conceivably, a bank can benchmark a hamburger chain on any situation that is similar to both industries.

Five types of benchmarking
1. *Internal benchmarking*
2. *Competitive benchmarking*
3. *Shadow benchmarking*
4. *Industrial benchmarking*
5. *Universal benchmarking*

In current usage, the word *benchmarking* refers to universal or world-class benchmarking. It points to the practice of identifying the best available procedures for delivering a certain aspect of service quality, no matter which organization we need to look at in order to benchmark excellence in the required aspect.

HOW TO CARRY OUT BENCHMARKING

Step 1. Identify the benchmarking variables. Use available research data, customer complaint files, or any other source that will identify customer expectations with regard to service quality. We might identify, for example, the following variables to be benchmarked: guaranteed delivery, customer waiting time at retail locations, and 24-hour customer service.

Step 2. Identify the organizations with the best reputation for each variable. Once you have chosen the items to be benchmarked, identify the organization that has the best reputation in an industry relevant to your company. For example, we could choose to benchmark Federal Express, McDonald's, and IBM for guaranteed delivery, customer waiting time at retail locations, and 24-hour customer service, respectively. At the preliminary stage, we may benchmark several organizations for each variable. We may later identify a single organization for detailed benchmarking, if we are convinced that the organization has been achieving outstanding results in a given area of interest.

Step 3. Collect relevant information on how they do it. This can be done through surveys, personal visits to the successful organization, telephone interviews, published reports, magazine articles, and the like. You also can use consultants to collect such information. Sometimes the CEO of an organization might contact the CEO of a company chosen for benchmarking and offer to share information on a reciprocal basis. This procedure can be used if the chosen firm is not a direct competitor.

How to carry out benchmarking
1. Identify the benchmarking variables.
2. Identify the organizations with the best reputation for each variable.
3. Collect relevant information on how they do it.
4. Review information and data to determine the level of success your competitors of achieving.
5. Determine your goals for each benchmark item.
6. Develop procedures for implementation.

Step 4. Review information and data to determine the level of success your competitors are achieving. For each benchmark item, find the level of success obtained by different firms. This process should identify the relationship between success and a given practice.

Step 5. Determine your goals for each benchmark item. After completing Step 4, if you find that customers are not satisfied by any organization, then you have the opportunity to be uniquely different, to offer something your competition does not. If customers are happy with a competitor, then you should set a target that will make you at least as good as the best in the field.

Step 6. Develop procedures for implementation. This step is not as simple as it might sound. Each organization is different. When we benchmark an organization, it is important to note that the structure of our organization can prevent us from fully implementing what we have learned. Another problem is that all the procedures used by a successful firm may not contribute to its success. It is important that we isolate *"differences that make a difference."*

HOW TO INTERPRET BENCHMARKING RESULTS

When interpreting benchmarking results, we need to remember that, though the same processes produce the same results, there could be substantial differences in the way your organization differs from the organization that is benchmarked. For example, suppose brokerage firm A benchmarks brokerage firm B, which offers more services at no additional cost. If firm B is owned by a larger financial institution, the additional services offered may be the result of this association. Firm A may not be able to replicate the success of firm B. In most instances, firm B will not qualify as a firm to be benchmarked to begin with. However, in some instances, the difference between the two firms may emerge after substantial work has been completed. So, we must always make sure that the conditions are comparable before implementing the results of benchmarking.

Benchmarking can be a major exercise. If you are embarking on a full-fledged benchmarking project, make sure that you understand the mechanics of benchmarking by reading further on the subject.

To know more

American Productivity and Quality Center (1993), T*he Benchmarking Management Guide.* Milwaukee: APQC Quality Press.

Bogan, C.E. and M.J. English (1994), *Benchmarking for Best Practices.* New York: McGraw-Hill.

Camp, R.C. (1989), *Benchmarking.* Milwaukee: ASQC Quality Press.

Codling, S. (1996), *Best Practice Benchmarking.* Houston: Gulf Publishing Company.

Harrington, J. (1997), *The Complete Benchmarking Implementation Guide.* New York: McGraw-Hill.

Mears, P. (1995), *Quality Improvement Tools & Techniques.* New York: McGraw-Hill.

Spendolini, M.J. (1992), *The Benchmarking Book.* New York: AMACOM Books.

DIMENSION REDUCTION TECHNIQUES

To operate efficiently, businesses develop several set procedures or systems. A good system increases efficiency, but not forever. Over a period of time, conditions change, or the system itself gets distorted. For example, efficient record-keeping systems developed during the precomputer years may be highly inefficient now. As a result, many systems that were developed to help us may indeed hinder us. Yet, it may be difficult for those who operate within a system to recognize its limitations. We need to address this problem of perceptual limitations. Perceptual limitations arise as a result of perceptual filtering and the adherence to the standard ways of looking at things (dimensionality). Systems that were helpful once become a hindrance at a later point in time because of our inflexibility or inability to identify and respond to the changing environment.

Systems that hinder

Service quality often is looked upon as something that we add to systems currently in place. It is seen as a process of making current systems better, faster, and more efficient. However, there are instances where the existence of a system itself can be a problem. We cannot add to the system or make it more efficient unless we change or eliminate the system already in place. Sometimes elimination of a hindrance may be all that is needed to improve the system. At a simple level, when we authorize every employee to replace any merchandise claimed to be defective by a customer, we are removing a hindrance to faster complaint resolution—having to seek approval from senior management each time a customer complains about merchandise.

There are instances where the existence of a system itself can be a problem. We cannot add to the system or make it more efficient unless we change or eliminate the system already in place.

Problems with current systems can be difficult to detect. Consider systems that become obsolete as a result of the changing environment. In most such cases, obsolescence takes place over a period of time, usually gradually. Even within an organization, what is obsolete in one part may not be in another. For example, some branches of a bank may have up-to-date computer terminals, while other branches still may depend on cumbersome manual procedures. Consequently, it is not always possible to know if or when a given procedure has become obsolete.

Two major principles may be used to help us understand this problem better: reduction of dimensionality and changing the viewpoint. The video camera technique discussed in the next section can be used to achieve both these objectives.

Perceptual filters

In general, the more we know about a given context, the more we understand it. We see more details in a three-dimensional representation than in a two-dimensional representation. Similarly, the more we know about a subject, the more easily we comprehend new material related to that subject. We find it easier to understand a badly written sentence in our native language than in a language with which we are less familiar. Prior knowledge is considered an asset, and it is an asset in most contexts. Paradoxically, prior knowledge also can result in perceptual filtering. We tend not to notice things to which we are constantly exposed. Prior knowledge can and does filter our perceptions in three ways: deletions, distortions, and generalizations. Once we get used to the way things are, we may, for example,

- not notice the fact that there aren't enough chairs for customers to sit in while they are waiting to be served (deletion);

- believe that there are more chairs than there actually are or believe that customers prefer to stand (distortion); or

- believe that no other company provides adequate seating for their customers (generalization).

What distorts our perceptions?
1. Deletion
2. Distortion
3. Generalization

Although few of us would admit that we habitually distort our perceptions, many of us are intuitively aware of such distortions. Often, consultants are called in "to take a fresh look" at problems, even when the consultant admittedly knows less than those working within the organization. What the consultant brings to the job is not necessarily additional knowledge, but a lack of preconceived ideas as to how things should be.

How do these perceptual filters apply to service quality research? Let us consider a few examples. Some of the procedures used in service organizations were established at a time when a different technology was in place. For example, not too long ago, computers were not universal. Extensive paper-based procedures were necessary. Filling in different forms for different services in the same institution made sense when operational procedures were manual. But, such procedures may not make sense now. Computers could conceivably eliminate duplication. Yet, prior knowledge-based, paper-based procedures often are carried into the new environment, and customers may be asked to provide personal information each time they use a different service, though such information can be accessed easily through the computer. Often, obsolete procedures will be defended as essential safeguards. Newer technology often is used as a faster and better way of doing the same things in the same way rather than as a tool for new ways of doing things.

Consider another example: A bank manager may argue that he or she knows exactly what a person who is close to retirement wants. Even when the manager's remarks are based on extensive experience, his or her experience may become outdated when the composition of this group changes (as might be the case when the affluent baby boomers get close to retirement). The manager could be dealing with customers on the basis of knowledge developed over the years. Yet, it may be irrelevant in the new context.

Lack of knowledge can be remedied relatively easily: The organization can conduct skill-building exercises for its staff; it can send employees to specialized courses and seminars; or it can hire external consultants. But, when the problem is due to deletions, distortions, and generalizations arising from being too familiar with a subject, corrective action is not easy to achieve.

One of the benefits of knowledge is the ability to generalize, to take the inductive leap—the ability to see connections that are missed by less experienced and knowledgeable people. Paradoxically, it is this inductive leap, based on prior knowledge, that leads to distorted perceptions in many cases. How does an organization cope with this problem? After all, past experience and knowledge are key components of success in any endeavor.

We may want to begin with an understanding of the dynamics of perceptual filtering. Many procedures that are in place in service organizations, such as banks, were devised for a time when technology was different. Procedures that enabled the institution to provide efficient service at one time may now interfere with providing quality service to customers. To avoid perceptual distortions, we do not need greater knowledge; rather, we need a way to see without perceptual distortions.

There are many methods by which perceptual distortions can be handled. Two particularly useful methods for "deleting the context" are the use of the as-if frame of reference and the video camera.

THE AS-IF FRAME

What is an as-if frame?

An as-if frame is a hypothetical context presented by the investigator to remove perceptual blocks and facilitate the participant in finding solutions to problems. A question such as "How would you manage the college if you could keep only 90% of the teaching staff?" posed to a college administrator is an example of an as-if frame. The main idea behind the as-if frame is to let a person solve a problem in an imaginary context. The problem solver may or may not know that the context is imaginary.

How to set up as-if frames

There are many different as-if frame techniques. One of the most common is the method of substitution. For example, in a study in which I was involved, a group of bank executives in Canada were asked, "If a highly skilled and intelligent McDonald's manager were asked to run your bank (the retail outlet) for one day, what would he or she ask the tellers to do to serve clients better?" Their answers produced many interesting ideas that could be applied directly to improve service quality. Yet, the same managers had maintained previously that their business was unique and they really could not learn anything about service quality from nonfinancial industries.

Exhibit 13.1
Four Techniques of the As-If Frame

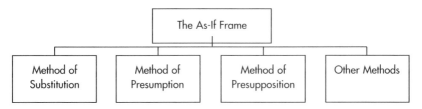

Another example of altering the context is to present management with the question, "What if alternative X were not available to you?" This is the method of presumption (or presumed constraints). Let us consider a situation in which a customer has to fill in a separate form for each service. The bank insists that it is absolutely critical that this be done. An exercise for management in this case would be, "What would you do if you were legally allowed to ask a customer information only once?" Most members of management will quickly come up with ideas for systems that would solve this problem easily.

This technique can be extended to every single operation. For example: If you were not legally allowed to _____ (fill in the operation whose elimination would improve customer service), how would you handle the situation?

Another variation of this technique is to present the problem as though it has already been solved by someone else (the method of presupposition). For example, "In Japan, a customer never fills out a deposit slip. How do you think they do it? Are we capable of doing it?" Chances are people will come up with several ways it could be done.

How to interpret the results

The most interesting aspect of the as-if frame results is that problems, which appear insurmountable in the current context, can be solved easily when the context is changed. The current context is governed by current knowledge and, thus, is resistant to new ideas. But changing the context or deleting a dimension removes the current knowledge associated with the problem and provides a greater opportunity to explore different solutions. Because of this, although skill is required to set up the as-if frame, interpretation is self-evident. If a number of equally efficient solutions are presented to solve the same problem, the best solution can be arrived at through the use of other techniques, such as the nominal group technique or cost-benefit analysis.

> **Usually the results are self-evident. In cases in which many equally valid alternatives are presented, the best can be chosen on the basis of other techniques, such as focus groups and cost-benefit analysis.**

The as-if frame is not a method unique to service quality measurement. It is one of the many techniques of problem solving. Any number of these techniques are available in books dealing with creativity. At the detailing stage, you may want to use more creative problem-solving/idea-generating techniques, in addition to or instead of the as-if frame (see the "To Know More" section).

Changing our perspective

Previously, we talked about two aspects of perceptual limitations: perceptual filtering and dimensionality. The as-if frame helps us deal with perceptual filtering. We can use the video camera technique to deal with the problem of dimensionality. When we change the dimension of a problem, we look at that problem differently, and this can change our perspective.

There are many ways of changing the dimensionality of a situation so that we evaluate things from a different point of view. The technique we use depends on the context. Let us consider the context of service from the point of view of the customer. In this case, we can use the video camera technique.

THE VIDEO CAMERA TECHNIQUE

What is the video camera technique?

The video camera technique refers to the video recording of transactions that usually involve the employee–client relationship. Although still cameras can be used in certain contexts, it is more common to use video cameras.

Why use the video camera technique?

The video camera technique achieves several purposes. First, it deletes a dimension. Second, it can be set up in such a way that every transaction can be seen through customers' eyes. Third, it enables us to view and replay specific segments for a better understanding of the processes.

How to use the video camera technique

To use the video camera technique, we simply mount a video camera and continuously record the process. This could be, for example, the reception desk at a hospital or the complaints counter at a supermarket. Several years ago, a manufacturing firm used this technique successfully. Their recording of housewives' trips to the refrigerator (with both hands full) resulted in their adding a foot pedal to the appliance. This technique can be very effective in understanding deficiencies in service quality.

How to interpret the results

Carefully following the sequence of a transaction can provide insights into the process being observed. Consider a customer who is being served by a customer service representative (CSR). It is common for the CSR to leave the counter to get the signature of a senior manager when a check exceeds a certain amount. Bank managers and other people in management are aware of this operation and pay it no attention. If this operation were to be filmed, however, several things would become obvious:

- It can take a long time for a CSR to get the signature.
- The customer is uncomfortable having to wait to get his or her own money.
- People behind the customer being served look annoyed.

To be sure, all of these signs can be seen without a video camera. But when things are observed firsthand, they appear natural and therefore not a problem. A video recording, on the other hand, removes a perceptual dimension and forces the observer to view the delay, see the discomfort of the customer, and recognize the effect it has on other people in the line. If we have any doubt about what we saw, we can view it again. Problems are presented in bold relief when we remove the context and one or more perceptual dimensions.

As an example, if we wanted to know how a customer is likely to feel about counter service in a bank, cameras would be mounted on the customer side—videos capture the situation (literally and figuratively) from the customer's point of view. The camera sees and records what the customer sees—such as employees talking among themselves while the customer is waiting or CSRs doing paperwork, which presumably can be done later. When examined from a customer's point of view, certain aspects of service become clearer. What appears logical and important from the employee side might appear as insensitive behavior when viewed by the customer. Employees could be talking about an important aspect of their work, yet the customer, who has been waiting in line for ten minutes, may perceive it as a social conversation.

Reduced dimensionality

We also can deliberately reduce dimensionality by confining the camera to a specific area. Thus, when a counter clerk goes to get the signature of a supervisor, all the camera records for (say) three minutes is an empty counter with customers fidgeting in line. Another way to reduce dimensionality is to suppress the audio recording completely. These techniques tend to enhance the tension level of the viewer and call attention to any discomfort the customer may feel.

In general, customers function with reduced dimensionality because they do not necessarily know the reasons for the delay while they wait in line. Artificial reduction of dimensionality while viewing is a way of approximating (however crudely) the effect of reduced dimensionality. When the camera records three minutes of an empty counter and fidgeting customers, and it is played back with no audio, the level of discomfort should indicate that an improvement is needed in that area. This leads to a number of logical questions, such as

- What happened during the three minutes when there was an empty counter?
- Can the actions that took place away from the counter be eliminated?
- Can the actions that took place away from the counter be shortened?

- Can the actions that took place away from the counter be done later?

- Can the actions that took place away from the counter be done beforehand?

In all probability, the actions that kept customers waiting were, at one time, a necessary part of the process. But, now they can be challenged: Are they still necessary? Do we have the technology or other procedures that will help us eliminate the steps that inconvenience our customers?

This example illustrates the numerous possibilities available through this technique.

1. By eliminating dimensionality, we call attention to factors that are normally overlooked as a result of closure (i.e., the human mind automatically providing the missing information).

2. By placing the camera on the customer side, we can view service in the same way as customers do.

3. By querying each procedure that causes discomfort, we can identify procedures that could be done differently or even eliminated completely.

Advantages of the video camera technique
- **Calls attention to overlooked factors**
- **Enables us to see as customers do**
- **Calls attention to unproductive procedures**

When applied properly (with management involvement), this technique can provide extremely valuable insight into service quality. Such insights can be used as input for further qualitative or quantitative research. It also is possible to use these insights to improve service quality without further research. This is especially the case when insights generated during this phase identify opportunities for greater efficiency that are direct, measurable, and meaningful.

To know more

The as-if frame is just one of many ways of solving problems by using creative techniques. There are many books on creative problem solving, and the following is one such book (no specific references are available for the video camera technique):

Michalko, M. (1991), *Thinkertoys*. Berkeley, CA: Ten Speed Press.

14

Detailing Techniques: Processes

P2D2: Processes and Detailing

PRODUCERS	PROCESSES	PEOPLE
Structural analysis Check sheets Mystery shopping Internal focus groups	Graphic techniques Run charts Stratification Flow charts	Complaint elicitation Content tracking Belief system analysis Pareto charts

Nominal group
  technique
Benchmarking
Deleting
  dimensionality
The as-if frame
The video camera
	Control charts	External focus groups
		Survey research
		Laddering
		Factor analysis
		Gap analysis
		Wish lists

Brainstorming Force field analysis Cost-benefit analysis	Fishbone diagrams Process mapping and evaluation	Tracking

We define service quality enhancement as a two-step process: making the service consistent and taking it to a higher level. The first aspect of service quality—*consistency*, or reliability—should be built into any aspect of service. Inconsistent service is not consistent with quality. This aspect is so important that quality experts such as Deming consider it to be a defining attribute of quality. Yet, in practice, consistency is little understood and, therefore, often ignored. The second aspect of service quality is to *achieve a higher level* of service.

The first aspect of service requires an understanding of the nature of variability and how to control it to achieve service that is consistent. It is a measure of *how well* we do what we do. McDonald's restaurants do not serve steak; they serve hamburgers. But if their service and product are consistent, then they fulfill the foremost criterion of quality. The second aspect has more to do with the quantity and nature of the service. It is a measure of *how much* we can provide to our customers. Contrary to what many people believe, *it is consistency, rather than level, that is the cornerstone of quality.* For example, an international courier service may deliver the mail faster (a lower average time) than the regular mail service, but if the courier delivery is inconsistent compared with the regular mail service, then the courier service does not fulfill the prime criterion of quality. Here, we demonstrate how we can measure the two components of variability in human performance.

Because consistency is central to the delivery of service quality, we must be able to understand and measure it. The standard measure of consistency is variability. The more consistent the service is, the less variable it is. Although we discussed variability previously, this aspect is so critical to the delivery of quality that we revisit the topic here in greater detail and discuss ways of measuring it.

COMMON CAUSE AND SPECIAL CAUSE VARIATIONS

Human performance will always show variability, from person to person and from occasion to occasion in the same person. Some of these variations are part of the system within which a person operates. For example, an employee's performance will vary depending on (1) the type and requirements of the customer with whom he or she happens to interact, (2) the availability of assistance when required, and (3) the equipment he or she uses, as well as other similar factors. These are common cause variations. By and large, an employee has no control over these factors. For example, if an employee has to share a computer terminal, he or she has no control over the waiting time while someone else is using it. This may affect the speed with which he or she serves customers. If a particular employee happens to deal with more customers with complicated requests, he or she may handle fewer customers compared with another employee who is exposed to more customers with simple requests. Variations of this type are said to be generated by the system within which an employee operates and over which employees have no control. If the speed with which an employee serves a customer is a performance measure, using the average time to serve a customer can be misleading. An efficient employee can be doing poorly on this performance measure because of factors that are beyond his or her control. The only way to effect an improvement in such cases is to pay attention to the system.

In contrast, people may vary in the way they perform a task, which may have little to do with the system within which they operate. Such variations have specific or assignable causes. For example, an employee may lack the skills required to do the job or may have received inadequate training. Variations that arise because of such assignable factors are called *special cause variations*. When the variation is identified as the result of special causes, it is not necessary to change the system but, instead, to pay attention to those causes that generate such variations and to help employees perform better.

> **Common cause variations are generated by the system. Employees have little control over them.**

Because these two kinds of variations call for different solutions, we need to identify the source of these variations. When we separate common cause variations from special cause variations, we can undertake suitable measures to reduce them and thus increase quality. As we have discussed,

> **Special cause variations are generated by causes that are specific and assignable.**

1. Common cause variations can be decreased by improving the system.

2. Tackling the identifiable causes that give rise to them can decrease special cause variations.

The importance of identifying common cause variations

A common mistake in evaluating people is to assume that a person's performance is related directly to his or her ability and efforts. As a result, many organizations are willing to reward or punish employees on the basis of scores achieved on some performance measure. However, such an approach ignores basic statistical principles, and, therefore, organizations may be rewarding or punishing employees at random. This is because not all differences in performance can be attributed to a person's ability and efforts. A large amount of variation in performance is generated by the system in which a person works. Many organizations ignore this important factor and treat all differences among employees as being generated by the employees themselves. Rewarding and punishing employees on this basis can, and often does, lower morale.

A great deal of variation found in any organization can be attributed to common causes, that is, to the system itself. It is not, as is commonly assumed, due to the ability and effort put forth by employees. It follows that exhorting employees to work harder or smarter to provide quality is not likely to improve quality—it can make it worse. Rewards and punishments do not have any effect on common causes. If common causes are the source of much of the variation, what is management to do?

The first priority of management intent on achieving consistent service is to identify how much of the variation can be attributed to common causes and how much to special causes. This can be accomplished by using simple statistical formulas. Common cause variations must be calculated statistically for each process and should not be decreed as some arbitrary figure. A policy statement that says "management will not tolerate more than a 10% deviation from the standard" is not very helpful (or even meaningful) if the common cause variation is 20% and employees are expected to operate within that system.

If the system is in a stable state (i.e., most employees are within control limits, which are discussed subsequently), it means that inconsistent performance leading to poor quality is the result of common causes and is a part of the system currently in place. Quality cannot be improved by any action that transfers the responsibility for service quality to the employees. Slogans, exhortations, rewards, and punishments may give an illusion of progress, but they will have no lasting effect on common cause variation. In such cases, the only element that can improve quality is management, because management, not the employees, is in control of the system.

Current management thinking, as Deming contends, is based on transferring the responsibility for quality from management (where it belongs) to employees (where it does not belong). Everyone "doing his or her best" will not result in superior service quality simply because most workers are already doing what they believe to be their best. What may be hindering them is the system that is already in place.

Considerable attention has been devoted to the performance of employees, but little attention has been paid to the causes that contribute to inconsistent service quality. Unless we understand the difference between common cause and special cause variations and act to reduce common cause variations, it is unrealistic to expect any improvement in service quality.

When common cause variations are treated as special cause variations
There is a general tendency to treat all variation from the standard as "arising out of special causes." What happens when management tries to fine-tune the employee's behavior, even though it is within the limits of common cause vari-

When we attempt to control quality when the performance measure is within control limits, the performance will deviate even more from the standard.

ations? The simple answer is that the variability in performance will increase. In other words, when management attempts to control quality when the performance measure is within control limits, the performance will deviate even more from the standard. The level of quality will go down.

The effects of tampering with a stable system

Let us consider complaint handling over the telephone. Assume that the average time for handling standard complaints in an organization is four minutes. The time range suggested by management for handling a complaint is between three and five minutes. The lower limit is to ensure that the customer does not feel rushed, and the upper limit is to ensure that complaints are handled as quickly as possible. Further assume that a particular employee takes an average of six minutes to handle a standard complaint. If management assumes that the extra two minutes over the company average indicates that the employee is a slow performer, then management is attributing all variations to the employee, whether he or she has any control over them or not. In this case, management may inform the employee to work more efficiently so that the average time does not exceed five minutes.

However, this is unlikely to produce the desired result, especially if the slow performance of the employee is due to common cause variations. When the variation is due to common causes, it simply means that the employee has no hand in his or her apparently slow performance. Within the system in which the employee operates, an average of six minutes is as likely to be produced by the system as, say, an average of two minutes. The variation between two employees with an average of two and six minutes may have nothing to with their ability or efficiency.

We assume the following for the sake of exposition. (We will see later how to calculate the two components of variations in performance.)

Average time to handle a complaint   4 minutes
Common cause variations: 4 ± 2 minutes

If this were the case, it would mean that as long as an employee takes anywhere between two (4 − 2) and six (4 + 2) minutes to handle a complaint, he or she is operating within the limits of the system. Nothing an employee does will result in better performance in the long run unless the system, as a whole, is improved.

Given this situation, what happens if employees are

warned to bring the time within the acceptable range whenever they go beyond this range? In broad terms, this is what happens:

The average for the system:	4 minutes
The variability of the system:	± 2 minutes (measured by statistical means)
Acceptable range:	± 1 minute (decreed by management)

Here, the acceptable range is lower than the variability in the system. As noted previously, the system, as it stands, can allow anywhere between two to six minutes to handle each complaint. Now, if Employee A takes six minutes to handle a complaint, he or she is asked to reduce it to five minutes. Because the average of four minutes in this case produces a value of six minutes as well, the only way to avoid taking six minutes is to bring down the overall average to, say, three minutes. Although the average time is now lowered, it carries with it the variability of ±2 minutes associated with the common cause. Now, Employee A will be producing results that range from one to five minutes (3 ± 2 minutes). If the employee is then asked not to dismiss a customer in one or two minutes, then he or she may move back to an average time of four minutes, once again generating some six-minute calls:

The range of the original system:	2 to 6 minutes
The range of the modified system:	1 to 5 minutes
The total range after modification:	1 to 6 minutes

As a result of tampering with the system, management has increased the range of complaint-handling time! In fact, constant adjustment to a stable system produces larger and larger variations. Tampering with a stable system, without changing it, results in higher variability and, consequently, in lower quality (see Exhibit 14.1).

Identifying common cause variations enables us to know whether the performance of an employee is within the range that is typical for the system. If it is, then we can concentrate our efforts on changing the system itself, rather than rewarding or punishing employees and thereby affecting quality adversely. Because the limits of variations cannot be set arbitrarily, common cause and special cause variations have to be specifically measured. Quality enhancement programs that ignore this measurement process stand a chance of creating a result that is completely opposite of what was desired.

When we identify the source of variation of a given level of performance, we will know where to look to improve employee performance. If the source of variation can be explained by common cause, then we will concentrate on

Exhibit 14.1
The Effect of Tampering with a Stable System

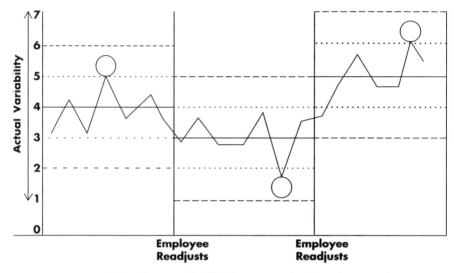

Employee Readjusts   **Employee Readjusts**

Note how variability increases (quality decreases) when we tamper with a stable system.

improving the system and attempt to make it more efficient. Conversely, if the source of variation cannot be explained by common cause, then we will concentrate on the individual (or other assignable causes) by focusing on the sources of deficiency, such as lack of training for the job, or tackling the sources of low morale.

CONTROL CHARTS

Control charts tell us whether a process (such as the performance of an employee) is on track or "within control." When a process is in control, it means that the performance of employees is within the expected range, given the system in which they are expected to operate. It implies that, as long as the process is in control, if we are to improve employee performance, we must change the system as a whole rather than the individual employee. When the control charts indicate that the process is "out of control," perhaps we must pay attention to individual employees whose performance

Control charts enable us to identify common cause and special cause variations.

falls beyond the control limits. In other words, when the performance is in control, the variations can be attributed to common causes, whereas when the performance is out of control, the variations are likely to be generated by special causes.

WHAT ARE CONTROL CHARTS?

Control charts are statistical charts used to monitor, control, and improve performance over time. They involve plotting performance figures on a graph and making a few minor statistical calculations to identify the lower and upper limits of common cause variations. By identifying the sources of variations correctly, control charts enable us to take appropriate action.

WHY USE CONTROL CHARTS?

Apart from the central benefit of enabling us to understand common cause and special cause variations, control charts help us monitor and identify variations and changes in performance over a period of time. (Control charts are, in fact, run charts with lower and upper control limits that define common cause variations.) Therefore, control charts can be viewed as an ongoing way of monitoring performance with regard to the delivery of service quality. In addition, these charts also can be used to spot ahead of time when the process gradually starts going out of control, so corrective action can be taken before the problem becomes serious.

HOW TO CONSTRUCT CONTROL CHARTS

There are several types of control charts, depending on the sample size and data used as input. For example, performance measures can be either attributes (such as the proportion of incorrect entries made by an employee) or variables (such as consumer satisfaction ratings). Although there are many types of control charts, two types—p-chart for percentages (or proportions) and XS-chart for continuous variables—are of particular interest to us. Because service quality data are usually based on large sample sizes (n > 50), we will not consider charts that are designed for small samples. Neither will we consider other special control charts that are of limited use in service quality and customer satisfaction measurement.

Control charts for percentages (counts data)

Consider an ongoing service quality study that is designed to track the billing errors of a utility company. Each month, a randomly selected sample of customers is asked whether it encountered any billing errors. This is a yes/no (attribute) type question that generates percentage figures. If, for the first month, 20.6% of the customers said they experienced billing problems, our defect rate is 20.6%. Data for 20 months are shown in Exhibit 14.2.

Exhibit 14.2
Data for a Control Chart

Month	No. of bills incorrect	No. of customers contacted	% defective
1	20	100	20.6
2	18	102	17.7
3	14	96	14.6
4	16	100	16.0
5	13	97	13.4
6	29	102	28.4
7	21	104	20.2
8	14	101	13.9
9	12	110	10.9
10	12	96	12.5
11	14	100	14.0
12	14	106	13.2
13	18	112	16.1
14	10	98	10.2
15	16	112	14.3
16	18	106	17.0
17	18	104	17.3
18	20	102	19.6
19	18	104	17.3
20	20	94	21.3
Total	335	2046	
Mean	16.8	102.3	

Note: p-charts are used for attribute-type (percentages) data.

To plot a control chart, we use the following steps:

Step 1. *Plot the proportion of data billing errors for each month.* The x-axis is time. Data for each month are plotted in sequence (20.6, 17.7, 14.6, and so on). (See Exhibit 14.3).

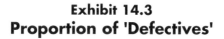

Exhibit 14.3
Proportion of 'Defectives'

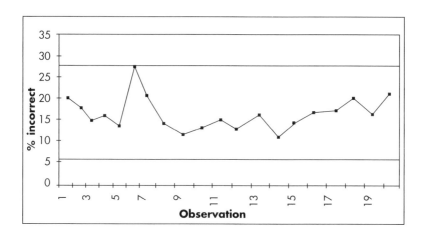

Step 2. Calculate the mean (P) of the series by dividing the total of all billing errors (defectives) by the number of observations.

P = Total defectives/Total number of observations
335 ÷ 2046 = 16.8%

Draw a line corresponding to this percentage. This is the center line around which we would expect the scores to fluctuate. (See Exhibit 14.4).

Exhibit 14.4
Proportion of 'Defectives' with the Mean Line

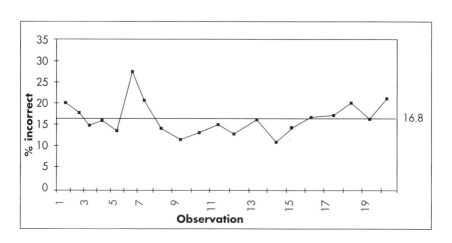

Step 3. *Calculate the control limit using the following formula:*

$$= 3 \sqrt{\frac{(100 - P)}{n}}$$

where n is the sample size. If the sample size varies from sample to sample (as it does in this case), use the average sample size, as long as the fluctuation in sample size is within reasonable limits (± 20%). If sample sizes are very different, more exact formulas must be used (see the reference at the end of this chapter).

$$= 3 \sqrt{\frac{16.8 \times 83.2}{102}} = 11.1$$

Step 4. *Set the lower and upper control limits using the following formulas* (see Exhibit 14.5):

LCL = (P − control limit) = (16.8 − 11.1) = 5.7
UCL = (P + control limit) = (16.8 + 11.1) = 27.9

Exhibit 14.5
Upper and Lower Control Limits

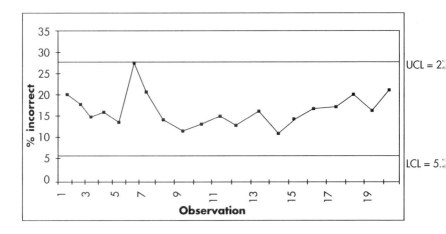

This means that as long the percentage of dissatisfied customers in any given month is between (approximately) 5.7% and 27.9%, the differences in performance cannot be attributed to any special cause. Thus, for instance, Month 16 cannot be considered as an improvement over Month 6, even though the billing errors dropped from 28.4% to 10.2%.

The control chart applied to our data suggests that all observations fall within the control limits. Because there is no evidence of special cause variations, asking employees to be more accurate (under the threat of punishment or the promise of rewards) is more likely to increase the variation in performance and make it worse than it was before. Therefore, if quality has to be improved, the system must be analyzed as a whole.

As we discussed previously, when the sources of variations are not understood and employees are rewarded or punished according to some predetermined performance measure, it is likely to increase variation in performance and result in lower, rather than higher, quality.

Control limits for variables (Continuous data)

In service quality research, data often are collected from a sample of customers. If a retail branch of an organization got an average satisfaction rating of 8.9 last year and 8.4 this year, should this be a cause of concern? Should rewards be given to another branch of the organization for which the average score went up from 8.4 to 8.9? In short, is the .5 difference entirely due to common cause variation, or should we look for special causes that might have contributed to the lower average rating?

The technique described in the previous section cannot be used to measure common cause and special cause variations in this context. To know if the average scores are under control or not, you should use what is known as the XS-chart (described here).

Suppose you are comparing the performance of 50 different branches of your organization in a region. Further suppose that the scores you are comparing are average customer satisfaction ratings, obtained through a survey of 100 customers for each branch. To obtain the LCL and UCL, follow these steps outlined:

Step 1. For each subgroup, calculate the mean and standard deviations.
Step 2. Calculate the mean of all means.
Step 3. Calculate the mean of all standard deviations.

Exhibit 14.6
Mean and Standard Deviations

Branch	Mean Rating	Standard Deviation	Sample Size (n)
1	8.7	2.1	100
2	7.9	3.1	101
3	8.5	3.6	98
...	...	...	
50	7.4	1.9	103
Grand Mean	**8.1**		
Mean SD		2.9	
Mean n			**100***

Note: Any spreadsheet or statistical program can compute mean and standard deviations.

* Mean sample size of 100 is used in these calculations because the sample sizes are close to 100. If the sample sizes vary widely from subgroup to subgroup (say, by 20%), then UCL and LCL have to be calculated individually for each subgroup.

Step 4. Calculate the UCL and LCL.

$$\text{UCL} = \bar{\bar{X}} + \frac{3}{\sqrt{n}} \times \overline{SD}$$

where $\bar{\bar{x}}$ = grand mean
$\overline{SD}$ = Average standard deviation

$$= 8.1 + \frac{3}{\sqrt{100}} \times 2.9 = 9.0$$

$$\text{LCL} = \bar{\bar{X}} - \frac{3}{\sqrt{n}} \times \overline{SD}$$

$$= 8.1 - \frac{3}{\sqrt{100}} \times 2.9 = 7.2$$

If the obtained mean for a branch is above 9.0 (the UCL), it means that there are special cause factors that contribute to the higher ratings. Conversely, if the obtained rating for a branch is below 7.2 (the LCL), there are special cause factors that contribute to the lower ratings. These calculations identify branches that are outside the control limits, either on the positive or on the negative side.

There also are formulas that identify standard deviations that are out of control:

$$\mathrm{UCL_{SD}} = 1 + \sqrt{\frac{3}{2\,(n-1)}} \times \overline{\mathrm{SD}}$$

$$= 1 + \frac{3}{\sqrt{2\,(102-1)}} \times 2.9 = 3.51$$

$$\mathrm{LCL_{SD}} = 1 - \sqrt{\frac{3}{2\,(n-1)}} \times \overline{\mathrm{SD}}$$

$$= 1 - \frac{3}{\sqrt{2\,(102-1)}} \times 2.9 = 2.29$$

This means that, as long as the standard deviation of any subgroup is between 2.29 and 3.51, the variability is under control. What does it mean if, for a subgroup, the mean is in control but the standard deviation is not? One possibility is that this subgroup could be offering a high level of service, but it may not be perceived in the same way by different groups of customers. There may be many reasons for this, including a segmented market such as varying levels of competence among employees.

These formulas apply only when the sample in each group is 30 or more. In the unlikely event that you are forced to work with a smaller sample, you should use a correction factor. (For details, consult the references at this end of the chapter.)

HOW TO INTERPRET CONTROL CHARTS

The basic interpretation of control charts is simple. As long as a process remains within the control limits, all variability is assumed to be due to common cause variations. When an observation falls outside this limit, we need to look more closely at the observation to determine the cause of the deviation. When the system is in a stable state, an observation outside the control limits likely is due to special causes.

If we are observing a phenomenon (such as performance) over a period of time, we need to watch for observations that fall outside the control limits. If, over a period of time, more and more observations start to fall outside these control limits, it also could mean that the system itself is becoming out of control (more variable and less efficient). Control charts also provide a number of insights into the process under observation, as illustrated in Exhibit 14.7.

- *Stability.* The process under observation is stable if all points are within the bounds, as defined by UCL and LCL. The process is in control.

Exhibit 14.7
Control Chart Patterns

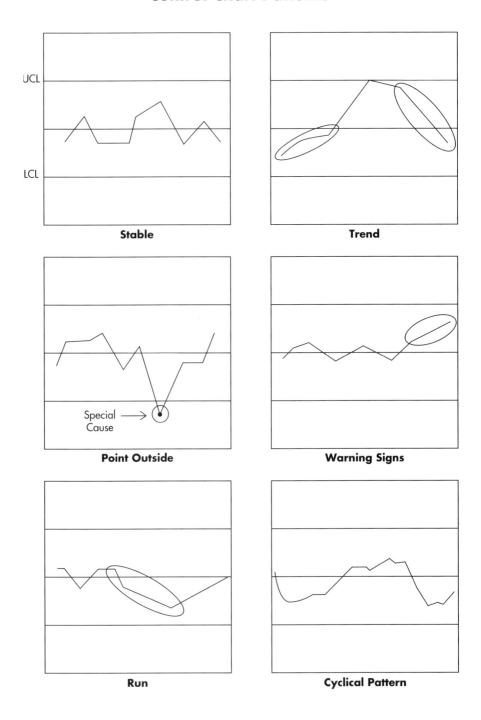

- *Instability*. When some observations lie outside these limits, then the process is unstable or out of control. This would point to special cause variations.

- *Warning signals*. When a number of successive observations lie above or below the mean, it is called a run. Even if these observations lie between LCL and UCL, runs should be watched closely because they might indicate the process is moving out of control.

- *Trends*. If the run continues to be strong (i.e., more and more successive observations continuously lie above or below the mean), it could mean that a trend is developing, either in a positive or a negative direction.

- *Cyclical patterns*. When patterns repeat themselves (e.g., the number of billing errors becoming higher during the beginning of the month rather than at the end of the month), we have cyclical patterns. A cyclical chart would point to a time-related extraneous factor, such as seasonality or workload.

Also note that, while dealing with percentage data, one chart is sufficient. However, when dealing with variables, we need control charts for means as well as for standard deviations.

Level of service

Once the variability is brought under control, it is relatively straightforward to improve the level. To control variability in a system requires an understanding of the factors that affect it. The knowledge that enabled us to control variability can be applied in order to improve the level. Let us consider the example of the customer service representative who is required to obtain the signature of a senior manager before processing a large transaction. Once we have eliminated variabilities due to special causes, then all the remaining variability can be attributed to common causes. Because common cause is inherent to the system, we attempt to act on the system. This might include increasing the dollar amount for which authorization is required or giving signing authority to more people in the organization. Such measures will decrease the variability. The level then can be increased by various means, such as adding more representatives during rush hours or having special counters for those with more complex transactions.

Many organizations fail to achieve quality because they

concentrate on level of service rather than on consistency of service. Yet, reducing variability is fundamental to improving quality. Corrective actions initiated as a result of misinterpreting variability can make the situation worse. In a vast number of cases, this can be achieved by manipulating the system rather than the employees. Measuring common cause variations using control charts is the first step toward achieving the goal of providing higher-quality service.

OTHER THINGS YOU SHOULD KNOW

Although creating control charts is not a difficult task, you must be prepared to encounter many practical problems. Some of these common problems include the following:

1. In setting control limits for percentage data, your lower control limit may turn out to be a negative number. If your data consist basically of counts, then negative numbers do not make sense. If this happens, treat 0 as the lower control limit.

2. In treating different subgroups (as in the case of evaluating the performance of different locations), we had assumed that the sample size is the same. If this is not the case, you may want to average out the sample sizes, as long as they are approximately the same (± 20%). If the sample sizes are too different, then more detailed calculations (one for each subgroup) may be needed.

3. If subgroups are not homogeneous, then the control limits are likely to be too broad. This means that the control chart will be less sensitive to changes. Whenever you suspect that subgroups are, in general, comparable, then you should stratify the subgroups and create separate control charts. For example, if you are creating control charts for waiting time, rural and urban outlets may be different enough to affect the control limits. In such cases, it might be preferable to treat urban and rural outlets as separate strata and analyze the data accordingly. If we do not do this, we may end up attributing most of the variations to common causes and fail to identify special causes.

If the process is in control, it does not follow that the service provided by the organization is satisfactory or even acceptable. All it means is that the service is consistent with what you would expect from the system as it exists now. This may have nothing to do with meeting the specification levels or customer requirements.

When an observation falls outside control limits, the causes should be identified. For example, on any given day, the average time to serve a customer may fall outside the control limits. Further investigation might identify the special cause to be a computer breakdown, leading to time-consuming manual operations. When a cause is identified, control limit calculations should be done as before. Recalculation of control limits is justified only when there is change in the process or the trend.

To know more

One highly recommended book on statistical process control is:

Wheeler, D.J. and D.S. Chambers (1992), *Understanding Statistical Process Control*. Knoxville, TN: SPC Press.

15

Detailing Techniques: People

P3D2: People and Detailing

	PRODUCERS	PROCESSES	PEOPLE
DIAGNOSING	Structural analysis Check sheets Mystery shopping Internal focus groups	Graphic techniques Run charts Stratification Flow charts	Complaint elicitation Content tracking Belief system analysis Pareto charts

DETAILING	Nominal group
	  technique
	Benchmarking
	Deleting
	  dimensionality
	The as-if frame
	The video camera
		Control charts	**External focus groups
			Survey research
			Laddering
			Factor analysis
			Gap analysis
			Wish lists**

DELIVERING	Brainstorming Force field analysis Cost-benefit analysis	Fishbone diagrams Process mapping and evaluation	Tracking

A s noted previously, service quality and customer satisfaction consist of any number of underlying dimensions or factors, depending on how they are derived. However, from a measurement perspective, the three-dimensional model mentioned in Chapter 5 appears appropriate.[1] Each dimension calls for a different set of techniques; the use of techniques that are inappropriate for a dimension can result in misleading interpretations.

- The first dimension of quality is the product or service itself. It is difficult to offer high quality if the underlying product or service itself is shoddy.

---

[1] The three-dimensional model is loosely based on a number of factor-analytic studies I carried out for a variety of clients in the service quality area. I have adopted this model here for its relevance to measurement techniques rather than for theoretical reasons.

- The second dimension of quality is dependability. This includes all soft attributes of service (e.g., friendliness, courtesy), as well as after-sales service. Offering excellent service to past customers, even when it is more lucrative to cater to new customers, is part of this dimension.

- The third dimension of quality is exceeding expectations. This dimension consists of those aspects of service that customers would not complain about if they did not receive them.

Exhibit 15.1
The Three Dimensions of Quality

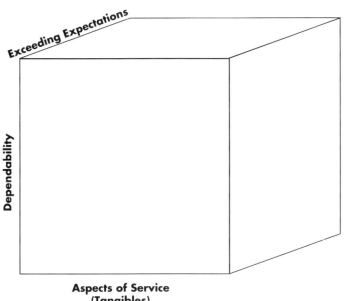

The bulk of customer satisfaction research involves measurement of these three dimensions. Each of these can use either qualitative or quantitative (or both) research techniques. For each dimension, we describe one qualitative and one quantitative technique.

MEASURING THE FIRST DIMENSION: ASPECTS OF THE PRODUCT OR SERVICE

The first dimension of service deals with aspects of the product or service. Does the product or service deliver all it is supposed to? If a hospital aims to admit patients within 30 minutes of their arrival, does it really achieve this objective? If a brokerage firm claims that its statements are easy to understand, do customers really agree?

Researching the first dimension is relatively straightforward. The research here is similar to researching a tangible product. Although each service poses its own methodological problems, in most cases, general research methodology used for products can be modified to suit service research as well.

Some examples of the first dimension

- **A clearly itemized statement**
- **Answering the phone before the third ring**
- **More personnel at peak times**
- **Not passing the customer to another service representative more than once**
- **Extending customer service hours**

The importance of the first dimension

Can a product or service survive, and even be successful, if its concept of quality is confined to the first dimension? The answer is a qualified yes. A product or service can survive, and even be successful, if it adequately fulfills the requirements of the first dimension, provided it is in a monopolistic market or in a market where demand exceeds supply. Many successful products of the past were developed in an environment of limited competition. Even when they delivered only those attributes associated with the first dimension, these products were enormously successful.

However, service that is satisfactory on the first dimension, but not on the second and third dimensions, is vulnerable to the emergence of new competitors. It also is vulnerable to substitute products. The first dimension is a necessary, but not a sufficient, condition of any service quality program. Soft dimensions of quality, such as dependability and exceeding expectations, have little meaning if the product does not deliver on hard dimensions.

Standard research techniques are adequate

Run-of-the-mill sample surveys, panel data, and standard focus groups usually are adequate to measure the first dimension of service quality. As mentioned previously, some aspects of the first dimension can be improved, even without specific reference to customers. Although the techniques of measuring the first dimension are the same as the ones used for product research, there are differences. For example, the scale used to measure service attributes appears to affect the results attained. For this reason, this aspect of service quality research will be explored in greater detail subsequently.

The next two sections describe the two most important techniques in measuring the first dimension:

- External focus groups (qualitative).
- Survey research (quantitative).

EXTERNAL FOCUS GROUPS

At this stage, we turn our focus to our customers. The objective is to measure customer satisfaction and expectations. A well-designed quantitative study is well-suited to this purpose. However, it may not always be advisable to launch a *quantitative* study without adequate exploratory work. Although we already might have done some exploratory work, we may still want to (1) explore further the expectations of our customers and noncustomers, (2) ensure that the proposed study is based on input from customers and noncustomers, and (3) ensure that the proposed study will include all major items that are of concern to customers and potential customers. External focus groups, or focus groups with our customers and/or noncustomers, are commonly carried out at this stage.

When we have no knowledge of where we stand and do not know where to begin, we may want to start with loosely structured discussions. The focus group is a good technique for this purpose. Focus groups provide an unstructured environment in which to clarify our thoughts on problems and possible solutions. Another context in which focus groups are useful is when people are reluctant or unable to offer their views in response to a pointed question (as in a quantitative questionnaire). For example, most consumers will find it difficult to articulate what service quality means to them, if they are simply asked a question. On the other hand, they might go to great lengths to explain the meaning of service quality in a focus group context. As we discussed in Chapter 8, focus groups do not necessarily lead to answers. Sometimes they can even mislead. However, focus groups are an excellent exploratory technique. They also are useful when the topic to be explored is complex or sensitive. External focus groups are similar to internal focus groups, both in structure and function.

HOW ARE THEY CONDUCTED?

External focus groups involve bringing together a small group of people (about 8 to 12), with a moderator who leads and guides the discussion. As with internal focus groups, the moderator is a trained professional in the art of group dynamics who ensures that everyone has an opportunity to contribute to the discussion and that no one individual dominates the group. The group discussion generally lasts between one and two hours, though other time frames are possible. The discussion is essentially unstructured. However, the moderator usually has a discussion outline that defines the areas of importance that must be covered.

External focus groups involve discussion of a specific topic among a small group of customers and noncustomers, with a moderator leading and guiding the discussion.

The participants may be users of a service, nonusers of a service, or even lapsed users. The groups are usually homogeneous, except in cases in which a group is structured deliberately to be otherwise. Where there are several distinct customer segments, the usual practice is to carry out several focus groups to cover these segments.

The objectives of external focus groups can be, for example,

- What customers' wants and needs are with regard to our services,

- How noncustomers perceive our services,

- What ideas employees have about improving service quality,

- Why noncustomers do not use our product or service,

- What attributes customers believe are critical and why, and

- What criticisms customers have with regard to our service.

A variation of this technique is to use one person at a time. This technique is known as the individual depth interview. Individual depth interviews are more expensive, because each person has to be interviewed separately. Depth interviews are useful when the issues are highly sensitive or we have reason to believe that participants are likely to be influenced unduly by the views held by other participants in a focus group.

External focus groups also can be used to test the clarity and adequacy of a proposed questionnaire to be used in a quantitative study. Focus groups are useful when we want to understand the breadth and depth of opinions held by the target groups. They are less useful and can be misleading, however, when used as a tool of quantitative measurement.

HOW TO INTERPRET THE RESULTS

By far, the most common way of interpreting the results is for the moderator to review the audio/videotape of the focus group interview and interpret the discussion in light of his or her experience. However, more formal methods of analysis, such as content analysis and neural networks, have received a greater amount of attention in recent years.

Focus group interviews are subject to several distortions. The competence of the moderator can be an issue. This is because, unlike in quantitative research, where skills such as sampling techniques, questionnaire design principles, and analytic techniques can be defined and taught, in qualitative research, the skills of a moderator are less clearly defined. A poorly trained moderator may unwittingly allow his or her views to influence those of the participants, permit a few participants to dominate the discussion, fail to probe when it is essential, or probe when it may be unwarranted.

Focus group discussions are interpreted by the moderator. Some formal techniques such as content analysis and neural networks also are used in interpreting the results.

Another factor that may distort focus groups is the way the respondents are chosen. Although focus groups are not expected to be completely representative of the population, they are not expected to be unrepresentative of the population either. If the participants hold views that are not common among the target audience, this may skew the findings.

Although focus groups are good at providing insights into customer thinking, the strength with which opinions are expressed can be a function of the group itself. In many cases, opinions expressed by focus group participants must be quantified through quantitative techniques.

In customer satisfaction and service quality research, focus groups can be of immense value in exploring customer grievances and identifying the factors that lead to satisfaction. However, this must be balanced with overemphasizing the views held by only a minority of our customers at the risk of ignoring the views of the vast majority. So it is almost always advisable to confirm the findings of focus group discussions by a well-designed quantitative study.

To know more

Some recent books on focus groups include the following:
Schwarz, R.M. (1994), *The Skilled Facilitator.* San Francisco: Jossey-Bass.
Templeton, J.F. (1994), *The Focus Group.* Chicago: Probus Publishing.

SURVEY RESEARCH

The results of the focus group cannot be generalized to the population from which the group is drawn. To do this, we need to carry out a quantitative study. A typical quantitative study involves survey research. Survey research involves interviewing a representative sample of our target audience to assess what we need to know. Thus, survey research can be performed on a sample of our customers to assess their satisfaction level. Survey research varies in its level of sophistication, depending on the study objectives and the resources available. A survey typically uses a set questionnaire.

A properly conducted survey enables us to make quantitative statements, such as "83% of our customers are happy with our counter service. This estimate has a margin of error of ±3% at the 95% confidence level." Such quantitative statements cannot be made on the basis of qualitative techniques such as focus groups.

HOW TO CARRY OUT SURVEY RESEARCH

Survey research is carried out generally by marketing research firms that specialize in and have resources to carry out research studies. Survey research can be fairly complex. Therefore, what follows is merely a bare outline of what is involved. Briefly, a properly conducted survey should follow the steps outlined here.

Step 1. Define the objectives of the project.
For example, your study objectives could be

- to assess the extent of customer satisfaction with your services,

- to assess the reasons for dissatisfaction when it exists, and

- to evaluate how your organization compares with others in the field.

Step 2. Define the target audience. For example, you might define your target group as your current and former customers.

Step 3. Decide on the length of the interview and how it will be conducted (in person, by mail, or by telephone). The length of the interview is determined usually by research needs, respondents' ability and willingness to answer, and the resources available. For example,

- Respondents will be contacted by phone.

- The survey will be 20 minutes in duration.

Step 4. Set the sample size. Sample size will depend on the level of accuracy needed, as well as the resources available. For example,

- The sample size will be 400 current customers and 400 former customers.
- This will have a margin of error of ±5% in each group.

Step 5. *Define a procedure for selecting the sample.* The results are generalizable only if the sample is chosen according to certain statistical principles. For example,

- We will stratify our customers as large and small, depending on the size of their purchase. We will sample 200 of each for each category.

Step 6. *Write a questionnaire that is suitable for the nature of the survey.* For example, a mail survey questionnaire will be structured differently from a telephone interview. The questionnaire should be of the right length in terms of the time it takes to administer (see Step 3).

- If you use a research firm, this function usually will be carried out by them, in consultation with you.

Step 7. *Administer the questionnaire.* Tabulate the results. These functions also will be carried out by the research firm.

Step 8. *Interpret the findings.* Survey results should be interpreted in terms of the objectives of the study. For example, one of our objectives (see Step 1) is "to assess the reasons for dissatisfaction when it exists." Consequently, interpretation of the findings would elaborate on matters such as the proportion of customers that are dissatisfied, the demographic groups that are highly dissatisfied, and the reasons for their dissatisfaction. The respondents for a survey can be current customers, lapsed customers, noncustomers, or any combination thereof. The field of survey research is fairly wide, and there are any number of marketing research books that describe the procedures involved.

How to carry out survey research

1. Define the project's objectives.
2. Define the target audience.
3. Decide on the length and type of interview.
4. Set the sample size.
5. Define the sample selection procedures.
6. Write the questionnaire.
7. Administer and tabulate the findings of the questionnaire.
8. Interpret the findings.

To know more

Survey research requires specialized knowledge. Most surveys are carried out by firms specializing in survey research. If you are not familiar with survey research procedures and would like to have more familiarity with these techniques, you may wish to read the following books:

Alreck, P.L. and R.B. Settle (1995), *The Survey Research Handbook*, 2d ed. Homewood, IL: Richard D. Irwin.

Chakrapani, C. and K. Deal (1993), *Marketing Research*. Scarborough, ON: Prentice-Hall Canada.

Fowler, Floyd J. (1993), *Survey Research Methods*, 2d ed. Newbury Park, CA: Sage Publications.

MEASURING THE SECOND DIMENSION: DEPENDABILITY

The second dimension—*dependability*—refers to attributes that are intangible, such as courtesy, trust, likeability, and after-sales service. It goes over and above the objective qualities of the product or service and deals with the way the customer is treated. This dimension covers a time frame that starts before a customer buys anything and extends beyond the purchase of the product or service. A broad range of attributes—attributes that are related to making the customer feel wanted from the beginning of a transaction to after-sales service—make up this dimension. This dimension can be the reason why people prefer to deal with one organization rather than another, even if the products and services offered by the two are comparable.

Whereas the first dimension of service (aspects of service) deals with tangible aspects, the second dimension is essentially an abstraction. It is a generalization made by the customer on the basis of what he or she observes. Consequently, measuring the second dimension poses some challenges.

The unitary nature of quality

When we deal with soft attributes of the second dimension, we essentially deal with abstract factors such as courtesy or politeness. Even though courtesy comprises such attributes as the employee smiling at the customer, being polite, and taking time to listen, it is essentially an abstraction. As a consequence, an employee may smile and be polite; yet it can be perceived as discourteous if the customer believes he or she is being rushed. The fact that the employee fulfilled most attributes associated with courtesy does not necessarily count. The evaluation is an abstraction and not an additive judgment. To be judged as courteous, an employee may have to deliver on all attributes related to a factor rather than on just some of them. So the challenge of research is to identify all underlying attributes related to any given factor.

These observations do not apply to the first dimension, which deals with the tangible attributes of a product or service. A bank that has convenient hours will be so perceived, no matter what other attributes it may or may not have. The attribute of longer hours (unlike the attribute of politeness) is not an abstraction but a measurable fact. Measuring the attributes that make up the second dimension should therefore take into account the unitary nature of the factors that make up the second dimension. Therefore, what we need is a system of measurement that treats related aspects of service as interconnected. The system of measurement essentially should recognize that the whole is not a sum of its parts.

Research techniques

The second dimension requires that the research and analysis be set up in such a way that they identify interrelated attributes. Two techniques are particularly well-suited to this purpose:

- *Laddering*, or a similar technique to identify basic motivations. Laddering can be used as a complement to factor analysis (qualitative).

- *Factor analysis* of attributes to identify the underlying factors (quantitative).

LADDERING

Suppose your average bank balance over a period of several years is $10,000. Then, one day you write a check that is $1 more than the amount you have in the bank, and the bank dishonors the check. What would your reaction be? The bank may explain to you that you did not have enough money to cover the check; that you had signed a contract stating that the bank has the right to dishonor your check when you do not have sufficient funds in your account. The bank has acted within the terms of the agreement. If you are like most people, however, you will be offended by the bank's action. You probably would say, "The bank could have at least called me." Most customers in such situations are likely to feel humiliated and upset. This is because service interactions mean more to customers than the transactions themselves. If a check has been rejected, it could mean any of the following to the customer:

- "You are not good for the money."
- "You are not important enough to be called before the check is rejected."
- "If you cannot manage your financial affairs, it's your problem."
- "You broke the rules. You face the consequences."

Thus, a rejected check is not just a rejected check. It could be a challenge to a customer's self-esteem, a threat to a sense of belonging that a customer may have felt in relation to the bank, or a challenge to the customer's self-worth. The apparent values that are offended are the means values; the ultimate values that are offended are the ends values.

Means and ends values

In service quality research, it is important to understand the ends values. Ends values refer to the underlying factors that give rise to a person's behavior in a given situation. Understanding ends values enables us to change service quality organically and in a logically consistent fashion. We need to understand the "more personal reasons why important attributes are important" (Reynolds, Cockle, and Rochon 1990).[2]

The technique that is particularly well-suited to elicit ends values is called *laddering*. According to the theory behind laddering, attributes of a product or service are not ends in themselves. Rather, the attributes of a product or service provide the means. The question is, What are the ends that a consumer is seeking to achieve through these attributes? We should not settle for the first reason given when the customer talks about service. Thus, laddering explores the underlying motives, or the ends.

HOW IS LADDERING CARRIED OUT?

Laddering is basically a qualitative research technique, even though quantitative analysis can be applied to the data collected. The interview procedures for laddering is similar to those conducted for focus groups or individual depth interviews. The main feature of the laddering technique is that the respondent is probed with one single objective in mind—identifying the ends value.

Laddering uses a variety of qualitative research techniques to probe individual customers in order to go beyond the surface (means) values to the underlying (ends) values.

In a typical session, the respondent is probed until he or she comes up with an ends value. Such probing leads the participant from surface attitudes to consequences to ends values (called the A-C-V

---

[2] Reynolds, T., B. Cockle, and J. Rochon (1990), "The Strategic Imperatives of Advertising: Implications of Means-End Theory and Research Findings," *Canadian Journal of Marketing Research*, 9, 3–13.

model). The moderator probes the respondent until ends values are arrived at, as the following example shows:

I like this bank's service.	(A–Attitude)
What do you like about the service?	
The employees know me by name.	(C–Consequence)
What is important about that?	
It makes me feel that I am known to the bank.	(C–Consequence)
Why is that important?	
It makes me feel important.	(C–Consequence)
So ...?	
I feel that I am treated with respect and feel good about myself.	(V–Value)

In this example, the interviewer has led the participants from an attitude to various consequences to an ends value (self-esteem). In actual practice, there may be several layers of consequences before ends values are reached.

HOW TO INTERPRET THE RESULTS

The data thus collected are analyzed using several techniques. Standard analysis results in a visual display of results, such as tables and charts.

Step 1. *Content analysis.* This involves going through the interview transcripts and identifying attributes, values, and consequences. An example is given in Exhibit 15.2.

Step 2. *Constructing the implications matrix.* In this step, the analyst constructs a matrix that shows how frequently each construct (be it an attribute, consequence, or value) is associated with every other construct (this looks like a correlation matrix). This matrix shows how each element leads to every other element. When the relationships are to adjacent elements, they are called direct relationships; when the relationships are to nonadjacent elements, they are called indirect relationships. Both relationships are represented in the matrix.

Step 3. *Constructing the hierarchical value map.* This is a visual representation of the implications matrix. It is a typical hierarchical map that shows how attributes, consequences, and values are related (see Exhibit 15.3).

Step 4. *Determining the dominant perceptual orientations.* In this step, the analyst tries to understand the pathways that lead to the top from the bottom (see hierarchical map). A formal numeric table that explains the dominant perceptual ori-

Exhibit 15.2
Laddering for a Financial Institution: Values, Consequences, and Attributes

Values	Consequences	Attributes
20. Success	8. Matches my needs	1. Less paperwork
21. Respect	9. Good advice	2. "They know me"
22. Belonging	10. Cheerful	3. Knowledgeable staff
23. Self-esteem	11. Efficient	4. Reasonable fees
		5. Clean environment
		6. Extended hours
		7. Flexible
		12. Avoids problems
		13. Courteous
		14. Brief waiting
		15. Waiting less unpleasant
		16. Easy to deal with
		17. Do not have to rush
		18. Impress others
		19. Socialize

entations can be created at this stage. These dominant perceptual orientations provide a basis for the marketer to tackle the service quality needs of customers. For instance, every aspect of current and proposed services can be assessed in terms of ends values. This tells us how a service—either by itself or by the manner in which it is delivered—fulfills ends needs and to what extent it does so.

WHEN TO USE LADDERING

Laddering can be used whenever we need to understand the real motives behind customers' actions. Laddering is particularly useful when nebulous concepts, such as "exceptional service," must be understood within business contexts. Although laddering clarifies the concepts being explored, it does not operationalize them.

Laddering can be used when we need an overall framework and a broader basis for understanding customer needs. Such understanding of customers serves two purposes. First, the overall framework lets us evaluate customer service from a global perspective. For example, if a bank knows that a bounced check threatens a long-term client's self-esteem, it may think of ways to prevent such a situation from arising as a part of its service strategy. Second, the broader basis for understanding and fulfilling customer needs provided by the technique enables the marketer to ask a different set of questions. For example, instead of asking what services the bank can provide to its

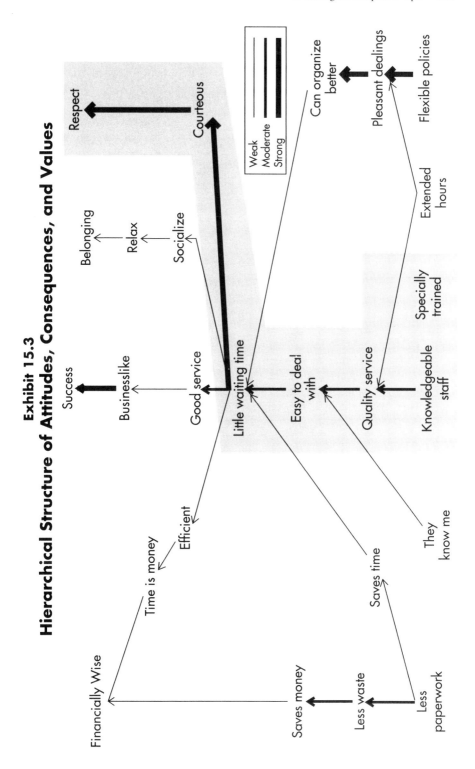

Exhibit 15.3

Hierarchical Structure of Attitudes, Consequences, and Values

customers, the marketer might ask, "Among the several services we can offer, which one will cater to our customers' self-esteem (or any other ends value)?" Therefore, whenever we must understand the values behind the needs of customers, we can use laddering. Although the laddering technique may not solve all service quality research problems, it provides a basis for evaluating the current status of service quality as well as a framework for improving it. It also provides a foundation for offering other services that are likely to be successful because they are in line with customer needs.

To know more

Reynolds, T.J., B.C. Cockle, and J.P. Rochon (1990), "The Strategic Imperatives of Advertising: Implications of Means-end Theory and Research Findings," *Canadian Journal of Marketing Research*, 9, 3–13.

———— and J. Gutman (1988), "Laddering Theory, Method, Analysis and Interpretation," *Journal of Advertising Research*, 28 (March), 11–31.

FACTOR ANALYSIS

Factor analysis is a technique that can be used to identify attributes that are related. A factor may be thought of as a collection of related attributes. For example, when a consumer thinks of a car's performance, he or she might think of its speed, its acceleration, its ability to handle different road conditions, the ease with which it corners turns, and so on. In this case, performance is a factor, and speed and acceleration are attributes that compose the factor. In product research, factor analysis is used for data reduction. Factor analysis provides the marketer and researcher with a compact way to describe and understand product attributes. It can be used for the same purpose in service quality research as well. However, its uses can be even more critical in service quality, as it relates to customer satisfaction.

We can hypothesize that the halo effect is less pronounced in tangible rather than in intangible attribute evaluation. For example, a customer is likely to identify that a car has moderate acceleration, although, once accelerated, it can reach a high speed. Even though both these attributes (moderate acceleration and high speed) may be related to high performance, the customers are likely to differentiate the two attributes clearly—they may evaluate the car as providing high performance except for its acceleration. On the other hand, when we consider intangibles such as courteous service, the situation can be different. An employee who smiles and is polite may not be perceived as courteous if, for example, he or she does not look at the customer while the customer is talking. It would appear that, when we deal with tangibles, a factor is an aggregation of related attributes; when we deal with intangibles, attributes are evidence of the existence of a factor. A car that does not accelerate quickly but delivers other attributes associated with performance is not "faking" performance, whereas an employee who talks politely but does not look at the customer could be faking courteous behavior. When an attribute belonging to a factor is not delivered, it may be construed that, in effect, all attributes belonging to that factor are not delivered. If we accept this hypothesis, then it would follow that, where intangibles are concerned, we should attempt to deliver all attributes that constitute a factor.

WHAT IS FACTOR ANALYSIS?

Factor analysis is a technique for grouping variables that are similar. For example, a questionnaire may contain customer satisfaction ratings on 20 different attributes. Some of these attributes may be correlated. (Attributes A and B are considered correlated if people who rate a product high on attribute A also rate it high on attribute B, and those who rate the product low on attribute A also rate it low on attribute B.) For example, if customers who rate a firm high on courteous service also rate it high on competent service, then these attributes are said to be positively correlated. In some cases, the correlation can be negative. This happens when customers who rate the firm high on one attribute, such as high prices, rate the firm low on another attribute, such as *a firm I would like to do business with.*

When many measures used in our survey are interrelated, they may be a reflection of a smaller number of underlying dimensions. Factor analysis identifies variables that are interrelated and reduces them to a smaller number of underlying dimensions called *factors.*

HOW TO CARRY OUT FACTOR ANALYSIS

In a typical exercise involving factor analysis, customers may be asked to rate a company or a service on a number of attributes. Each attribute is then correlated with every other attribute to identify the structure of the underlying relationships. The correlations (or covariance) thus derived are analyzed using factor analysis. The resultant output shows the attributes that are highly correlated with each factor. Generally speaking, attributes that are loaded highly on a factor will exhibit some commonality. The researcher then can name the factor, depending on the common theme.

How to Interpret the Findings

We can illustrate the interpretation of the findings through an example. In this example, consumers rated the importance of several attributes with regard to an organization's service. The attribute ratings were subjected to factor analysis (see Exhibit 15.4):

Exhibit 15.4
Factor Loadings

	Factor I	Factor II	Factor III
Work done correctly	.8	.1	.2
Technician courteous	.9	.0	.1
Employees always willing to help	.7	.3	.3
Manager trustworthy	.7	.3	.0
Takes time to explain	.6	.4	.3
Handles nonroutine requests	.9	.0	.1
Sales staff courteous	.8	.1	.3
Reasonable waiting time	.3	.9	.3
Waiting area comfortable	.1	.7	.1
Location convenient	.0	.8	.4
Clearly itemized invoices	.4	.1	.6
Technician competent	.3	.1	.7
Good credit	.1	.1	.8
Work done on time	.1	.2	.6
Convenient hours	.2	.1	.9
Knowledgeable service personnel	.1	.1	.6
Manager trustworthy	.2	.1	.6
Bill too high	.1	.2	.6
Waiting area comfortable	.1	.2	.5
Counter staff courteous	.3	.2	.6
Location inconvenient	.1	.1	.7
Technician competent	.2	.3	.6
Good credit	.1	.4	.6
Convenient hours	.3	.2	.6
Provided prompt attention	.1	.2	.7

Looking at the factor loadings (correlation between a factor and each variable), within each factor we see that the attributes indeed are logically grouped and can be named accordingly (namely, dependability, convenience, and functionality). Naming the factors is done by inspecting the attributes that constitute each factor. Each factor then can be used as the basis for quality enhancement. After identifying these factors, we may want to improve our performance on the factor; if we want to be perceived to be dependable, we may want to deliver on all aspects that constitute dependability.

When we complete a factor analysis, factors can replace the variables. Suppose we carry out factor analysis on 30 variables and arrive at five factors. Then we can replace 30 original ratings by five-factor scores for each respondent. These factor scores can be used as input for further analysis of data.

Exhibit 15.5
Attributes and Factors

Attribute	*Factor*
Work done correctly	**Dependability**
Technician courteous	
Employees always willing to help	
Manager trustworthy	
Takes time to explain	
Handles nonroutine requests	
Sales staff courteous	
Reasonable waiting time	**Convenience**
Waiting area comfortable	
Location convenient	
Clearly itemized invoices	**Functionality**
Technician competent	
Good credit	
Work done on time	
Convenient hours	
Knowledgeable service personnel	
Manager trustworthy	
Bill too high	
Waiting area comfortable	
Counter staff courteous	
Location inconvenient	
Technician competent	
Good credit	
Convenient hours	
Provided prompt attention	

Factor analysis identified three underlying factors and produced the following factor loadings, correlations
between a factor and the attributes. The loadings
help us identify the factors.

Factor analysis can be used whenever we need to understand how different attributes are interrelated in the minds of the consumer.

Factor analysis also has several limitations, such
as the following:

1. When the underlying relationships are not
   strong, the factors produced by factor analysis may not be stable.

2. The way the factors are named can distort the way
   the data are interpreted.

3. Sometimes different factor-analytic procedures may
   produce different results.

To know more

Klein, P. (1996), *An Easy Guide to Factor Analysis*. London:
Routledge.

MEASURING THE THIRD DIMENSION: EXCEEDING EXPECTATIONS

Researching the third dimension—exceeding expectations—
is probably the most difficult of all. But this dimension can
contribute substantially to the perception of quality. Exceeding expectations has two meanings. We can exceed expectations in a quantitative sense. For example, if we expect that
we will be served in 15 minutes, and we are served in just 10,
then the service has exceeded our expectations. Our expectations also can be exceeded in a qualitative sense. For
example, the president of a company can telephone a customer to find out more about his or her recent complaint.
The third dimension of quality deals with exceeding expectations in a qualitative sense rather than in a quantitative
sense.

Measuring expectations from a qualitative point of view
poses special challenges:

- How do we know what customer expectations are?
- How do we know how we can exceed such expectations?
- How can we track the extent to which we have
  exceeded expectations?

Obviously, we cannot ask the customer what it is that he or
she is not expecting so that we can provide it. We need spe-

cial techniques to elicit ideas about tasks, which, if carried out, will result in our exceeding customer expectations.

Research techniques

There are many creative techniques that can be used to identify the attributes that will help us exceed customer expectations. We discuss two of these techniques here:

- Wish lists (qualitative).
- Gap analysis (quantitative).

WISH LISTS

There are two reasons why customers cannot tell us what their expectations are:

1. Customers themselves are not aware of their expectations.

2. Customers are more likely to know about what they are not getting than to be able to express what exactly they expect in a given situation.

Yet, if we are to exceed expectations in the qualitative sense and deliver something that the customer is not expecting, we must identify the needs of which customers themselves are not aware.

Focus groups tend to be used for this purpose. However, standard focus groups are not structured to find out what customers are not expecting to get. In most focus groups, the initial part of the discussion is used to set the stage and create rapport. Focus group discussions of service tends to revolve around what customers currently get and what they would like ideally in the future. Unfortunately, this approach limits what the participants will say about what they would like in the future. Perception of what would be good to have is often limited by what is perceived to be reasonable. Thus, a customer will not talk about longer banking hours if he or she perceives that it is not reasonable to expect the bank to offer longer hours.

A wish list can be considered as a variation of a focus group. From an operational point of view, it is a focus group. We simply alter the structure and content to concentrate on a single theme—what the customer would like if there were no restrictions—the wish list technique. The whole discussion here revolves around the following basic question:

"If there were no limitations, if you could have whatever you want, and if everything were possible, what would you expect from your (bank/hospital/airline ...)?"

By not having any other objective—by not giving any other framework that may indirectly limit what might be possible—we increase the chances of eliciting benefits that customers would not mention normally, even in a standard focus group.[3]

The wish list technique explores, usually in a focus group setting, what the customer would like if there were no restrictions.

Wish lists are useful when our aim is to explore a means of providing exceptional service, going beyond using reactive approaches such as gap analysis. A wish list is a proactive technique that attempts to go beyond the expressed needs of customers and to understand the normally unexpressed needs, needs of which even customers are not clearly aware. As mentioned previously, a considerable amount of creativity may be needed to identify the wishes that are capable of being translated into an action plan.

A typical group that is based on the wish list approach could produce between 100 and 300 benefits. Participants usually start with reasonable benefits. However, as the moderator starts writing these benefits on flip charts, participants come up with more and more benefits that are far removed from the current business context. These are perhaps the most valuable part of the wish list and normally cannot be identified using quantitative techniques.

HOW TO INTERPRET THE FINDINGS

What we look for in wish lists are opportunities to create service that exceeds expectations. Wish lists are not likely to lead to direct action, but they may point to new directions. For example, the wish list generated by Coastline Hotels contained the wish:

"When I travel, I wish I could move around without care, rain or shine."

Although the hotel was in no position to control the weather, it started providing disposable raincoats and umbrellas to its guests. Judging from the guest comment cards, this gesture was appreciated, because the hotel was

---

[3] Although this sounds like a minor variation of the standard focus group technique, results that we get using this approach tend to be considerably different from the ones we get using standard focus groups.

located in a frequently rainy city. Two things are worth noting: First, it is unlikely that customers would have specifically suggested that the hotels provide umbrellas or disposable raincoats because this is not a standard practice for hotels. Second, the wish was not phrased in a way suggesting what the hotel should do, but what the customer ideally wanted. Most unexpected benefits are phrased this way. It is for us to assess whether the benefits sought by customers can be translated in some way and operationalized into an action plan.

Many of these wishes cannot be implemented or even operationalized. However, such discussions tend to produce some good ideas. Creative thinking can help us translate what may appear to be a farfetched idea into a concrete action plan.

OTHER THINGS YOU SHOULD KNOW

There are at least three reasons why these "wish list" groups work:

1. The absence of other objectives and related discussion focuses respondents' attention firmly on the benefits—real and imaginary.

2. The process that concentrates on quantity discourages participants from embellishing their choices with reasonable explanations.

3. The process of writing their responses on flip charts without comment or criticism—either from the moderator or the other members of the group—encourages the participants to come up with new ideas. They are not likely to come up with these ideas in standard focus group situations, in which the moderator or other participants can potentially comment favorably or unfavorably on the ideas generated.

Many focus groups incorporate the process of wish lists into their discussion. However, for the reasons mentioned here, it is better to use focus groups exclusively devoted to the wish list idea.

To know more

The skills required to carry out a wish list technique are similar to the ones required to carry out a standard focus group or a brainstorming session. No specific published references are available for this technique.

GAP ANALYSIS

Service quality programs do not always produce the expected results. There are several reasons for this. The most important is the difference between what customer expectations are and what management delivers. Despite its best intentions and effort, management may fail to deliver what the customer wants or expects. Gap analysis is a set of techniques that identifies the difference between what is achieved and what needs to be achieved. These differences occur at different points in the system. The following are some common gaps (Parasuraman, Zeithaml, and Berry 1985).

Service quality gap. The gap between what customers expect and what they perceive they are getting. For example, customers may expect to be served within 15 minutes when they go to a retail location, but they may perceive the average service time to be close to 30 minutes. (See Exhibit 15.6.)

Understanding gap. The gap between customer expectations and management's perception of customer expectations. For example, management might think that "efficient service" means that customers have to be served promptly, whereas customers could interpret it to mean "knowledgeable service."

Design gap. The gap between management's perception of what the customer expects and the translation of this perception into service standards. For example, when customers complain that they do not have enough time to pay their bills, they could mean that they need at least two weeks to pay. Management might interpret "enough time to pay the bills" to mean one week's lead time. So, although management may be under the impression that it has made progress in terms of customer expectations, customers themselves may not think so.

Some common gaps
1. **Service quality gap**
2. **Understanding gap**
3. **Design gap**
4. **Delivery gap**
5. **Communication gap**

Delivery gap. The gap between service standards intended by management and service standards delivered. For example, management might intend to keep billing errors under 1%, but the actual rate of error could be 2%.

Communication gap. The gap between what is delivered and what is communicated to customers as being delivered. For example, a courier company can promise 9 A.M. delivery by the following day. The customer might believe that this service is available

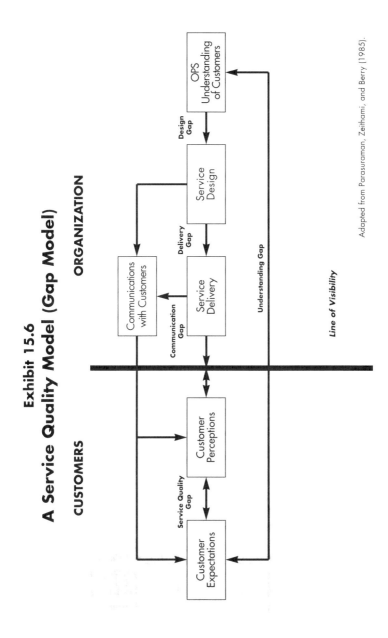

Exhibit 15.6
A Service Quality Model (Gap Model)

Adapted from Parasuraman, Zeithaml, and Berry (1985).

throughout office hours, whereas the service may not be available after 3 P.M. Although the company may correctly claim that it guarantees 9 A.M. delivery, this is not what is understood by the customer.

Consider a situation in which the customer has had no difficulty in expressing what he or she wants. In such cases, we simply create a framework within which the customer can, for each attribute, express how much of this attribute he or she would like and where the organization stands with regard to his or her expectations.

One technique that is well-suited to this purpose is known as the semantic differential. Here, customers indicate, on a bipolar scale, how much of a given attribute they ideally would like and how the company performs on that attribute.

Expectation	1	2	3	4	5	
Extremely discourteous	__	__	__	__	__	Extremely courteous
Service extremely slow	__	__	__	__	__	Service extremely fast
Staff very standoffish	__	__	__	__	__	Staff very friendly
Performance						
Extremely discourteous	__	__	__	__	__	Extremely courteous
Service extremely slow	__	__	__	__	__	Service extremely fast
Staff very standoffish	__	__	__	__	__	Staff very friendly

Gap analysis can be carried out using a wide variety of techniques. It involves collecting information on customer expectations as well as on their perception of current services. The difference between the two is the "gap."

The difference between expectation and performance can be seen as the gap to be filled. A common way of depicting the previous information is through the use of line charts that show the difference between expectation and performance.

Gap analysis is not restricted to semantic differential or quadrant analysis. Parasuraman (1987), for example, suggests the following approach, which uses three questions for each attribute:

1. Compared to my minimum service level when it comes to _____ (e.g., prompt service), service performance is

Lower		The same			Higher	No opinion	
1	2	3	4	5	6	7	8	9	N

2. Compared to my desired service level when it comes

Exhibit 15.7
Quadrant Chart

Opportunity Matrix

Adapted from *Ontario Public Service* (1992).

to _____ (e.g., prompt service), service performance is

Lower   The same   Higher   No opinion
1   2   3   4   5   6   7   8   9   N

3. My perception of Company X on
_____ (e.g., prompt service),
service performance is

Lower   The same   Higher   No opinion
1   2   3   4   5   6   7   8   9   N

These three ratings for each attribute show where a company stands.

- If (3) is higher than both (1) and (2), then the company provides a service that exceeds not only the customer's minimum expectation, but also the desired
  level.

- If (3) is above (1) but below (2), then the company
  provides a service that meets the minimum customer
  requirement, but falls short of the desired level.

- If (3) is below both (1) and (2), then there may be a
  serious problem in that the company fails to provide
  even the minimum level of service expected by customers.

Depending on where the gap occurs, we can use different techniques (which could include any of the techniques from focus groups to brainstorming) to assess that gap.

Gap analysis can be used in situations where the organization needs to pinpoint areas in which they lag behind customer expectations.

A careful gap analysis is a must for instituting and monitoring a quality program. When people complain that "service quality programs don't work; we tried it," the chances are very good that the reason why the quality program did not work was because there was a critical difference, at great expense, between what consumers expected and what management delivered.

WHEN TO USE GAP ANALYSIS

This technique is useful when the relevant attributes are well-known and well-defined. When a bipolar scale is used, it is assumed that, unless customers indicate the extreme points, neither extreme may be desirable. For example, extreme courtesy by staff may be interpreted as being overly solicitous and may make customers uncomfortable. Gap analysis is used to determine how to meet customer expectations. It also can be used to bridge the gap between the standard and current performance.

The main advantage of this type of analysis is that it pinpoints the areas in which actions are needed. For example, if the analysis shows that there is an understanding gap (the gap between what customers are getting and management's perception of what they are getting), then our corrective action could be the sharpening of the information flow between customers and management. If the analysis shows that there is a delivery gap (service standards intended by management and those delivered), then our corrective action could be to pay more attention to internal processes and internal communication.

Gap analysis solutions are likely to be remedial rather than creative.

Bridging the gap essentially is remedial in nature. It is debatable whether excellence can be achieved by continually remedying what is perceived as a deficiency by our customers or by ourselves. It is helpful to think of gap analysis as the minimum we may need to do as well as a tool to monitor our performance rather than as a proactive tool to deliver customer satisfaction.

To know more

Brassard, M. and D. Ritter (1994), *The Memory Jogger II*. Metheun, MA: Goal/QPC.

Mears, P. (1995), *Quality Improvement Tools & Techniques.* New York: McGraw-Hill.

Parasuraman, A., V.A. Zeithaml, and L.L. Berry (1985), "A Conceptual Model of Service Quality and Its Implications for Future Research," *Journal of Marketing*, 49, 41–50.

Tague, N.R. (1995), *The Quality Toolbox.* Milwaukee: ASQC Quality Press.

APPENDIX: SAMPLE DISCUSSION GUIDE

Subject: Customer satisfaction. *Target group:* Lapsed Green Circle customers.

1. INTRODUCTION

Welcome
Roles (moderator's, participants')
Disclosures (audiotaping, one-way mirror)

General overview: In our discussion this evening, we'll be focusing on health insurance coverage. We'll be discussing what's important to you and what's not regarding health insurance coverage, and how you feel about various plans.

First name introductions: Tell me a little about yourself—your first name and what you do.

2. BACKGROUND

Tell me how you are now covered for health insurance. Describe your present coverage to me. What plan do you have, what does it cover, why do you have it, and who pays for it?

Did you ever have a Green Circle health insurance plan? How long ago was this? How long did you have it? Whom did it cover (self, self and spouse, family)? What did it cover?

Why did you switch from your Green Circle health plan to the one you have now? (Probe reasons extensively.) How long ago was this? (Find out how many now have an employer-paid plan or another individual/family plan or who have no coverage at all.) For those who switched to another individual/family plan: How did you find out about your present plan? In the past, did you ever have a health plan that was paid for by an employer? If so, how long ago was this? What did this plan cover?

3. SATISFACTION WITH THE APPLICATION PROCESS

Setup: I want you to think about your present plan in relation to the Green Circle health plan you formerly had. And I want you to take me through various comparisons. I want to explore who does the best job in your opinion—your present insurer or Green Circle. We'll examine a number of different areas.

What were you looking for when you bought your Green Circle health plan? Were you looking for specific kinds of coverage? If yes, what kinds of coverage were you looking for? (Probe for specific kinds of coverage.) Why were you looking for this kind of coverage? When you bought your present plan, were you looking for the same kinds of coverage?

When you bought your Green Circle health plan, how did you go about getting information on the coverage? Did you get any brochures/pamphlets? Was this printed information clear and easy to understand? Where did you obtain these brochures/pamphlets? Did you have telephone conversations with anyone at Green Circle? (If so, whom? Why? Impressions? Results?) Did you have different plans from which to choose? Were the differences between these plans clear? Did you find the kind of coverage you wanted?

With your present plan, how did you go about getting information? (Continue with the same line of questioning as above.) When did you first think of switching from Green Circle to your present plan? How long did it take you to make up your mind to switch? When you bought your Green Circle plan and your present plan, did you consult with anyone in making up your mind? (Spouse? Friend? Agent/broker? Business partner?) Were you clear on what you were buying when you bought your Green Circle plan? (Were you aware of what was included and excluded?) Were there any areas where you were uncertain about what was covered and what was not?

Are you clear on what your plan covers? Are the plans (your Green Circle plan and your present plan) the same with respect to prescription drug coverage— do they have the same annual maximum? Do they cover the same kinds of drug prescriptions? Are the plans the same with respect to dental benefits? Do they both pay the same percentage of your dental bill? Why did you eventually buy the plan you now have?

In both cases, did you buy what you wanted, or did you have to make trade-offs? If so, what trade-offs? Did you buy more than you wanted? Less than you wanted? (If so, why?)

With respect to your Green Circle plan, how would you describe the cost? (Probe unaided responses first.) Is the cost fair? Reasonable? Is it affordable (or do you have to forgo other purchases to afford it? If so, what other purchases have you forgone?) Does it seem like a good value to you?

Now, with respect to your present plan, how would you describe the cost? (Continue with the same questions as above.)

Overall, how was the application process for both Green Circle and your present plan? Did they differ? Was the process in both instances easy and uncomplicated? Was the process in both instances clear? Straightforward?

Are you familiar with the phrase "medical underwriting"? Were you or any of your family medically underwritten? If so, how long did the process take? Was the time frame what you were expecting? (Probe: Longer? Shorter? Just what was expected?)

4. SATISFACTION WITH UTILIZATION

(Review: You have told me that you all have had your present plan for ... and your Green Circle plan for ... before that.) Take me through your claims experience, both with respect to your present plan and with Green Circle. (Set up chart on a flip chart) How many of you have made claims under your present plan and with Green Circle in the following areas?

	present plan	*Green Circle plan*
*drug		
*dental		
semiprivate/private		
vision care		
counseling services,		
registered specialists,		
and therapists		
home support services		
ambulance services		
other (devices that assist,		
medical equipment and supplies,		
accidental dental, hearing aids)		

*How were these claims submitted (to Green Circle/present plan)?

(With respect to areas mentioned in which claims have been filed)

Tell me about your experience filing claims. What was good about it? What was not so good? What was your experience with respect to both Green Circle and your present insurer (dental claims, drug/prescription claims, and so on)? (With respect to factors mentioned that were not so good, go over several specifically: How strongly do you feel about...?)

Was it easier or harder to make a claim than what you expected? When you were making a claim, did you ever have to call your insurer (Green Circle or your present insurer)? (If so, what was your impression? Were they helpful? What was the result?) Are there any areas you think insurance companies could improve upon when it comes to making claims (if not already mentioned)? Has anyone had a claim refused or only paid in part? If so, what was your reaction? (Probe for insurer and for subscriber's comprehension of the reason and clarity of explanation.) Did you find the explanation satisfactory?

5. SATISFACTION WITH RESPECT TO:

A. Phone servicing

Have you ever telephoned Green Circle or your present insurer? Why? What were your impressions of the way you were treated? Was it easy to get the information/action you required? Are there areas of telephone servicing that insurers could improve upon? (Probe unaided responses first.) What should be their hours of service? What days of the week?

B. Billing

How do you pay for your present plan? (Probe: How many use preauthorized payment service and quarterly billings?) How did you pay when you had Green Circle coverage? Are you satisfied with this way of paying for your coverage? Do your present insurer and Green Circle differ with respect to their billing processes?

Suppose an insurance company were to let you pay by using your credit card. How would you feel about that? Suppose an insurance company were to bill you every six months or just once a year. How would you feel about that?

C. Communication

Did you receive any information from Green Circle? If so, what did you receive? Do you remember what it was about? Do you receive any information from your present insurer? If so, what do you receive? Do you remember what it was about? Are there topics you'd like to receive information on from an insurance company? (If so, what are they?)

6. SATISFACTION WITH RESPECT TO THE PLAN OVERALL

Is the plan you now have providing you with the coverage you now want/need? Are there kinds of coverage you now wish you had? Are there kinds of coverage you now wish you could drop? In general, how happy are you overall with the plan you have (on a rough scale of 1–10, where 10 is "very happy" and 1 is "not happy at all")? Would you say you have the plan that's ideal for you right now? (If not, what's missing?) Would you recommend the plan you have to a friend or family member? Have you, in fact, done so? How long do you expect to keep your present individual health insurance plan?

7. SATISFACTION WITH RESPECT TO SPECIFIC PARTS OF THE PLAN

I'd appreciate your taking a few minutes to complete this questionnaire. It's anonymous. Please just fill it in with respect to the plan you have. (While respondents complete this questionnaire, check with the client group for any additional questions.)

Questionnaire

* Satisfaction Rating: Use a scale from 1–10, where 10 = "very happy"; 5 = "so so" or "neutral"; 1 = "not happy at all".

Important to you? Coverage	If yes, how important? Yes	Satisfaction No	Nice to have	Essential to have	Rating*
prescription drug	___	___	___	___	___
dental services	___	___	___	___	___
vision care	___	___	___	___	___
counseling services	___	___	___	___	___
registered specialists and therapists	___	___	___	___	___
home support services	___	___	___	___	___
ambulance services	___	___	___	___	___
accidental death and dismemberment	___	___	___	___	___
medical equipment and supplies	___	___			
hearing aids	___	___	___	___	___
preferred hospital accommodation (semiprivate, private)	___	___	___	___	___

If you have marked any area above with a satisfaction rating of 5 or less, please indicate why:

_____

_____

_____

_____

____

_____

_____

What would be the single most important consideration that would make you switch to another company's plan?

_____

_____

_____

____

Background:
Occupation:_____
Age: ___ 20–29 ___30–39 ___40–49 ___50–59 ___60–69 ___70+
Gender: ___ male ___ female
Coverage: ___ self ___self + spouse ___family
Annual household income: ___up to $35,000 ___$35,000–$60,000 ___$60,000–$100,000 ___
over $100,000

8. AWARENESS ISSUES

Are you aware of any recent or proposed changes to your health insurance? (If so, what?) Are you likely to continue with your present plan? (If not, why not?) Are you aware of any Green Circle advertising on television? (Probe unaided awareness—What do they recall? What are their impressions?)

9. FINAL

(Check with the client group behind the mirror for further questions during completion of the questionnaire.) Thank you for coming out this evening and for sharing your opinions candidly about this important topic.

Source: Adapted from Dr. Barrie Wilson's notes (personal communication).

16

Delivering Techniques: Producers

P1D3: Producers and Delivering

	PRODUCERS	PROCESSES	PEOPLE
DIAGNOSING	Structural analysis Check sheets Mystery shopping Internal focus groups	Graphic techniques Run charts Stratification Flow charts	Complaint elicitation Content tracking Belief system analysis Pareto charts

DETAILING	Nominal group
	  technique
	Benchmarking
	Deleting
	  dimensionality
	The as-if frame
	The video camera
		Control charts	External focus groups
			Survey research
			Laddering
			Factor analysis
			Gap analysis
			Wish lists

DELIVERING	**Brainstorming** **Force field analysis** **Cost-benefit analysis**	Fishbone diagrams Process mapping and evaluation	Tracking

Once we go through the measurement process, we are left with the task of translating what we know into what we need to achieve. Measurements can be formalized in many different ways, depending on the conceptual framework within which the measurements are obtained. We must focus our efforts more sharply at this stage, so that our resources are spent effectively. In addition, we need to understand and cope with forces that will resist change. The next few chapters will describe a number of techniques that will move us toward a more focused orientation. Although these techniques are specific and well-defined, we also will be faced with more complex issues from time to time. These issues may have no standard solutions, or they may be applicable

183

only to a particular organization. Sometimes the solution may be obvious, but we may lack the resources to implement it.

BRAINSTORMING

Brainstorming is one of the techniques we can consider at the implementation (delivery) stage of a service quality program. Brainstorming is a way of tapping the brain power that is already within an organization.

WHAT IS BRAINSTORMING?

Brainstorming is a method for generating a large quantity of diverse ideas on a given topic in an atmosphere that is free of criticism and judgment. It is similar in structure to internal focus groups. Like focus groups, brainstorming sessions have a moderator and a group of participants. It is carried out in a setting akin to focus groups, and it enables participants to build on one another's ideas while staying focused on the common goal. It provides an opportunity for everyone to participate and break free from standard modes of thinking. There are two methods of brainstorming: structured and unstructured.

Structured brainstorming

Step 1. *The moderator starts with an informal discussion of the problem and then writes it on a flip chart.* The discussion is continued to make sure that each participant understands the problem in the same way. For instance, the problem can be stated as "The biggest source of customer dissatisfaction is the unduly high response time it takes for our service personnel to respond to complaints." Our objective for this session is to increase customer satisfaction by finding ways to reduce our response time.

Step 2. Each participant offers a solution in turn. There may be several rotations. There is no direct interaction among participants at this stage, except for the purpose of idea clarification. Ideas are not praised, criticized, or evaluated at this time. For example, participants might suggest such ideas as the following:

"We should employ more service people."
"A more efficient computer systems could help us to speed up response time."
"Outsourcing some service activities is a solution."
"We should concentrate on our product so we do not have as many complaints to deal with."

Step 3. *The moderator writes down the ideas in the participants' own words.* When necessary, the moderator checks with each participant to ensure that what was written is exactly what was said. Often, several sheets of paper are required to write down the ideas. All sheets are displayed like posters, so that all ideas are visible at all times. This process, which normally takes between 20 and 30 minutes, is continued until participants are unable to produce any more ideas.

How to carry out brainstorming

1. **The moderator starts with an informal discussion of the problem and then writes it on a flip chart.**
2. **Each participant offers a solution in turn.**
3. **The moderator writes down the ideas in the participants' own words.**
4. **The moderator, in consultation with the participants, eliminates duplicate and illegal ideas.**
5. **As an option, the process can be continued.**

Step 4. *The moderator, in consultation with the participants, eliminates duplicate and illegal ideas.* For example, a suggestion such as "We should tape-record our conversation with our customers without their knowledge" may be eliminated if it is illegal to do so.

Step 5. *As an option, the process can be continued.* Ideas can be discussed in greater detail, and, if appropriate, the participants may arrive at a consensus with regard to the most productive ideas.

Unstructured brainstorming

Unstructured brainstorming is identical to structured brainstorming with one exception. During Step 2, any participant may offer any idea at any time, rather than waiting for his or her turn. This procedure has the advantage of not embarrassing those who have few ideas. However, the procedure also has the disadvantage of inhibiting participants who are reluctant to volunteer their opinion unless they are asked specifically to do so.

HOW TO INTERPRET THE FINDINGS

As the examples in Step 2 indicate, the suggested solutions may deal with people, equipment, management, product improvement, or any other aspect that can have a bearing on the problem. Diverse solutions give us many options. If our aim is to narrow the solutions, then brainstorming can reduce the options by eliminating the less effective ones. The source of each idea provides some clue as to how the problem is viewed by different strata within the organization and what difficulties might occur when implementing alternative solutions. If the ideas or solutions are a reduced set of alternatives, then they can be tested further using techniques, such as cost-benefit analysis, which are discussed subsequently.

Brainstorming can be used at any stage of the service quality measurement program. The main advantage of this technique is that it is nonthreatening, because ideas are not criticized. Because all ideas are written down and displayed, brainstorming can expand the vision of the participants by exposing them to alternative viewpoints and nonstandard solutions.

To know more

Brassard, M. and D. Ritter (1994), *The Memory Jogger II*. Metheun, MA: Goal/QPC.

Mears, P. (1995), *Quality Improvement Tools & Techniques*. New York: McGraw-Hill.

Tague, N.R. (1995), *The Quality Toolbox*. Milwaukee: ASQC Quality Press.

FORCE FIELD ANALYSIS

In any organization, there are always forces that favor change and those that oppose it. An organization that is interested in delivering service quality must understand the opposing forces, so that it can deal with them appropriately. Force field analysis is designed to achieve this objective. Understanding the opposing forces will help an organization to reinforce positive changes and minimize or eliminate negative ones by addressing the genuine concerns of those who oppose change. The purpose of force field analysis is to compare positive and negative forces, enable decision makers to consider all the implications of proposed change, create an honest balance sheet, and elicit honest reflection on the effects of change.

> **Force field analysis *is a* technique aimed at understanding the forces that lead an organization toward change and the forces that oppose that change.**

Change can be viewed as a struggle between driving and restraining forces. The driving forces are those that help the change occur; the restraining forces are those that attempt to block the change. Force field analysis is the technique designed to make explicit the driving and restraining forces that exert pressure on a proposed change.

HOW TO CARRY OUT FORCE FIELD ANALYSIS

Step 1. The moderator, in consultation with participants, defines the problem. A large "T" is written on a flip chart, with the problem to be analyzed on the top left-hand side and the ideal solution on the top right-hand side.

Problem
We have too little control
over our suppliers. There are too
many of them.

Desired Change
Have no more than two or
three suppliers of the
same service.

Step 2. *The moderator brainstorms with the participants to understand the positive forces.* These are then listed on the left-hand side of the flip chart.

Step 3. *The moderator brainstorms with the participants to understand the negative forces.* These are listed on the right-hand side of the flip chart.

Step 4. *The discussion is continued and the driving and restraining forces are prioritized.* This can be accomplished in several different ways. For example, each participant may be given ten points that he or she can assign in any proportion to one or more of the driving forces. Each participant also is given another ten points to assign similarly to the restraining forces. The final assignment of number by the groups will be used to prioritize the forces.

- **Define the current problem.**
- **State the desired goal.**
- **Identify the forces that drive and restrain the achievement of the goal.**
- **Continue the discussion and prioritize the driving and restraining forces.**
- **Discuss and agree on the solutions.**

Step 5. *Solutions are discussed and agreed on.* Solutions are proposed by participants on how the driving forces can be strengthened by addressing the concerns of those presenting the restraining forces. Consider a situation in which the main driving force for adding more employees to a service department is to reduce the turnaround time. The main restraining force is that, during slow periods, the service department will be overstaffed. By understanding the concerns expressed by those opposing change, the organization may decide to employ additional staff on a part-time basis. This addresses the concerns of both driving and restraining forces. The agreed-on actions that address the concerns of the restraining forces then are written down.

Action to be Taken

1. Find a mechanism to track and monitor the competitiveness of our suppliers.

2. In selecting the two or three suppliers, make sure we have choices. Develop a list of "standby" suppliers.

3. Monitor price, quality, and turnaround time on a continual basis to ensure that they confirm to our requirements.

The process of working through opposing forces tend to bring the two sides closer together by exposing each side to a differing point of view. Increasing the driving forces, decreasing the restraining forces, or both can create change.

HOW TO INTERPRET THE FINDINGS

Once we identify the positive and negative forces, decision makers prioritize the driving forces that can be strengthened and identify opposing forces that should be eliminated to achieve movement toward the ideal state. Pushing the positive force by itself is unlikely to effect the desired change if negative forces are stronger. Force field analysis compels the decision maker to pay attention to those who oppose change as well as to why they do so. In addition, addressing negative forces can point to the potential pitfalls that must be avoided if the change is to be implemented. In cases in which the opposing forces have a legitimate point of view and a strong case, a cost-benefit analysis of the system can be undertaken to resolve the issue. (See Exhibit 16.1.)

Present this analysis to the decision makers so that a consensus can be reached over the main restraining forces.

Because force field analysis deals with forces that are for and against change, it is most useful when an organization is on the threshold of making major changes. Force field analysis should be undertaken before implementing changes, so that opposing forces will have input on the decisions being made.

It is important to note that silencing or crushing the opposition is not the purpose of force field analysis. Rather, it is to learn from the opposition. By addressing the genuine concerns of the opposition, we can arrive at better decisions, avoid potential pitfalls, and convert potential opponents into allies when implementing the change.

To know more

Force field analysis, originally used by Kurt Lewin, is a standard quality improvement technique. Most books that deal with quality improvement contain reference to this technique, such as the following:

Mears, P. (1995), *Quality Improvement Tools & Techniques.* New York: McGraw-Hill.

QIP, Inc./PQ Systems Inc. (1995), *Total Quality Tools.* Miamisberg, OH: Productivity-Quality Systems Inc.

Tague, N.R. (1995), *The Quality Toolbox.* Milwaukee: ASQC Quality Press.

Exhibit 16.1
Force Field Analysis

It is customary to indicate the driving and restraining forces with arrowheads facing opposite directions.

DRIVING FORCES		RESTRAINING FORCES
1. We can control the quality of service.	▶ ◀	We may not get competitive prices.
2. We can save time.	▶ ◀	We will have fewer choices.
3. Fewer suppliers can be made accountable.	▶ ◀	They might become complacent.
4. They will be more loyal and more productive.	▶ ◀	They may take us for granted.
5. Turnaround will be quicker.	▶ ◀	Turnaround will be poor.
6. They can be cheaper.	▶ ◀	They can be more expensive.

COST-BENEFIT ANALYSIS

When we start exploring different courses of action aimed at improving service quality, some questions inevitably arise. What will a proposed improvement cost? How will it benefit us? When we consider several alternative courses of action, which alternative is optimal in terms of return on investment? Cost-benefit analysis provides answers to these questions.

Cost-benefit analysis is a formal method of analyzing the costs and benefits of each proposed course of action. The objectives of the analysis are to assess (1) whether a proposed course of action is worth undertaking, given the cost, if we are contemplating a single course of action; and (2) which one of the possible courses of action will be most beneficial, if we are contemplating choosing a course of action among several alternatives. There is another advantage of doing a cost-benefit analysis. Because the analysis requires us to examine the contemplated courses of action, we are forced to identify hidden costs and benefits of a given course of action.

HOW IS COST-BENEFIT ANALYSIS CARRIED OUT?

A cost-benefit analysis is carried out by people who work in an organization, such as employees and management. You can carry out cost-benefit analysis by following the steps outlined here:

Step 1. Calculate the primary costs of the proposed courses of action. For example, you could be considering

a. installing a video booth in which customers can register complaints, and

b. employing a designated person to receive customer complaints.

The primary cost of installing a video booth is $150,000 a year, and the cost of employing a person is $80,000.

Step 2. Use other techniques, such as flow charting, to identify the secondary costs associated with the proposed course of action. The secondary costs of the video approach include such expenses as the videotapes, the maintenance required throughout the year, the space the booth occupies, and the expense of hiring an employee to watch and summarize (if necessary) the nature of the complaints. These items are listed, and the costs are estimated. Similarly, the secondary costs of employing a designated person for handling complaints could include the office space he or she occupies, the benefits associated with the job, someone else filling in when the complaint-handling person is away on holidays, and the expense of training the person in charge.

How to carry out cost-benefit analysis
1. Calculate the primary costs.
2. Identify secondary costs.
3. Calculate the benefits.
4. Review the list.
5. Attach values on a common scale to each cost and benefit.
6. Subtract benefits from costs.

Step 3. Calculate the benefits to be derived from the proposed changes. For a video booth, these could include reduced cost, improved customer satisfaction, and less time wasted attending customer complaints. Assigning a designated employee also could generate the same benefits. The video booth has the added benefit of being accessible 24 hours a day. Assigning a designated person has the added benefit of providing a personal touch. In adding up the benefits, make sure that you also take into account the long-term benefits of a proposed course of action.

Step 4. Review the list to make sure nothing significant on the cost or benefit side has been overlooked.

Step 5. Attach a positive or negative value on a common scale to each cost and benefit. This could be a monetary scale. You can assign actual financial costs and savings, where possible. Where the benefits are intangible (such as a personal touch), the costs and benefits can be converted into a monetary scale on the basis of their implied worth.

Step 6. Subtract benefits from costs. The remainder is the objective of the analysis. When several alternative courses of action are being considered, the one with the largest remainder will be the one that should be favored.

HOW TO INTERPRET COST-BENEFIT ANALYSIS

The results of cost-benefit analysis are self-explanatory. When a cost-benefit analysis identifies many alternatives with a similar cost-benefit ratio, we can use several criteria to choose the next course of action. Such criteria include the following:

- The alternative that is acceptable to most people,
- The alternative that is least disruptive, and
- The alternative that is simpler to implement.

Assessing costs and benefits forces us to look into the proposed course of action more closely. However, unless it is carried out objectively, it may simply reinforce our preconceptions because some of the benefits that are expected to accrue will have to be estimated. Such estimates can be influenced easily by our own preconceptions. One way to minimize such biases is to ask more than one person (including a possible outsider) to do the analysis and reconcile the estimates through discussion.

To know more

Cost-benefit analysis is a standard technique used in financial analysis. The analysis need not always be elaborate or formal. However, if the level of investment is high, it is advisable to do a formal analysis of costs and benefits. Many books, such as the one listed here, are available for this purpose:

Leyland, R. and S. Glaister (1994), *Cost Benefit Analysis*, 2d ed. Cambridge, UK: Cambridge University Press.

17

Delivering Techniques: Processes

P2D3: Processes and Delivering

	PRODUCERS	PROCESSES	PEOPLE
DIAGNOSING	Structural analysis Check sheets Mystery shopping Internal focus groups	Graphic techniques Run charts Stratification Flow charts	Complaint elicitation Content tracking Belief system analysis Pareto charts
DETAILING	Nominal group technique Benchmarking Deleting dimensionality The as-if frame The video camera	Control charts	External focus groups Survey research Laddering Factor analysis Gap analysis Wish lists
DELIVERING	Brainstorming Force field analysis Cost-benefit analysis	**Fishbone diagrams Process mapping and evaluation**	Tracking

Afferter having considered various courses of action, and the costs and benefits associated with them, we also need to consider the processes of delivery in detail. Our aim here is not to consider the mechanics of delivery. Rather, our interest is in understanding more precisely the causes of the problems we face and the actions we must undertake to remove the obstacles to achieving our goals. We consider two techniques here: the fishbone diagram and process mapping and evaluation.

THE FISHBONE DIAGRAM

Suppose research reveals that the problem that bothers most customers is the rudeness of employees. An organization committed to service quality may "solve" the problem by immediately firing the offending employees. But, as we saw before, this may not solve the underlying problem. The problem could have resulted from a number of factors, such as people, policies, procedures, or even equipment. It is helpful to think of a problem in terms of *effects, symptoms,* and *root causes:*

- *Effect* is the situation we find ourselves in. Thus, a billing error is an effect.

- A *symptom* is a condition that is evidence of an underlying problem that gives rise to the situation. For example, billing errors are a symptom of some underlying problem.

- *Root cause* is the main stimulus that gives rise to the problem. The root cause may be made up of many less important causes. In our billing example, incorrect computer input could be the root cause of the problem. Other less important causes could include lack of program checks and the failure to act on customer feedback.

When we analyze a given problem by studying all the probable factors that could have contributed to it, we are using the cause-and-effect method. The cause-and-effect model can be presented as a fishbone diagram, with the problem represented as the fish's head and the causes represented as the fish skeleton (see Exhibit 17.1). This type of diagram also is known as the *Ishikawa diagram* or the *cause-and-effect diagram*.

The fishbone diagram is a graphical technique in which a problem is represented as a fish's head. The purpose of the diagram is to identify probable causes of the problem.

The fishbone diagram is used to identify

1. the probable causes of a problem by classifying and visually displaying them,

2. the conflicting requirements within the system that led to the problem, and

3. the probable underlying causes of a problem.

So, whenever we confront a problem that might have been caused by a variety of factors, we may want to formalize our thinking and identify the source of the problem with the use of the fishbone diagram.

HOW TO CONSTRUCT A FISHBONE DIAGRAM

A fishbone diagram is constructed using the following steps:

Exhibit 17.1
Fishbone Diagram Outline

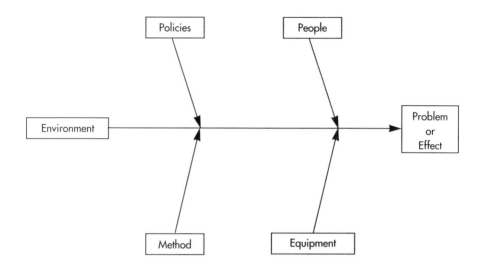

Step 1. Identify the problem that needs solving and place it in the box on the right-hand side (the "head of the fish"). The problem may be identified in any number of ways. Research into customer satisfaction is one method preferred by many organizations. Problems also may be identified by other methods such as observation. Suppose we identify the problem to be rudeness of employees. This is the problem, or the effect.

How to construct a fishbone diagram

1. **Identify the problem that needs solving and place it in the box on the right-hand side (the "head of the fish").**
2. **Write in the main factors that potentially could cause the problem.**
3. **Generate the probable cause under each category.**
4. **Write in summary form the cause on each horizontal fishbone that intersects the appropriate fish rib.**
5. **Refine the diagram by emphasizing the most probable causes.**

Step 2. Once a problem is identified, place it in the box on the right-hand side. Write in the main factors that potentially could cause the problem. In this example, they are people, procedures, policies, and equipment (see Exhibit 17.2).

Step 3. Generate the probable cause under each category. Brainstorming (with managers and employees) and/or internal research could be used for this purpose. The main objective here is that we not overlook any possible cause.

Step 4. Write in summary form the cause on each horizontal fishbone that intersects the appropriate fish rib. Make sure you write causes rather than symptoms (see Exhibit 17.2).

Step 5. Explore the diagram by asking a series of "why" questions to identify the root causes. Refine the diagram by emphasizing the most probable causes. For example, brainstorming

Exhibit 17.2
Fishbone Diagram: An Example

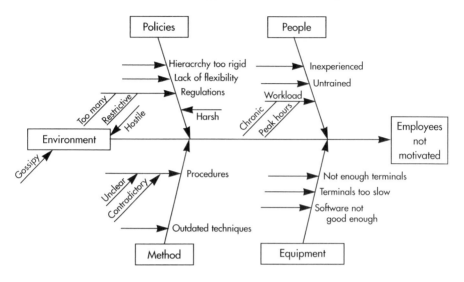

with employees might reveal that, though there are a number of reasons why they are rude to customers, the root cause is the unrealistic demand placed on the employees in expecting them to serve more customers than they can handle satisfactorily. The brainstorming session also may show that simply increasing employees' salary, training them to be courteous, and rewarding them for more courteous handling of customers will not solve the problem, because they are not the root causes.

HOW TO INTERPRET THE FISHBONE DIAGRAM

The value of a fishbone diagram is that it shows at a glance (1) which parts of the system contribute the most to the creation of the problem and (2) how two perfectly reasonable expectations from two sources within the system create conflicts that lead to the problem.

For example, management policy may stipulate that the customer be provided with quick service. However, many employees may fail to provide such service. Instead of immediately disciplining the employees, if we construct a fishbone diagram, we may be able to solve the problem better. We may be able to understand why employees are not following management's stipulation. It could very well be the result of the equipment they have to work with. We may find that many people have to share the same computer terminal. (This might have come about as a result of another perfectly legitimate goal: keeping costs down.) This means, depending on the demand for the terminal, that a customer may or may not be accorded quick service. Again, inadequate training may conflict with employees' ability to bend the rules to 'satisfy customers with special needs.

We look for possible corrections to the system and possible conflicts within the system.

Consequently, a fishbone diagram will provide us with a reasonable hypothesis as to why the problem arose in the first place. Such hypotheses could fall into one of the following three categories:

1. *There are aspects of the system that can be corrected to solve the problem.* For example, employees may lack proper training in some aspects of their jobs. We can remedy the problem by simply providing the required training.

2. *There are conflicts among different parts of the system, for reasons that do not contribute to the goals of the organization.* This is a common phenomenon in many organizations. Policies and procedures may exist in different departments that are the result of how these departments evolved over a period of time. However, these same policies and procedures may not contribute to the overall goals of the organization. For example, a customer service representative may be frustrated by the fact that he or she had to ask the customer for information that had already been provided to the organization in a different context. This procedure may have been developed when computers were not common and continues to be used, even when it can be avoided.

The fishbone diagram is used to identify
- **the probable causes of a problem by classifying and visually displaying them,**
- **the conflicting requirements within the system that led to the problem, and**
- **the probable underlying causes of a problem.**

3. *There are conflicts between the objectives of different parts of the system that can be solved by prioritizing the objectives.* For example, the objective of economy may conflict with the objective of having adequate resources required to do the job effectively. In this case, management should prioritize its objectives. Thus, if the priority of management is to offer quick service, then economy will become a secondary objective, to be aimed for once the primary objective has been achieved.

Whenever there is a conflict in the system, it could frustrate the employee who has to deal with it. He or she may express this frustration by transferring it to the customer. The fishbone diagram, by explicitly exploring the antecedents, is likely to throw light on why a problem arose in the first place and implicitly suggest solutions.

OTHER THINGS YOU SHOULD KNOW

The main purpose of the fishbone diagram is to broaden our perspective, so that we can identify causes that may not be immediately obvious. Extensive input to the diagram, therefore, is very important. When the issue is sensitive, a huge blank diagram may be displayed in a common area for many days, so that anyone who has something to contribute can write his or her ideas on the diagram. Whenever possible, ideas should be combined. Although we emphasize generating as many potential causes as possible, eventually it is the quality of these ideas that results in a satisfactory solution to the problem. Once the ideas have been generated, our aim should be to combine similar ideas and identify the existence of each proposed cause and the effect in question.

To know more

The fishbone, or the cause-and-effect, diagram was initially introduced by the quality expert Kaoru Ishikawa in 1943. Since then, it has become a standard quality improvement tool, and most standard books that deal with quality management include this technique, such as the following:

Brassard, M. and D. Ritter (1994), *The Memory Jogger II.* Metheun, MA: Goal/QPC.

Kaminsky, F.C., R.D. Davis, and R.J. Burke (1993), *Statistics and Quality Control for the Workplace.* Milwaukee: ASQC Quality Press.

QIP, Inc./PQ Systems Inc. (1995), *Total Quality Tools.* Miamisberg, OH: Productivity-Quality Systems Inc.

Tague, N.R. (1995), *The Quality Toolbox.* Milwaukee: ASQC Quality Press.

PROCESS MAPPING AND EVALUATION

Even when we take normal precautions, we may find that the system does not work as well as it should. When a system that is supposed to work efficiently breaks down, it may not always be clear to management what caused the breakdown. Process mapping and evaluation are techniques that attempt to identify the causes of such a breakdown. A process map shows how a transaction is facilitated or impeded, while process evaluation introduces and evaluates possible solutions.

Process mapping is a technique for examining a process to determine where and why major breakdowns occur within a system. Process evaluation is the process of finding solutions to the problem so identified.

From a conceptual viewpoint, process evaluation is similar to constructing a flow chart, which was described previously. The purpose of the flow chart is to identify the sequence of events in order to eliminate the elements that are no longer necessary or to adopt more efficient procedures to accomplish the goal. But when we hypothesize that there still might be some bottlenecks in the system, we can use process mapping and evaluation procedures.

To apply process mapping, we simply follow a transaction from the beginning to the end, as we do in constructing a flow chart. However, a flow chart involves concentrating simply on the sequence. Process mapping, on the other hand, is concerned not only with the sequence, but also with the "behind-the-scenes" information, usually related to time. For instance, in the following example, in addition to simply mapping the events, as we do in flow charting, we also pay attention to other things that happen in a given sequence. Such evaluation shows that there are four points of delay. By following a number of transactions and analyzing them logically, we can identify recurring patterns that contribute the most to inefficiencies in the system.

1. Customer presents the check.
2. The account is checked on a computer.   *A terminal sometimes is not immediately available.*
3. The check is presented to an officer.   *Sometimes an officer is not readily available.*
4. The customer presents a large number .   *Large number of deposits delays other customers.*
   of deposits
5. The total deposit amount needs   *A terminal sometimes is not immediately available.*
   to be input into the computer.

HOW TO CREATE A PROCESS MAP

Step 1. Create a process map worksheet. For example, we may want to create a worksheet for exploring why check processing is frequently delayed. Start with this, for example:

Process Map Worksheet

How a Transaction Is Processed	(Process Mapping and Process Evaluation)
Sequence of events (mapping)	"Behind-the-scene" look (evaluation)

Step 2. Define the key elements in the process. Such key elements could refer to possible reasons for the gap between consumer expectations and your performance. In our example, the key elements include such factors as access to computers, officers with signing authority, and the complexity of the transaction.

Step 3. Define the major work units of the process. Note them on the left-hand side of the process map. Identify what happens during that phase of the process. Write this on the right-hand side of the chart.

Process Map Worksheet

How a Transaction Is Processed (Process Mapping and Process Evaluation)

Sequence of events (mapping)   *"Behind-the-scene" look (evaluation)*

1. Customer presents the check.
2. The account is checked on a computer.   A terminal sometimes is not
   immediately available.
3. The check is presented to an officer.   Sometimes an officer is not readily
   available.
4. The customer presents a large number   Large number of deposits delays other
   of deposits.   customers
5. The total deposit amount needs   A terminal sometimes is not
   input into the computer.   immediately available.

How to create a process map
1. Create a process map worksheet.
2. Define the key elements.
3. Define the major work units.
4. Identify the activities.
5. Indicate the activities that flow from the internal customers.
6. Consider the best course of action to achieve the goal.

Step 4. Create a chart that follows the process flow, moving from left to right.

Step 5. Indicate activities that flow to the internal customers with an arrow. As with flow charts, process mapping should follow the actual observed sequence of events and not a secondhand description or an idealized model.

Step 6. Consider the best course of action to achieve the goal. We can achieve this goal by using the process evaluation technique described here.

HOW TO EVALUATE A PROCESS MAP

To evaluate a process map, we look for "problems" behind the scenes. In the previous example, if our aim is to reduce the average processing time from seven to four minutes, we can evaluate each aspect of the map. (See Exhibit 17.3).

- A terminal is not immediately available   *Can we have more terminals?*
- An officer is not available   *Can we do away with this procedure?*
- There are a large number of transactions   *Can we have a separate counter for this?*

Not all solutions are easy to implement or cost-effective. What we get at this stage is an indication of possible courses of action to achieve our goals.

Process mapping, like flow charting, calls attention to frequently overlooked aspects of a system. In general, process mapping and evaluation do not lead directly to action but provide potential solutions that may have to be tested further.

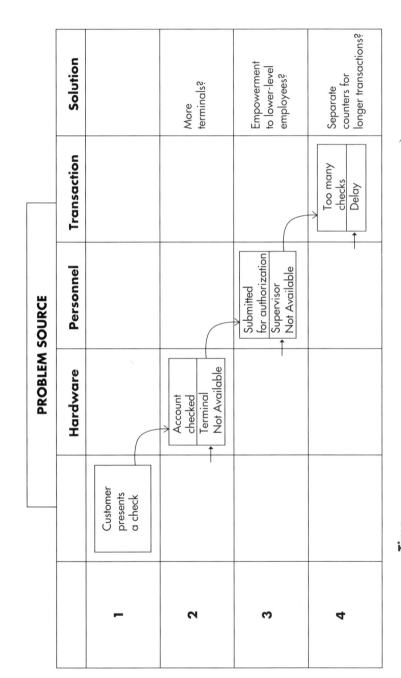

Exhibit 17.3
Process Flow Chart

OTHER THINGS YOU SHOULD KNOW

As with flow charts, the real value of process mapping and process evaluation is in the formalization of the process. The careful listing of the steps involved in a given process forces us to take note of the weak links in the system. It also provides definite clues as to where the bottlenecks are and which part of the process provides the greatest opportunity for improvement. It is usually helpful to create a process map that is very detailed, so that the cause of the problem or the area to be improved can be precisely identified. Another variation of this technique would involve creating a detailed flow chart of the process (as described in Chapter 11) before creating a process map.

To know more

Process mapping and process evaluation are commonly used techniques. The following book contains a description similar to the one provided here:

Whiteley, R. (1991), *The Customer Driven Company*. Reading, MA: Addison-Wesley.

A somewhat different and detailed exposition can be found in the following book:

Chang, R.Y. (1994), *Continuous Process Improvement*. Irvine, CA: Richard Chang Associates.

18

Delivering Techniques: People

P3D3: People and Delivering

	PRODUCERS	PROCESSES	PEOPLE
DIAGNOSING	Structural analysis Check sheets Mystery shopping Internal focus groups	Graphic techniques Run charts Stratification Flow charts	Complaint elicitation Content tracking Belief system analysis Pareto charts
DETAILING	Nominal group technique Benchmarking Deleting dimensionality The as-if frame The video camera	Control charts	External focus groups Survey research Laddering Factor analysis Gap analysis Wish lists
DELIVERING	Brainstorming Force field analysis Cost-benefit analysis	Fishbone diagrams Process mapping and evaluation	**Tracking**

T his stage of service quality measurement—delivering and people—refers to making sure that the quality program implemented by the organization is working the way it should. It is a way to ensure that the organization receives continual feedback, so that it can act should a program not work the way it was intended, and to alert the organization to the changing needs of the customer.

TRACKING

When a service quality program is implemented, it is important that it be kept on track. When market conditions change, so do customer expectations. New customers may have different expectations. Gaps between customer expectations and management perception can develop at any time. It is also possible that, as time goes by, the processes put into place may work less efficiently. We need constant feedback to avoid such eventualities.

Tracking is a method of continually evaluating our performance. It can be reactive or proactive.

Tracking can be proactive or reactive. *Reactive tracking* involves watching for problems that develop through an analysis of customer complaints and other telltale signals. *Proactive tracking* can be active or passive. *Passive proactive tracking* involves setting up a standardized research project, which provides management with continuous feedback. Active proactive tracking involves senior managers actively contacting a certain number of customers and getting their feedback on the service that is delivered versus the service that is expected.

HOW TO TRACK

Most conventional tracking studies fall under the category of passive proactive tracking. This type of tracking is usually carried out with the use of a standard questionnaire.

Step 1. Select the appropriate questions. Use only those questions that matter, those questions that discriminate. To identify such questions, you might want to do a preliminary large-scale study to understand which questions are salient and which are not. Techniques such as quadrant analysis, regression analysis, and discriminant analysis can be useful here. Salient attributes can be identified through direct questioning or derived importance scores.[1]

Step 2. Keep the questionnaire short. It is best to keep the questionnaire short, so that the quality of response is high and the cost is low. Lengthy tracking questionnaires have several drawbacks, such as lower response rates, lower quality of responses, and higher costs.

Step 3. Use appropriate scales. Be careful about the scales that are used. Use only scales that are sensitive to the measurement. Use simple scales, if possible. For a discussion of the different types of scales used in customer satisfaction research, see Chapter 20.

Step 4. Use at least one open-ended question. Tracking, by definition, is carried out over a period of time. During this

---

[1]Derived importance scores are scores calculated using statistical methods without directly asking the customer. For a more complete explanation, see the section on derived importance scores (Chapter 20).

time, conditions might change. What was satisfactory service at one point in time may not be satisfactory at some other point in time. When satisfaction scores decline, we need to know whether market conditions have changed. One or two open-end questions will help us achieve this purpose.

How to carry out tracking
1. Select the appropriate questions.
2. Keep the questionnaire short.
3. Use appropriate scales.
4. Use at least one open-end question.
5. Rotate the panel.
6. Use adequate sample sizes.

Step 5. Rotate the panel. If you are using a panel of customers to provide you with feedback, continually retire a portion of panelists to make room for new customers, as well as to eliminate habituation effects.

Step 6. Make sure that the sample sizes are adequate. Small samples cannot detect small differences. For example, if the sample size is 100, then a 6% change in customer satisfaction is not likely to be statistically significant, meaning that the change could be attributed to chance. So either your sample should be large enough to detect smaller differences, or you should use other techniques such as moving averages.

HOW TO INTERPRET TRACKING

- *Beware of sampling error.* If you use a new sample each time, allow for sampling error. Small increases or decreases in average are not likely to mean anything unless there is a trend.

- *Use control charts.* Use control charts to identify changing patterns. Unless there is evidence of an identifiable trend, do not interfere with the process and fine-tune it.

OTHER THINGS YOU SHOULD KNOW

It is preferable to track attributes, such as customer satisfaction, on a frequent basis. If resources are limited, then a more frequent, but smaller, "rolling sample" can be used instead of an infrequent larger sample. For example, instead of using a sample of 1,000 annually, we can use 100 per month, cumulating 12 months' sample for analysis and tracking purposes.

Part IV

Measuring Customer Satisfaction

19

Customer Satisfaction Measurement

S
o far, we have treated measurement of customer satisfaction as a part of measuring service quality. More specifically, techniques discussed under the People column of the P3D3 matrix mostly deal with customer satisfaction research. There are, however, several issues that are of specific interest to those who are involved in customer satisfaction research. In this part of the book, we explore in greater detail aspects of customer satisfaction measurement, which were briefly touched upon under service quality measurement.

There is widespread criticism of customer satisfaction measurement (CSM). The main problem with CSM is that it "does not work." In other words, CSM does not seem to relate to important business variables such as repeat purchase, customer retention, and profitability. It is logical to suppose that if customers are satisfied with us, they will return to us. They will be less inclined to switch. It also would follow that if fewer customers switched, then the cost of marketing would be lower, making the company more profitable. Almost by definition, we would expect customer satisfaction to relate to loyalty and profitability. If customer satisfaction does not accomplish these, then from a business point of view, there would be little point in tracking it. There is enough evidence to show (e.g., see *Fortune* 1995) that customer satisfaction, as currently measured, does not relate to crucial business variables such as repeat purchase and loyalty.

What are we to make of this? One possible conclusion is that customer satisfaction is irrelevant to business. This statement lacks face validity and does not make intuitive sense. Why would satisfied customers not buy from us again? Why would they not stay longer with us? Even Reichheld (1996), who contends that customer satisfaction is "one of the least reliable and most common [measures in use today]," admits that it "is not that customer satisfaction does not matter; it matters a great deal. It is the manner, context, and pri-

ority of satisfaction measurement that has become a problem."
A more rational hypothesis would be that it is customer
satisfaction, as measured currently, rather than customer satisfaction itself, that is unrelated to loyalty and profitability. In
fact, that is the hypothesis on which this section is based.
Customer satisfaction should relate to loyalty and profitability, and if it does not, it is the measurement that is at fault.
We start with a discussion of why customer satisfaction measurements often do not work.

MEASURING THE WRONG THINGS

We measure the wrong things when our measurements are
unfocused or when too many trivial measures are included.

Unfocused measurements

Not all companies have the same goals and objectives. Not all
companies aspire to be price-competitive or state of the art. In
fact, Treacy and Wiersema (1995) argue that a company needs
to excel in only one of three aspects—innovation, product leadership, or customer intimacy—and be only acceptable in the
other two. In other words, if a company's mission is not to be
the most innovative company in the field, it is not necessary to
measure this aspect in great detail. Detailed measures of satisfaction in areas in which a company does not intend to excel is
similar to measuring the trivial many, since they are not really
actionable as far as the company is concerned.

Using too many measures

In an attempt to make measurements comprehensive, many
researchers fall into the trap of including far too many variables, making the trivial many dominate the vital few.
Although this approach might be useful at exploratory stages,
it is inappropriate usually at later stages of measurement.
Measuring the trivial many, as opposed to the vital few, variables has several disadvantages: It can diffuse our focus and
distract our attention away from important to "interesting"
variables, make the data collection process more difficult, put
burden on the data collection process, and as a result,
decrease the quality of the data collected.

USING INTERNAL MEASUREMENTS THAT ARE DETRIMENTAL TO EXTERNAL CUSTOMER SATISFACTION

Organizations eager to deliver customer satisfaction often
tend to ignore the very people—their employees—who are

charged with the responsibility of delivering it. It is assumed that rewards and punishments that are based on performance are all that is needed to motivate employees. This tacit assumption leads to internal measurement that works against external customer satisfaction.

Using measurements that create imbalance

Quality in service is created by the interaction of three distinct forces—producer, processes, and people. Many organizations make the mistake of emphasizing customer satisfaction to the exclusion of employee satisfaction. When employees are simply rewarded and punished on the basis of what may be faulty measurements of customer satisfaction, it introduces fear, which is one of the fundamental enemies of quality (Deming 1986). As Deming repeatedly points out, attempts to achieve quality through employee intimidation are bound to fail. Customer satisfaction has to be balanced with employee satisfaction. Employees are internal customers, and in the long run, employee satisfaction is critical to customer satisfaction. The purpose of customer satisfaction measurement should be to improve customer service and not to intimidate employees. As McConnell (1991) puts it, "as long as fear prevails, your people will continue in a survival mode, and the implementation of a quality approach to management will remain an impossible dream."

"Chicken efficiency"

Another problem related to internal performance measures is what Brown (1996) calls "chicken efficiency." Fast-food restaurants cook their food so that customers can be served quickly. However, when the food is cooked but not sold within a given period of time, it has to be thrown away. When the chain managers are judged on the basis of the number of chickens that are thrown away, they may become "efficient" by not cooking the chicken until a customer shows up. This might increase the "efficiency" of the outlet at the expense of the customer, who may have to wait longer to be served. Such measures drive the wrong performance. To use another example, if employees are judged on the basis of the number of mistakes they make in dealing with customer complaints, they might find subtle ways of avoiding customers altogether.

USING REARVIEW MEASUREMENTS

Key measures change over time. Services that were once considered exceptional can become standard at a later point in time. For example, many automobile features that were optional until a few years ago, such as CD players and air bags, are now often standard. Such changes can make what once were key drivers into cost-of-entry variables. High prices may have little bearing on customer satisfaction under certain economic conditions, and yet, price can be the driver under other economic conditions. Variables that once contributed to customer satisfaction may no longer do so. This is particularly true in the current context. Rapid technological developments can change key drivers within a short period of time.

Unless key drivers are tested on a continual basis for their contribution to satisfaction, we could be using variables that no longer drive satisfaction.

MEASURING THE WRONG AUDIENCE

Most CSM systems avoid the mistake of grouping customers with obviously dissimilar needs. For example, experienced researchers would probably develop different measurement systems for domestic and commercial users, even though the service being measured is the same (e.g., telephone services). However, there are several instances in which such intergroup distinctions are not so obvious. Questions relating to emergency admissions are relevant only to a small proportion of people using medical services. Sophisticated financial services offered by a bank may be of little interest to those whose needs rarely go beyond basic deposits and withdrawals. Attributes that relate to a variety of services provided by a hotel may not mean much to those who never, or sparingly, use these services. As a result, CSM of these services will not truly reflect the discontent of those who use the services on an ongoing basis, unless the relevant subgroups are specifically identified and the data carefully segregated and analyzed. Even then, we may not have a sufficient number of cases that will enable us to interpret the data adequately. Yet, most CSM is global.

The inclusion of several customers whose views are not critical to the service in question can obscure the views of the few that are. For example, if 90% of the businesses are not time-sensitive, then a courier firm that delivers on time and one that doesn't may get similar satisfaction ratings. However, if most of the courier firm's profits come from time-sensitive clients, then CSM would miss the point by diluting the views of the vital few customers.

MEASURING THINGS THE WRONG WAY

Even when we measure the right things, we may go wrong by using the wrong measurement techniques. For example, we could be measuring our performance versus that of our competition using an 11-point scale. If such a scale turns out to be inconsistent or insensitive in detecting differences, then, even though we are measuring the right thing, our measurement will be flawed. Similarly, customers' stated importance of a given attribute may have little to do with their satisfaction. Using metrics that are not tested for their validity and reliability also can provide misleading measurements of customer satisfaction.

Social measurements can never be as precise as physical measurements. Consequently, the criterion for a good customer satisfaction metric is not accuracy but usefulness. Is the metric sensitive enough to detect differences in service quality offered by two companies? Can the metric spot the changes in customer satisfaction between one time period and the next? When we do not pay enough attention to such aspects of measurement, we are likely to end up with scores that are useless at best and misleading at worst.

From another point of view, as we discuss in Parts II and III, using the wrong techniques can result in distorted measurements as well.

HAVING NO KEY MEASURES OF SATISFACTION

Not all measures contribute to customer satisfaction. Even those that do so do not contribute to the same extent. When we don't specifically identify key satisfaction measures, we accord equal importance to key measures and trivial measures, to measures that are of marginal importance and those that are not. Key measure can be a priori, a posterior, or both. An organization can decide on the basis of its mission what the key measures are. Alternatively (or in addition), it can derive the importance of the attributes being measured. Customer satisfaction measurements tend to be less effective when there are no key measures.

THE USE OF THE CUSTOMER SATISFACTION INDEX

One of the most widely used measures of customer satisfaction is the customer satisfaction index (CSI). The CSI is a single number that management believes will tell it how the company is doing as far as customer satisfaction is concerned.

The movement of this number is watched eagerly by those who are charged with the task of keeping customers happy. (The CSI does not have to be a single number. Some companies use more than one index. But the basic idea is the same—summarize large quantities of data into few numbers, typically one.) In fact, many companies use the CSI to compensate employees (Naumann and Giel 1995). Although it is enticing to have a single number that will tell us at once how satisfied our customers are and how well we are delivering satisfactory service, the CSI can be highly misleading. Considering the importance that many companies attach to this number, it is time we took a closer look at this measure. We discuss this in greater detail in the next chapter.

TOWARD AN ACTIONABLE CSM SYSTEM

Customer satisfaction measurement systems that suffer from one or more of these shortcomings tend to be less effective. In some cases, they can be misleading. What we need, then, is a customer satisfaction system that is actionable, one that can overcome or will minimize the impact of the problems we have discussed so far. The model proposed in the next chapter details steps toward achieving that goal.

20

A Step-by-Step Guide to Measuring Customer Satisfaction

Measuring Customer Satisfaction

	TEN STEPS TO CREATING AN ACTIONABLE CUSTOMER SATISFACTION STUDY		
CONCEIVE	1. Gather background data	2. Choose attributes to measure	3. Choose the right audience
DEVELOP	4. Choose the basic CSM questions	5. Choose the right metric	6. Make analysis action oriented
INTERPRET & TRACK	7. Consider segmenting the market	8. Interpret the measures correctly	9. Use results cautiously
	10. Create a tracking system		

This chapter discusses in detail how to set up a customer satisfaction measurement system. The focus of the discussion is on conducting surveys that will measure and track customer satisfaction. The approach presented here takes into account the common mistakes in measuring CSM and suggests ways to eliminate or minimize such mistakes.

STEP 1. GATHER BACKGROUND DATA

When starting a CSM program, it is always helpful to begin with some qualitative research. Techniques such as *focus groups* (pp. 153–55), *brainstorming* (pp. 184–86), *nominal group technique* (pp. 117–20), and *laddering* (pp. 164–69) can be used for this purpose. Preliminary measurement of customer satisfaction may also involve *eliciting* and *analyzing complaints*. We already have discussed techniques that are useful for these purposes. Data obtained through internal and external focus groups, and insights gained from customer complaints, can provide useful input for developing a CSM system. In addition, we also may want to specify how the information we collect will be used. We have two purposes at this stage: (1) to gather effectively all preliminary information we have and need and (2) to bring focus to the measurement system by defining how the information will be used.

STEP 2. CHOOSE THE ATTRIBUTES TO MEASURE

For a CSM system to be effective, we need to measure the right things. This means choosing attributes that are relevant. Nobody purposely sets out to measure irrelevant attributes, but one often ends up measuring things that do not contribute to the understanding of customer satisfaction. More specifically, measuring the right attributes means four things:

1. Measuring attributes that are relevant to the mission of the organization;

2. Measuring attributes that contribute to customer satisfaction;

3. Avoiding measures that are no longer valid; and

4. Avoiding measures that are detrimental to customer satisfaction.

START WITH THE PURPOSE: MISSION STATEMENTS

The first aspect of creating focused measurements relates to the organization's mission. What is the mission of the organization? Is it to provide exceptional service? Is it to offer the most competitive price? Is it to be the most innovative company in the field? No matter what the company's primary mission, it should be explored in greater detail than should other attributes. The main reason for this is that it is unrealistic to expect the company to excel in all aspects that contribute to customer satisfaction. For example, if an organization wants to be highly innovative and provide the highest-quality service, it is unlikely that the organization will have the lowest price. If a firm expects to excel in an area, it follows that we need more information about customer reaction in that specific area than in other areas in which the organization proposes to provide only adequate service. When attributes measured pertain to customer satisfaction in areas in which the firm wants to excel, they provide specific input to the firm.

Derive the importance scores: Measure attributes that matter

Measuring only those attributes that contribute to satisfaction constitutes two aspects: including attributes that contribute to satisfaction and eliminating those that do not. Measuring the things that do not contribute to satisfaction cannot be considered harmless. Irrelevant attributes provide an illusion of comprehensiveness, and when there are too many of them, they may overshadow the relevant attributes. We can get measurements on only those aspects of service we choose to measure. So, it is critical that we choose all the measures we need and eliminate those we do not need. While using our mission statement is one way of choosing the right attributes, it also is important that the attributes we measure do, indeed, contribute to satisfaction.

Customers often are asked to evaluate an organization on specific attributes such as "How well did organization X do in terms of quick response?" Even if an organization gets a high score on a positive attribute, it does not follow that this attribute is important to consumers.

A derived importance score is any importance score that is calculated on the basis of a respondent's answers to a set of questions using techniques such as coefficient of determination (R-squared), multiple regression, and discriminant analysis.

We can, of course, ask a corresponding question on the importance of each attribute (e.g., "How important is it to you that an organization is quick to respond?") and plot importance against performance. This approach has two disadvantages. First, certain answers are inherently more probable. For example, people might state that it is important that they not wait in line, and yet, this may not necessarily affect their satisfaction level. Second, it increases the length of the questionnaire, because we need to ask an importance question for each attribute question. To overcome these problems, we can use what are known as "derived importance" scores by relating the way customers rate an attribute to their level of satisfaction.

What are derived importance scores?

A derived importance score is any importance score that is calculated on the basis of a respondent's answers to a set of questions. In other words, a customer does not have to tell us directly how important different attributes are in deter-mining satisfaction. The term *derived importance score* is a generic term and does not necessarily imply the use of any specific measure. However, in customer satisfaction research, three techniques are commonly used: coefficient of determination (R-squared), multiple regression, and dis-criminant analysis.

Coefficient of determination

The coefficient of determination is the correlation squared. Correlation is a simple statistic that measures how well two attributes are (linearly) related. For example, we can ask cus-tomers about a retail establishment the following question:

"Overall, how do you rate the quality of service provided by this company?"

and follow this by a series of evaluative questions such as "How would you rate this establishment in terms of

- promptness of service,
- courteousness of staff,
- adequately trained personnel,
- knowledge level of staff?"

We then can correlate each of the rating questions with over-all satisfaction.

Attribute	Correlation with overall satisfaction
• Promptness of service	.73
• Courteousness of staff	.80
• Adequately trained personnel	.65
• Knowledge level of staff	.40

Although correlation measures how well each attribute is related to overall satisfaction, it is not a good enough measure for assessing the importance of an attribute to overall satisfac-tion. The reason for this is that correlation is not a linear mea-sure. For example, a correlation coefficient of .4 is not twice as large as a correlation of .2. This makes the comparison of the importance of different attributes intrinsically difficult.

A better measure of derived importance is the coefficient of determination, or R-squared. This measure is obtained by taking the square of the correlation, which is a linear mea-sure.

Attribute	Correlation with overall satisfaction	R-squared	% variance (explained $R^2 \times 100$)
• Promptness of service	.73	.53	53%
• Courteousness of staff	.80	.64	64
• Adequately trained personnel	.65	.42	42
• Knowledge level of staff	.40	.16	16

The coefficient of determination (R-squared) refers to the amount of variance explained, and it is interpreted linearly. Thus, we can state that courteousness is four times as important as knowledge in determining overall satisfaction, because R-squared is four times as large (16 versus 64).

Multiple regression analysis

If our aim is to assess the core set of attributes that contributes to customer satisfaction, we can use another technique known as *multiple regression analysis*. Given a set of attributes that influences customer satisfaction, multiple regression analysis identifies the fewest possible attributes that contribute to customer satisfaction, as well as their relative importance. The input for this analysis could be customer ratings of overall satisfaction for a given firm and the ratings of the same firm on performance attributes.

The output produced by multiple regression analysis includes the following:

• The attributes that contribute the most to customer satisfaction;

• The percentage of variance explained by the attributes that contribute to customer satisfaction (the higher the percentage, the greater the contribution of the chosen attributes to customer satisfaction); and

• The relative importance of the attributes included in the model (commonly known as the beta weights).

However, there are many weaknesses in this model. For example, if two attributes are both highly related to customer satisfaction and if they correlate highly between themselves, then only one of the two will appear to influence customer satisfaction. For example, if fast service and efficient service are highly correlated with each other and with customer satisfaction, then only one of the two (say, efficient service) will be highly related to customer satisfaction. The other variable (fast service) is likely to be only weakly related to satisfaction. This problem is known as multicollinearity. As long as this problem exists, weights derived from multiple regression analysis cannot be used to indicate the relative importance of attributes.

Simple regression analysis

In simple regression analysis, we carry out a regression for each attribute separately, with some criterion variable such as overall customer satisfaction. Because we analyze one variable at a time, the problem of multicollinearity does not arise. What we get is a measure similar to coefficient of determination.

Discriminant analysis

Why do customers prefer one organization over another? What attributes contribute to this choice? To what extent do they contribute? Questions such as these are answered by discriminant analysis. In structure, as well as in its basic objective, discriminant analysis is similar to multiple regression analysis. In multiple regression analysis, our aim is to understand the extent to which a set of variables (such as different performance ratings) affects another variable (such as customer satisfaction). In discriminant analysis, our aim is to understand the extent to which a set of variables (such as different performance ratings) affects a customer choosing one firm over another.

Limitations of derived importance scores

Although it looks attractive to use derived importance scores, they can be seriously misleading. Consider an attribute on which all firms are rated high or all firms are rated low. When this happens, attributes that show little variance will have low derived importance. The reason for this is that all firms are rated the same, irrespective of how they are rated on overall satisfaction. For example, consider the following illustration:

Firm	Overall rating	Convenient location
A	9	8
B	3	8
C	5	7
D	8	7

Although B scored low on overall satisfaction, it is perceived to be as good as any other firm as far as convenient location is concerned. Although the overall ratings vary, the ratings on convenient location are more or less constant. Therefore, the derived importance of convenient location will be low. But it does NOT mean that convenient location is not important. So, when we compute derived importance, we also should look for attributes that show low variance. In such cases, it is the stated importance, rather than the derived importance, that is more reliable.

What technique to use?

If we simply want to understand the relative importance of different attributes, correlation is preferred, because it is not affected by other variables in the set. If, on the other hand, we want to build a model to predict customer satisfaction with the least number of variables, multiple regression may be a better method. Finally, if we want to know why a customer chooses to belong to one group (e.g., customer of our firm) versus another (e.g., customer of our competitor), we use discriminant analysis.

What if this is your first CSM quantitative study?

The previous discussion assumes that you have done some preliminary quantitative research from which the results can be used to derive the importance weights. If no such research data are available, then derived importance scores cannot be used to select the salient attributes. In such cases, a larger number of attributes may be included in the questionnaire, based on qualitative research and the objectives of the firm. Once some quantitative data become available, we can derive the importance of attributes and eliminate the attributes that do not contribute to customer satisfaction from the next study.

What criterion measure to use?

Most customer satisfaction studies use overall satisfaction as the criterion measure. The derived importance scores are simply a measure of how strongly each attribute contributes to overall satisfaction. This is an acceptable approach. However, CSMs have been criticized as being unrelated to behavioral variables such as repeat purchase. In such cases, there is no reason why the criterion variable could not be repeat purchase, revenue from current customers, or even market share. If repeat purchase data are not available, we also can use some proxy variables such as intent to buy the product the next time. We can use both hard (such as repeat purchase) and soft (such as overall satisfaction) measures and derive more than one set of derived importance scores.

To know more

Derived importance score is not a statistical term but a generic expression for importance weights obtained by a number of methods. Any applied book on statistics covering the techniques discussed in this section can be used to obtain further information. Some such books include the following:

Grim, L.G. and P.R. Yarnold (1995), *Reading and Understanding Multivariate Statistics.* Washington, DC: American Psychological Association.

Sharma, S. (1996), *Applied Multivariate Technologies.* New York: John Wiley & Sons.

Be current: Avoid measurements that no longer work

Over a period of time, the marketing environment changes. Even if we have been careful in choosing the attributes that relate to our mission and contribute to customer satisfaction, it does not follow that these attributes will be equally effective across time. Rapid technological changes can quickly change the factors that contribute to satisfaction. What contributes to a satisfactory transaction in a bank? Research once might have shown that efficiency and pleasantness of the employee with whom the customer interacts are the most critical factors. As more people start using electronic transactions, efficiency and pleasantness of the employee may become less critical. At the same time, the ease and quickness with which the customer can access his or her account and carry out the required transactions can be more important in contributing to customer satisfaction. Therefore, it is vital that we not completely rely on the derived importance scores of the past but continually test them to make sure that they stay current.

Use relevant measures: Avoid detrimental measures

In measuring customer satisfaction, we should avoid measures that create a conflict between external and internal customers. A Canadian hotel chain had this sign posted at the check-in counter: "You are checked in within 60 seconds, or your room is free." It is unclear whether customer satisfaction is substantially affected by the fact that customers are checked in within 60 seconds as opposed to 2 or 3 minutes. Yet, such a stringent standard (with uncertain benefits to the customer) is likely to create stress in the employee, leading to employee dissatisfaction. A measure such as this can potentially create a conflict between the employee and the customer, where the customer is perceived as a challenge to be coped with. As Deming repeatedly emphasizes, dissatisfied or fearful employees can seldom be expected to provide quality service that leads to customer satisfaction.

STEP 3. CHOOSE THE RIGHT AUDIENCE TO BE MEASURED

Marketers and researchers are familiar with the concept of target audiences. Seldom would a competent marketer or researcher measure the wrong audience. However, in measuring service quality, measuring the wrong audience happens in subtle ways. It comes about by the inclusion of respondents whose responses are not relevant for the survey under consideration. As a result, we tend to get high customer satisfaction scores. To appreciate this problem, we must understand the nature of customer expectations, especially in the service industry. An examination of customer needs points to the following observations:

1. *Most customers have only nominal and predictable contact with us.* For example, most people who use a bank do so to deposit and withdraw money in predictable patterns. People who use multiple services and those with unusual requests form a minority.

2. *Customers who have nominal and predictable transactions tend not to be dissatisfied.* Even when customers who have nominal and predictable contacts do complain, the nature of their complaints tends to be predictable and easily remedied. If a person's main contact with a bank is confined to depositing his or her paycheck twice a month, there is little to be dissatisfied about, except perhaps the time he or she has to wait to be served and the impoliteness of the employee.

The first point (most customers have minimal contact) is in line with customer buying behavior, which tends to follow a negative binomial distribution (Ehrenberg 1972). High-quantity buying is limited to a small group of buyers. This is the commonly observed Pareto phenomenon. From a logical point of view, there is no reason for someone who has minimal and predictable contact with us to be dissatisfied (rating us a 3 on a 10-point scale), unless the service is noticeably bad.

Or, to use another example, let us consider internal customer satisfaction with the legal department. Most employees or department heads may have no reason to contact the legal department and, as a result, will rate it more positively than negatively. Even if we isolate internal customers who have had some actual contact with the legal department, the problem of measurement still might persist. Suppose that 95% of those who contacted the legal department did so to obtain routine material such as employee contract forms. Assuming such requests were handled with ordinary efficiency, we would expect the customers to be satisfied with the response they received. Further suppose that the remaining 5% needed some serious legal advice, and they were highly dissatisfied with the quality of the service they received. Now, even if we aggregate customer satisfaction scores of only those who had some contact with the legal department, the voice of the 5% of dissatisfied customers will be completely drowned out by the voice of the 95% of satisfied customers. Yet, it is the view of the 5% who had genuine legal problems that might be critical in determining how satisfactorily the legal department is functioning.

Customer dissatisfaction is usually localized

We start with the hypothesis that dissatisfaction usually is localized. Late delivery may be a problem for some customers, but not for all. Not all customers wait in line for a long time; customers who arrive early and during off-peak hours are served faster. Minor discrepancies in amounts billed bother some customers more than others. As a result, serious customer dissatisfaction seldom arises across the board. Dissatisfaction usually is localized and limited to a small proportion of customers. Consequently, aggregate measure of customer satisfaction is of limited value at best and highly misleading at worst.

This is not to imply that dissatisfaction does not arise across the board. It does, but it is much more likely to arise in small groups that are exposed frequently to a given service. Such scenarios include the following:

- Billing problems affecting 1% or 2% of your customers,
- Delivery problems confined to a small region and affecting no more than 1% of your customers, and
- The technical department failing to provide satisfactory service only with certain types of problems, which may arise in less than 5% of all cases.

These scenarios are more probable than

- billing problems affecting 90% of your customers,
- delivery problems arising in every region and affecting more than 80% of your customers, and
- the technical department failing to provide satisfactory service no matter what the problem.

Dissatisfied customers may be few, but they may be important

As a result, aggregate CSM data will not identify developing problems. Small numbers of dissatisfied customers are easily overshadowed by large numbers of "satisfied" customers. The argument often is made that we should probably be happy if a vast majority of our customers are satisfied. The fallacy in this argument is that it confuses input with output. Dissatisfied customers may be a minority, but they may be knowledgeable; they may be heavy users; and they may be highly profitable to the organization. There is also the possibility that discontent may spread.

Therefore, we should avoid thinking of customers as an amorphous group and think of them as a collection of groups of customers with different needs and expectations. For example, if we are doing an internal customer satisfaction study with regard to the technical services department, then we should keep in mind the following:

1. We should avoid surveying everyone who is a potential customer of technical services. Positive feelings held by employees who have not had any significant dealings with the technical department have no bearing on the performance of the technical services department. In fact, they dilute the evaluations provided by more knowledgeable evaluators.

2. Neither should we believe that surveying only those who have had dealings with the technical department will solve the problem. It is very likely that most of those who contact the technical department do so for relatively minor and routine services. There may not be much at stake and, as a result, the dissatisfaction level may be low.

3. We should avoid asking general questions that can mean different things to different customers. Consider a question such as "How satisfied are you with the timely response of technical services?" This question looks sufficiently precise and focused and, yet, it may tell us nothing about how prompt the service has been. If most people who approach the technical department have requirements that are not time-sensitive, a week's turnaround time may not affect the customer satisfaction level. But, if the request is time-sensitive, even a few hours' delay can cause considerable dissatisfaction.

Two measurement filters

Our first priority, then, is not to think of customer satisfaction in general terms, but to view it as a measure that has to be put through at least two other filters.

Filter 1. What specific product or service are we measuring customer satisfaction against? For example, it is not enough for a financial institution to measure satisfaction with "retirement products." What, precisely, is being measured? Mutual fund sales? Advice on asset allocations? We cannot possibly increase customer satisfaction if we do not know exactly what a customer is not satisfied with.

Filter 2. Is this customer a user of such a product or service? If we measure customer satisfaction in relation to the mutual fund advice we offer, we need to confine ourselves to those who have the experience of buying mutual funds from us.

These two factors then can be filtered further in terms of heaviness of usage and the seriousness of the problem. Most users of CSM do segment the market by using demographics, psychographics, usage, or geodemographics. Unfortunately, these segments do not necessarily relate to the service on which satisfaction measurement is sought.

We need to understand before we aggregate

This is not to say that we should not aggregate customers. Rather, we should first understand customers and then, on the basis of their needs, group them later. In practical terms, this means that the starting point for customer satisfaction measurement is the service on which the measurement is sought. When we think in terms of specific services, our questionnaire itself will have different versions. To continue our illustration, we will not ask for satisfaction on "timeliness." When we are measuring satisfaction, the rating on timeliness may not have much meaning if the customer is mainly using services that are not time-sensitive, such as requesting upgrades for computers. In such cases, we may want to ask how long the turnaround time was and whether that was satisfactory. If we are asking about a time-sensitive service, such as fixing a computer that "crashed," then timeliness, rather than the elapsed time, is critical. Once we start to think of the specific aspects of service on which satisfaction measurement is sought, then questions become focused and specific. The measurements we derive from specific questions provide important input to quality improvement.

Think in terms of processes

One of the fundamental tenets of the quality movement is that excellence is achieved through focusing on processes rather than on people. When we blindly segment the market and try to understand customer satisfaction by segment, we are concentrating on people. But when we look at each service and relate it to customer satisfaction, our focus is on the process. We will know if customers are dissatisfied and, if so, *why* they are dissatisfied. Because satisfaction is related to a specific service and process associated with it, we also will have input to help us improve the quality of service.

If we want to make customer satisfaction measurement work, we should move away from using customer satisfaction as a proxy measure for employee performance, simply because it is not. If we use CSM as a measure of how the processes are working, rather than how employees measure up (or as a progress report of our performance), then our questionnaires will relate customer satisfaction to the processes under consideration. As quality experts from Deming to Crosby point out, the most effective way to improve customer satisfaction is to improve the processes through which services are delivered, not to coerce employees to deliver it.

For example, in an internal customer satisfaction study, if, on "timely response," the legal department gets a score of 8 and the technical department gets a 7, what exactly are we measuring here? What conclusions can we draw? That the technical department is tardy? What if the workload of the technical department is four times heavier than that of the legal department? Even if it is true that the technical department is tardy, what do we know about the context? What processes are they supposed to improve? Is it a question of resources or competence? How serious is the problem? The more we consider such questions, the less meaningful the standard measures of customer satisfaction begin to look.

Processes determine the audience

This step is about choosing the right audience. Yet, much of our discussion has been centered on the dangers of routine aggregation of data and processes that are to be measured. This is because it is the processes that determine the audience, so aggregation has to be done carefully. To choose the right audience, you must do the following:

- *Think in terms of subgroups.* We should think in terms of subgroups of customers. A measure such as prompt service can mean different things to different customers, depending on the heaviness of their usage.

- *Think in terms of processes.* Our measurements should be in terms of processes. This means that we should be wary of using a standard measure across different services. While comparability is a good thing, it should not come at the expense of meaning. If we need to use standard attributes, they should be followed by questions— probably open-ended ones— that will quantify the ratings.

- *Think in terms of feedback rather than a progress report.* Treating customer satisfaction measurement as a progress report is the main reason why there is widespread use of standardized measures. When we eliminate the need to standardize, we can concentrate on the real business of measuring customer satisfaction.

In many cases, we may not know precisely who the right audience is. In other cases, we may have to determine the right audience after the fact. For these reasons, it is important to ask the right CSM questions (which are discussed in Step 4).

STEP 4. DECIDE ON THE BASIC CSM QUESTION COMPONENTS

Five basic questions relate to the basis of customer satisfaction measurement: incidence, frequency, importance, performance, and an overall criterion measure. It is not absolutely essential to ask all five types of questions, but they must be given sufficient consideration before deciding to discard one or more of the five measures.

Incidence

This variable relates to the relevance of a given service or the incidence of a given problem. The following are examples of incidence questions:

- "Did you use an electronic search service in the past year?"
- "Did you have any problem with your telephone service in the past three months?"

These questions act as filtering variables for further questions, as well as provide the basis for defining the relevant audience.

Frequency

When we identify a customer as the user of a service or as one facing a problem, we then need to assess the frequency with which the service is used or the problem is encountered. Once again, the purpose of this variable is to separate frequent from causal problems and to relate customer satisfaction to the frequent recurrence of the problem. Examples of frequency questions include the following:

- "How often did you use an electronic search service in the past year?"
- "How often did you have a problem with your telephone service in the past three months?"

Frequency questions usually are asked only of those who reply in the affirmative to the incidence questions.

Importance

A problem that is frequent (e.g., the elevator is always crowded) may not necessarily be considered important by customers who face it. Conversely, a service that is not used frequently by the customer (e.g., emergency procedures in a hospital) may be vitally important. Therefore, we need a measure of importance in addition to the frequency measure. Examples of importance questions include the following:

- "How important is it to you that your computer problems be fixed in the same day?"
- "Is it important to you that our service be available to you online?"

Performance

The previous three types of questions are a prelude to the central issue of performance. How satisfied is the customer with our performance? How does our performance compare with that of our competitors? In some cases, we may split this variable into two parts—one relating to how well we performed and the other relating to how satisfied the customer is with our performance. Examples of performance questions include the following:

- "How do you rate our ability to provide same-day service?"
- "How satisfied are you with our same-day service?"
- "How would you rate Company B [competitor] on this service?"

Overall criterion measure

It also is useful to have an overall criterion measure, such as overall satisfaction with the service provided. The overall criterion measure provides us with a means of computing the importance of the individual attributes (see the section on derived importance scores at the beginning of this chapter).

These five aspects of measurement—incidence, frequency, importance, performance, and overall criterion measure—

are basic to all CSM systems, though they may not be explicitly included in the questionnaire. For example, if we interview only those who made more than ten long-distance calls last month, based on telephone company records, we already know the incidence and frequency. Again, in some cases, we may avoid asking direct importance questions and decide to use derived importance scores instead. So, it is not always necessary to ask explicit questions to cover these five aspects relating to customer satisfaction.

STEP 5. CHOOSE THE RIGHT METRIC

Attributes we choose to measure can be measured on a number of different scales. What type should be used? Do we use a numeric scale (e.g., a 10-point scale), a verbal scale (e.g., good, average, or poor), or a binary scale (e.g., satisfied or not satisfied)?

The measuring instrument we use influences satisfaction scores. For example, if the average rating of overall satisfaction is 7.8 on a 10-point scale, what average rating can we expect the same attribute to have if it is measured on a 5-point scale? The current evidence is that different scales provide different ratings, and they are not directly comparable. This suggests that we should be careful about the metric we choose to measure customer satisfaction. The second problem is that many metrics produce inflated scores. On 10-point scales, most customers do not use the lower points of the scale; when there is no midpoint on a scale, most neutral customers tend to move up rather than down (positive bias). So we must look at measurement scales with two issues in mind:

1. *Weaknesses of measurement scales.* Most scales used in CSM have inherent weaknesses. We cannot avoid them, but we can choose a scale that introduces the least amount of bias for the problem under consideration.

2. *Inflated ratings.* We seem to get inflated ratings when we use standard numerical scales such as the 10-point scale. As noted elsewhere, this is likely due to extraneous influences, such as regression toward the scale, midpoint of the scale, respondents' tendency to truncate the scale, and the prevalence of a high proportion of low-use customers.

These two points are discussed in greater detail subsequently.

a. Problems with measuring instruments

The first problem relates to the type of scales used in CSM studies. Some scales produce more reliable results than do others. The problems of scales used in marketing research include response bias, lack of clarity, and the inability to differentiate among the objects rated. Scales are sometimes rejected because they lack face validity (i.e., they don't appear "reasonable" to the user). Sometimes a scale that works well in a face-to-face interview may not work in the same way in a mail or telephone survey. Other scales may be somewhat more difficult for respondents to use. Improving measuring instruments is an ongoing process. Therefore, the following comments should be taken as representing the current state of knowledge and not as definite solutions to problems of measurement. The following observations are based on the results of a number of studies, the most prominent of which are by Bellcore Measurements Research (Devlin, Dong, and Brown 1993). The results thus far indicate that there is no "best scale" that will provide the most appropriate results under all circumstances. As Devlin, Dong, and Brown (1993) succinctly put it, "There is no perfect scale, only bad and better ones." It is best to experiment with a short list of different scales before settling on the ones that are best suited for your purposes.

Most scales that are used in service quality research fall into three major categories: verbal scales, numeric scales, and comparison scales

Verbal scales

Verbal scales of evaluation use words, rather than numbers, to describe various scale points. Although, typically, numbers are assigned to different scale points (e.g., 4 = Very good; 3 = Good; 2 = Not good; 1 = Poor), respondents using the verbal scale depend on words, rather than numbers, to evaluate the service. Verbal scales can be binary scales, rating scales with a midpoint, or rating scales without a midpoint.

> *Binary scales.* Binary scales have two alternatives, such as
> - Acceptable – Unacceptable
> - Good – Not good
> - Satisfied – Dissatisfied.

Binary scales are excellent when the distinctions are clear in a customer's mind. They also force customers to examine their attitudes more closely and decide one way or the other. However, binary scales tend to make the customer's task difficult when he or she believes that the true answer lies between the two alternatives offered. For example, the service offered may not be considered "unacceptable," but neither is it "acceptable" in the sense that the customer is satisfied with it. Therefore, binary scales are suitable only when we believe that the respondents have clear-cut perceptions.

Rating scales without a midpoint. Examples of rating scales without midpoints include

- Acceptable – Somewhat acceptable – Somewhat unacceptable – Unacceptable
- Excellent – Good – Poor – Very poor
- Very satisfied – Satisfied – Dissatisfied – Very dissatisfied.

Scales such as these tend to suffer from a positive response bias. Studies show that those who have neither a positive nor a negative opinion about something tend to choose the lowest positive descriptor rather than the lowest negative descriptor. There is some evidence to show that this bias is not uniformly distributed across the population. This poses an additional problem. The differences in evaluation between two subgroups may be a function of their bias toward a positive response, rather than of genuine evaluative differences.

Rating scales with a midpoint. The previously noted scales may be changed to include midpoints. The following is an example of a verbal scale with a midpoint:

- Acceptable – Somewhat acceptable – Neither acceptable nor unacceptable – Somewhat unacceptable – Unacceptable
- Excellent – Good – Average – Poor – Very poor
- Very satisfied – Satisfied – Neither satisfied nor dissatisfied – Dissatisfied – Very dissatisfied

As long as these types of scales are unambiguous, they seem to work in most situations, though ambiguity often arises in the way in which a question is framed.

Subjective versus objective scales

Rating scales can be phrased either from a subjective viewpoint or from an objective point of view. Subjective scales refer to a customer's personal feelings, as in this example:

- Very satisfied – Satisfied – Neither satisfied nor dissatisfied – Dissatisfied – Very dissatisfied

An *objective scale*, on the other hand, attempts to elicit from a customer an "objective" evaluation, as shown in this example:

- Excellent – Good – Average – Poor – Very poor

Which is better—subjective scales or objective scales? Again, empirical research seems to support objective scales. Why is this so? One possible hypothesis is that objective scales tend to suffer less from positive bias. An objective rating gives the customer a chance to dissociate his or her feelings—however mild—from the evaluation itself. *"Poor" [service]* sounds less like a complaint than *[I am] dissatisfied [with the service]* and, as a result, less subject to positive bias. Devlin, Dong, and Brown (1993) state that the relationship between these two scales is complex (see Exhibit 20.1).

Numeric scales

Numeric scales, such as 10-point scales, appear to have inconsistent discriminating power. More often than not, they are poor discriminators. Another problem with these scales is the ambiguity of what, for example, 7.5 means in words. Although an average of 7.5 sounds high, what if averages for all institutions tested range from 6.5 to 8.5? What if the aver-

Exhibit 20.1
Examples of How Respondents Use Different Scales

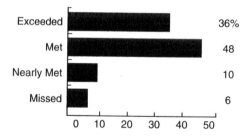

Exceeded	36%
Met	48
Nearly Met	10
Missed	6

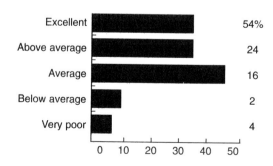

Excellent	54%
Above average	24
Average	16
Below average	2
Very poor	4

Source: Devlin, Dong, and Brown (1993).

ages range from 7.5 to 9.5? There does not seem to be a consistent relationship between numbers on this scale and how a person would describe that number in words. Devlin, Dong, and Brown (1993) report that the distances between points on a 10-point scale, as measured by verbal categories, are not equal (see Exhibit 20.2).

Exhibit 20.2
Where Do People Place Response Categories on a Scale of 0–10?

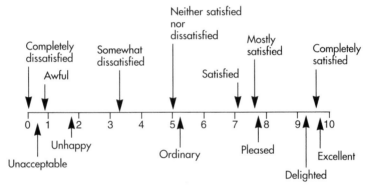

Source: Devlin, Dong, and Brown (1993).

Scales with a large number of points, such as a 10-point scale, tend to be particularly poor discriminators. In several studies of customer satisfaction, the analysis of results shows that customers tend to mentally truncate the scale[1] to the upper range, which thus makes all average ratings highly positive.

My own examination of several studies shows that the failure of numeric scales to distinguish between competing products is much more pronounced for service quality/customer satisfaction than for product quality/product satisfaction measurements. It is not clear why this is so. However, we can hypothesize that the intangible nature of service (as opposed to a product) makes the rating seem "subjective," and this, in turn, leads to a positive bias.

---

[1]Based on studies by Randy Hanson of Maritz Marketing Research (see Gleason, Devlin, and Brown 1994).

Comparison scales

Comparison scales compare actual performance to some other measure, such as a person's expectations, as shown in this example:

The competence of the staff was

- Much better than what I expected.
- Better than what I expected.
- About what I expected.
- Worse than what I expected.
- Much worse than what I expected.

Comparison also can be done between one company and another that is perceived to be the industry standard.

On responding to customer complaints

- Company A is much better than Company X.
- Company A is better than Company X.
- Company A is about the same as Company X.
- Company A is worse than Company X.
- Company A is much worse than Company X.

Comparison scales tend to distinguish companies and services better than the other two types of scales. This generally seems to be the case, whether the comparison is between a person's expectation and what is being delivered or between the performances of one company and another.

Importance of testing

The previous comments are based on exploratory research on scales used in service quality and customer satisfaction research. They should be considered as preliminary findings. Not all researchers will agree with the comments contained in this chapter. (For a taste of the controversy surrounding this area, refer to the references at the end of this section.) No matter what scale is being used, the researcher should be on the lookout for difficulties faced by respondents in comprehending the scale. It might be worthwhile to monitor a number of interviews. If many respondents have difficulty in understanding the scale, then perhaps it is too confusing to them (and others who did not ask for clarification).

Our discussion is intended as a general guide to scales. Although I tried to steer clear of controversy and reported only generalized findings, not all researchers will agree with these comments. For a flavor of controversy surrounding this topic, see Grapentine (1994), Wittink and Bayer (1994), Schmalensee (1994), Gleason, Devlin, and Brown (1994), Crum and Wilburn (1993), and Rust (1993).

b. Making the best of inflated scores

When a customer satisfaction survey produces high average scores for all the organizations studied, it is quite likely that the scores are artificially inflated. This is not an uncommon situation in customer satisfaction studies. We can minimize this problem by choosing the right metric. If we find ourselves in a situation in which all institutions score high, we may choose to place less emphasis on the average score and concentrate instead on measures of variability. A common measure of variability is standard deviation.[2] A high standard deviation would indicate that there are many customers who score considerably lower (or higher) than the mean. In such cases, we may want to plot the actual distribution of ratings to understand the nature of such deviations.

Suppose we carry out a survey that measures the customer satisfaction level with four different organizations. If we find that all the average ratings are high (say, higher than 7.5), and the organizations are not distinguished, we may want to understand the extent of agreement among customers with regard to the average ratings. Coefficient of variation is a suitable measure if we want to understand variability across different organizations or different attributes. It is calculated as follows:

1. Calculate the standard deviation of the ratings. (Almost any program that deals with data analysis—including common spreadsheets—will calculate standard deviations.)

2. Calculate the coefficient of variation (CV). CV = (Standard deviation/Mean) × 100.

3. If the CV is high (say, higher than 30%), then plot the scores. This is done by using the discrete points of the rating scale as the x-axis and the percentage of respondents giving a specific rating on the y-axis.

4. If the distribution is bimodal or multimodal (i.e., has more than one peak), then the market is probably segmented. Different groups of people have different

---

[2]Most statistical programs and spreadsheets have the capability to calculate the standard deviation. The reader who is unfamiliar with the concept of standard deviation will find it explained well in almost any basic book on statistics.

degrees of satisfaction, and this may be related to their needs. You may want to stratify people into different groups and study their specific characteristics.

5. If the distribution is almost flat, with a large standard deviation, this could mean that there is no real agreement among customers about the type of services you provide. It also could mean that there is considerable variability in the type of services provided. In either case, such results suggest that you should examine the process much more closely.

6. If no specific patterns are found, you may decide to ignore the mean score and concentrate instead on customers who show dissatisfaction (for example, customers whose ratings of the service are in the bottom quartile).

If no specific patterns are found, you may decide to concentrate on customers who show dissatisfaction.

To know more

Crum, K. and M. Wilburn (1993), "Customer Satisfaction Measurement: Some Pitfalls and Solutions," paper presented at the American Marketing Association's ART Forum, Monterey, Calif.

Devlin, S., H.K. Dong, and M. Brown (1993), "Selecting a Scale for Measuring Quality," *Marketing Research*, 5 (Spring), 12–18.

Gleason, T.C., S.J. Devlin, and M. Brown (1994), "In Search of the Optimum Scale," *Marketing Research*, 6 (Fall), 28–33.

Grapentine, T. (1994), "Problematic scales," Marketing Research, 6 (Fall), 8–13.

Rust, R.T. (1993), Customer Satisfaction Measurement: Some Pitfalls and Solutions," paper presented at the American Marketing Association's ART Forum, Monterey, Calif.

Schmalensee, D.H. (1994), "Finding the Perfect Scale," *Marketing Research*, 6 (Fall), 24–27.

Wittink, D.R. and L. Bayer (1994), "The Measurement Imperative," *Marketing Research*, 6 (Fall), 14–22.

Step 6. Make analysis action oriented

Once we have collected the data, it is important to use the right analytic techniques. We have already discussed a variety of these, such as the following:

- Use factor analysis to identify the underlying dimensions, and group attributes in a logical way.

- Use correlation and regression analysis to identify how different attributes contribute to overall satisfaction.
- Use discriminant analysis to find out what contributes to dissatisfaction.

Our aim in data analysis is to derive actionable information. We already saw how we can do this with the use of gap analysis. But, if used mechanically, even a simple technique can mislead. To illustrate this point, let us look at one of the simplest and most frequently used techniques of customer satisfaction research: the quadrant analysis.

QUADRANT ANALYSIS

Quadrant analysis is a technique that displays the status of an attribute in two dimensions simultaneously. For example, suppose we collect information on the frequency and importance of different service quality problems faced by customers. We can plot this information in the form of a graph, as shown in Exhibit 20.3. This is a simple x-y graph. The center lines represent the mean, or median, for each variable. The use of the figure is immediately obvious. For example, we may avoid spending our resources on problems that are considered to be neither frequent nor important (bottom-left quadrant). These problems give us the least leverage in terms of resources invested in them. Problems that are important to customers and are frequent (top-right quadrant), on the other hand, provide the highest leverage. Next in importance is the top-left quadrant, which represents problems that are important, though not frequent.

> **Quadrant analysis *is a technique that displays the status of an attribute in two dimensions simultaneously.***

Quadrant analysis also can be used in many other contexts in which we need to understand the relationship between two attributes.

How to do quadrant analysis

Quadrant analysis assumes that we want to study how two variables relate to each other.

> **Step 1.** *Select two variables to be plotted.* Consumers rate a number of service quality attributes on how important they are to them and how well a company is performing on those attributes. We now have two basic attributes: importance and performance.

Exhibit 20.3
Quadrant Analysis

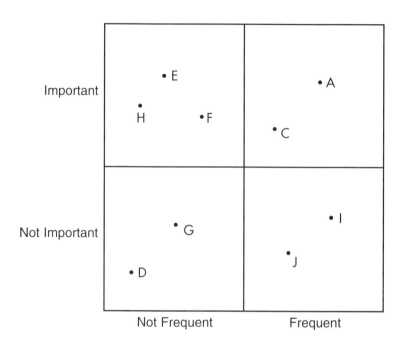

Step 2. *Assign one variable as "x" (to be plotted on the horizontal axis) and the other as "y" (to be plotted on the vertical axis).* Plot importance on the x-axis and performance on the y-axis.

Step 3. *Assign scale values to these axes on the basis of the original scale values.* If the scales used to collect the data are on a 10-point scale, the axes should be calibrated accordingly. (The data can be of any type: yes/no, percentages, rating scales, etc.)

Step 4. *Plot the items of interest in the intersection of x- and y-values.* If the importance of "billing accuracy" is 8 and the company's performance rating on this attribute is 6, then billing accuracy is plotted at x = 8, y = 6. Other attributes are plotted similarly.

Step 5. *Draw the horizontal and vertical dividing lines to identify the quadrants.* For the x-axis, the line is drawn vertically from the mean of the variable plotted along the x-axis; and, for the y-axis, the line is drawn horizontally from the mean

How to create quadrant charts
1. Select two variables to be plotted.
2. Assign one variable to the x-axis and the other to the y-axis.
3. Assign scale values to these axes based on the original scale values.
4. Plot the items of interest in the intersection of x- and y-values.
5. Draw the horizontal and vertical dividing lines to identify the quadrants. The dividing lines represent the averages.

of the variable plotted along the y-axis. For nominal type variables, the median, rather than the mean, is used.

Now you should have a quadrant chart very similar to the one shown in Exhibit 20.3. (In the exhibit, points indicated by A, B, C, and so on refer to variables such as billing accuracy and timely response.)

How to interpret the chart

Interpreting a quadrant analysis chart is fairly straightforward. A properly created and labeled chart should be self-explanatory. To continue with our example, we can state the following:

> The top-right quadrant consists of attributes that are of above-average importance to customers, and our performance also is above average. The top-left quadrant consists of attributes that are not important to customers, but our performance is above average. The bottom-left quadrant consists of attributes that are not important to customers; neither do we deliver on these attributes. The bottom-right quadrant consists of attributes that are important to customers on which our performance is below average.

Where can it be used?

Because most data interpretation involves attempts at understanding the relationship between two attributes, quadrant analysis can be used in a number of situations in which it is important for us to study such relationships. Quadrant analysis is a simple technique. Its main power lies in the fact that it enables us to examine an object on two dimensions simultaneously. Quadrants visually highlight what is important and what is not.

How even a simple technique can mislead

It is important to remember that even a technique as simple as quadrant analysis can mislead. For example, the dividing lines provide an illusion of separation between the highs and lows of each attribute. In reality, the dividing lines are far from definitive. For example, if we include one more attribute or eliminate one that we already have (especially if it happens to score very high or very low in either or both dimensions), the center lines will move, and attributes will change quadrants. An attribute that appears in the top-right quadrant (the best position) easily can be placed on the bottom left (the worst position) if the attribute is too close to the quadrant dividers. For example, if the analysis is based on 400 customers, the results will have a margin of error of ±5%. Consequently, any attribute that is close to a divider could easily fall in another quadrant. Because quadrant analysis does not involve any statistical procedures, the dividing lines are arbitrary and can mislead. It is best to view quadrants as directional indicators rather than precise formulations.

The purpose of this discussion is to show that (1) even a simple technique can provide actionable input and (2) if we are not careful, even a simple technique can seriously mislead. Although we should make our analysis action-specific, we always should be on the lookout for ways in which we can go wrong.

Analyses can be considered action oriented if the conclusions drawn point to one or more courses of action. Steps such as deriving importance scores, placing attributes on a quadrant map, and identifying gaps in levels of service contribute to action orientation. They all attempt to show which of the several alternative courses of action we should pursue. A report that simply lists customer satisfaction ratings, on the other hand, cannot be considered action oriented.

To know more

Pia, K.L. (1993), *"Evolution of Quadrant Analysis: The Good, the Bad, and the Ugly,"* paper presented at the American Marketing Association's 14th Marketing Research Conference, Chicago (October).

STEP 7. CONSIDER SEGMENTING CUSTOMERS

Customer satisfaction often is related to the benefits sought by customers. However, all customers may not be seeking the same benefit. Some may be driven by convenience, while others may place greater emphasis on the quality of service. Averaging the rating of all customers is likely to average out the differences. For this reason, it may be worthwhile to carry out a segmentation analysis on benefits sought. Techniques such as cluster analysis and a classification tree can be used for this purpose.

STEP 8. INTERPRET THE MEASURES CORRECTLY

It is important to interpret the customer satisfaction measures correctly. More specifically, we must differentiate common cause and special cause variations. If we are tracking customer satisfaction, we may want to plot the results on a run chart, use upper and lower control limits, and interpret the results, as explained previously.

STEP 9. USE RESULTS CAUTIOUSLY

Many organizations that institute a CSM program also create a Customer Satisfaction Index (CSI). What exactly is a CSI? It is simply an average of all attributes that are believed to contribute to customer satisfaction. Because different attributes can contribute differently to overall customer satisfaction, the individual attributes are weighted to reflect this reality. This is the essence of a CSI. Everything else is detail.

A CSI does not have to be based solely on survey data. It can take into account factors such as repeat buying, volume of purchase, complaints recorded, and market share. No matter what it includes, the basic idea is the same: A CSI is a weighted combination of different attributes.

Some common ways of creating CSIs

A CSI can be based on a single measure of satisfaction or a combination of several measures. The latter is more common than the former. Let us start with the example of a bank that regularly asks customers of different branches to rate these branches on 20 different performance attributes such as

- Employee characteristics
  Knowledge
  Courtesy
  Efficiency
- Service adequacy
  Speed
  Access
  Product availability
- Management responsiveness
  Complaint handling

To make comparisons among different branches easier (as well as for employee compensation purposes), the bank decides to develop a CSI, which would summarize the information in just one number.

How is a CSI created? There are no standard procedures for creating a CSI. However, here are some ways by which a CSI is created.

An Unweighted CSI

The unweighted method of a CSI simply averages all attributes that are considered relevant to customer satisfaction. The main weakness of this method is that an attribute that is only weakly related to customer satisfaction will get the same weight as one that is key to customer satisfaction.

Weighted CSIs: The a priori method

In this method, management (or anyone who is responsible for creating the index) assigns different weights to different attributes. For example, if employee characteristics are assumed to be twice as important as management responsiveness, then we can assign a weight of 1 to employee characteristics and .5 to management responsiveness. The measures are multiplied by the assigned weights and then combined to arrive at an overall index. The main weakness of this method is that the weights assigned can be arbitrary. How do we really know, for instance, that management responsiveness is only 50% as important as employee characteristics? If our assumption is incorrect, our CSI will be incorrect as well.

Weighted CSIs: A posteriori methods

These methods usually use statistical techniques to assess the relationship between a given attribute and customer satisfaction. The following are some of the most commonly used techniques.

Correlation analysis. In this method, each attribute is correlated with some criterion measure, such as overall satisfaction with the branch. Attributes that correlate highly to this overall measure will receive high weights, and those that correlate poorly will receive low weights. The main weakness of this method is that two or more attributes that contribute to satisfaction may be correlated highly among themselves. For example, if quick service and efficient service correlate highly with overall satisfaction, we assign large weights to both attributes. But if customers do not distinguish between these two attributes, we are effectively measuring the same attribute twice, thereby doubling the weight given to these attributes.

Coefficient of determination. Coefficient of determination is the square of the correlation, commonly referred to as the R-squared. The advantage of using R-squared is that it is expressed on a linear scale. For example, an attribute that has an R-squared of .40 can be said to be twice as important as another that has an R-squared of only .20. Because of this property, R-squared is preferred usually to straight correlation.

Factor analysis. To avoid the problem of correlated variables distorting the weights (as discussed previously), we can apply factor analysis to the attributes. Factor analysis groups attributes into theoretically uncorrelated groups. We then can apply weights on this basis. The weakness of this approach is that we may not always get robust factors, and often it is not clear what the factors are or what to do with the variance that is left unexplained by factor analysis.

Modified correlation analysis. In this approach, we simply eliminate all attributes that strongly correlate among themselves. We may, for example, arbitrarily define all correlations above .6 as "high" and, if two variables are correlated above this level, choose only one in the set. The drawback of this approach is that two highly correlated attributes cannot automatically be considered redundant. For example, effectiveness and speed may be highly correlated, but they may not be redundant variables and can measure two different aspects of service. There may be several instances in which what is considered effective service may, indeed, be slow. Eliminating one of the two variables from the index can be misleading if the ratings on these variables begin to diverge.

Principal components analysis. Given a set of attributes, such as customer satisfaction measurements, principal components analysis creates the best possible linear combination of those attributes. The result is a weighted combination of attributes that explains the maximum amount of variance in the data. The weakness of this approach is that, while the weights might be best representative of the underlying attributes, we have no way of knowing whether the attributes themselves are relevant to customer satisfaction.

Multiple regression analysis. This is an extension of correlation analysis. Multiple regression analysis can be used to compute the simultaneous relationship between a number of attributes and customer satisfaction. This analysis eliminates redundant variables and produces what are known as "beta weights," which shows how important a given attribute is in relation to other attributes in contributing to customer satisfaction. The greatest weakness (and pitfall) of this method is the elimination of highly correlated variables (multicollinearity). We can, and often do, end up with a measure that may exclude some important variables.

There are many related methods by which CSIs can be created.

Why CSIs mislead

While discussing different CSI procedures, we note that each technique is subject to one or more limitations. There are no perfect measures, and we often need to work with imperfect ones. The problem with the use of CSIs, then, is not the shortcomings of each procedure discussed so far. It is more fundamental than that.

CSIs are intuitively appealing. So is the logic of creating them: We choose only those variables that contribute to customer satisfaction; we take into account the importance of each attribute by weighting it appropriately; we avoid the problem of multicollinearity; and we validate it on a new sample. So what is the problem? Why is it that we cannot use CSIs to gauge our performance and to compensate our employees? The fact is, CSIs are riddled with many serious problems and cannot be used as a consistent guide to implementing service quality.

CSIs are insensitive

The greatest weakness of CSIs is that most of them are insensitive. This weakness is inherent in the process of creating the index itself, irrespective of the competence and sophistication of the index creator. This is best understood with the help of an example. Let us consider a fictitious CSI, which is assumed to have been creating using standard statistical procedures and competent research. (In this illustration, only customer survey data are used. But even if the CSI is based on other variables, such as repeat purchase, the implications are the same.)

> Customer satisfaction index =
> .50 × satisfaction with on-time delivery
> +.25 × satisfaction with after-sales service
> +.10 × satisfaction with product quality
> +.08 × satisfaction with responsiveness
> +.06 × satisfaction with service availability

If the average ratings on the five attributes are 8.8, 8.1, 8.5, 8.7, and 7.9, respectively, then, by using this formula, we will arrive at a CSI score of 8.4 (.50 × 8.8 + .25 × 8.1 + .10 × 8.5 + .08 × 8.7 + .06 × 7.9). The index shows that on-time delivery is the most highly weighted in determining overall customer satisfaction and, hence, the CSI. In fact, on-time delivery is more important than all other variables combined. This being the case, we would assume that any serious problem associated with on-time delivery would be reflected in the CSI. Unfortunately, this is not so. Suppose there is a serious problem with on-time delivery, and 20% of customers are seriously affected. Assume further that those who are affected lower their rating by 2 full points, an unmistakable change in ratings. For the sake of clarity, let us also assume that all other ratings remain exactly the same. This will bring down the average rating of on-time delivery from

8.8 to 8.4 (8.8 × 80% + 6.8 × 20%). The CSI now will be 8.3.

So, here we have a situation in which 20% of customers suddenly lowered their ratings by an unmistakable margin of 2 full points on an attribute that is more important than all other attributes combined. Yet, the CSI shows hardly any movement, a barely noticeable shift from 8.4 to 8.3. Any institution that uses the CSI as a major measure to track customer satisfaction or to spot problems before they become disasters can hardly hope to achieve its goals this way.

Many CSI reports also contain the averages of component variables, usually in the form of bar charts. Without proper analysis, such bar charts may not alert us to the serious problems that might be affecting customer satisfaction. In the previous example, while the CSI shows barely any movement, the critical variable—on-time delivery—hardly shows any alarming movement either. The average on this variable has dropped .4 points, a drop that may be of some concern, but hardly points to the seriousness of the problem.

Is this an alarmist discussion of the dangers of using CSIs to track customer satisfaction? The logic of the CSI shows that it is not. If anything, this illustration understates the danger. Most CSIs use a considerably larger number of variables. An important variable that may be going out of control with a portion of our customers will be completely overshadowed by other variables that show no change.

In the previous example, it also is possible that the CSI actually can go up, even though 20% of our customers are seriously upset about not receiving the product on time. This can happen if the averages of some of the nonaffected variables go up through random fluctuations.

Using the CSI as a sole—or even as a major—measure of customer satisfaction can mislead us by hiding the problem until it becomes so big that it cannot be hidden. By then, it may be too late. Using the CSI this way is akin to driving while using an aerial map as a guide. Just as an aerial map does not show one-way streets or smooth sharp turns and minor breaks in paved roads, the CSI does not show what is affecting customers, will not smooth customer dissatisfaction that is currently brewing, and will not warn us of the dangers ahead.

CSIs are subject to model estimate errors

We have discussed how the CSI can remain invariant and hide potential problems. It also can do the reverse—show movements when everything is static. Such movements can occur either upward or downward. When CSIs are used to compensate an employee, department, or branch office, the resulting index and, thus, the allocation of compensation do not relate at all to customer satisfaction. How so?

Consider how CSIs are created in the first place. They are simply weighted combinations of component variables. No matter how they are assigned, the weights are estimates of the influence of the constituent variables. (The parameter values of the weights are, of course, unknown.) If the estimated weight for a given variable is, say, .32, the parameter value could be different. Depending on how far our estimates are from our parameter values and in which direction, the actual weights could be higher or lower. Thus, Branch A, whose CSI is higher than that of Branch B, could indeed be no better. Yet, most CSIs do not report the error band but seem to assume that the coefficients used are error-free.

CSIs are subject to measurement errors

When we measure customer satisfaction using customer attitudes, the measurement is subject to sampling errors. A nominal scale measurement that is based on 100 customers could have a margin of error of $\pm 10\%$, or an error band that is 20 percentage points wide. Thus, if 50% of customers report that they are highly satisfied with your company, this "true" figure could be anywhere between 40% and 60%. If so, how can we be confident that a department that received an endorsement of 55% of customers is superior to a department that was endorsed by only 45% of customers? That is difficult enough. But, when we weight this by another estimate that is subject to its own error and combine it with other variables that also are subject to similar errors, we complicate the problem. In addition, there are other sources of distortion such as bias.

Errors are inherent in measurements, and they should not deter us from using measures that can be potentially useful. If bias is minimized—if the researcher is careful when creating an index and has done pretesting, replication, and rigorous statistical analysis—chances are that the many random errors (but not the biases) would cancel each other out, and we would get an approximate answer. But the key word here is "approximate." We cannot assume that *all* errors are canceled out and the final index is precise, no matter how many tests we have carried out. It follows, from elementary sampling theory, that all estimates and all sampling results have error bands attached to them. So, when a company decides to reward the top 10%, some employees who contributed significantly to customer satisfaction will not make the list, and some who did not will make the list. Many employees will be rewarded arbitrarily and at random. Many will be punished (i.e., will not receive the reward) arbitrarily and at random. Random rewards and punishments are not conducive to generating the desired result. Therefore, a compensation system that is based on CSIs can be potentially destructive.

CSIs, a measure with limited usefulness

Is the CSI completely useless? Probably not. It can be useful under limited conditions. For example, it can identify major trends. It may be able to pinpoint customer dissatisfaction, if that dissatisfaction is strong and widespread. CSIs can chart our progress over the years.

Yet, the problems associated with CSIs are both serious and real. Currently, CSIs are frequently used for the following purposes:

1. To assess if customers are happy with us,

2. To be forewarned about problems, and

3. To compensate employees, departments, and branch offices.

As we have noted, the CSI does not necessarily detect customer dissatisfaction, does not necessarily identify potential problems or discontent, and is an ineffective (and probably demoralizing) way to compensate individuals or groups.

One of the reasons why customer satisfaction measurement does not work is because it focuses on a potentially misleading measure: the CSI. To accord more than cursory attention to the CSI is to ignore the real effort involved in understanding the customer. We cannot ensure customer satisfaction when we use a measure that is riddled with problems, which is what the CSI is. A good customer satisfaction measurement system, then, should concentrate on specific diagnostic measures, rather than one overall index that can seriously mislead (Chakrapani 1996).

Why, then, create a CSI at all? If it cannot guide us in improving customer satisfaction and if it cannot give us any feedback on our performance, is it worth computing? Think of the CSI as an aerial photograph mentioned previously. An aerial photograph cannot show us the details, such as where the one-way streets and hidden intersections are. Consequently, it is useless as a guide to driving. However, it is useful in that it provides an overall view of the area and enables us to understand the nature of the terrain. Similarly, the CSI is a poor measure for driving a CSM system. All the same, the CSI can be useful as a historical measure. It is a rough-and-ready way of tracking where we are going in very general terms. Although the CSM is too inconsistent a measure to be used as a proxy for detailed CSM measurements, it may be adequate as a historical measure.

STEP 10. CREATE A TRACKING SYSTEM

Measuring customer satisfaction is an ongoing process. We already discussed the details of creating a tracking system. It is preferable to track customers on a continuous basis (such as every month or every quarter) rather than at longer intervals (such as once a year). If there are budget constraints, we might measure fewer customers more frequently rather than a large sample of customers less frequently. If we employ smaller samples, we can use rolling averages to smooth out small sample fluctuations and identify the underlying trends.

It also is important to remember that standard tracking is reactive in nature. It does not provide any input to creative service. Combining the standard tracking with proactive tracking (e.g., senior officers of the company calling customers on an ongoing basis and having semistructured conversations) might provide greater input in terms of current customer satisfaction levels and what we must do to keep our customers satisfied.

APPENDIX: MODELING AND MEASURING CUSTOMER SATISFACTION—AN EXAMPLE

When we measure customer satisfaction, it is important to have an underlying model or "a theory of knowledge," as Deming calls it. The reason for having an underlying model is that it enables us to test the validity of our assumptions, which lead to constant improvement in our measurement procedures. As an example of an explicitly specified model, here is a brief description of CSMpact, which was developed by Gordon S. Black Corporation. This exposition is not evaluative. Rather, it is intended to show how a model is put together and how it is used to solve marketing problems.

Satisfaction as a function of "events"

The methodology treats satisfaction as a resultant attitude formed on the basis of a number of events. It is the purpose of the research to identify the events that lead to increased satisfaction. The study provides two types of measures:

1. Diagnostic measures, which highlight the improvements that increase customer satisfaction; and

2. Descriptive measures, which document the performance of the schools.

Descriptive measures are collected on a 0- to 10-point rating scale. Customer experiences are measured on a binary scale.

Measured events as a subset of relevant events

The events to be measured in the final questionnaire are the result of preliminary studies, including focus group interviews, to eliminate redundancy and duplication and to avoid the multicollinearity problem. Items are chosen to optimize two conflicting requirements: the need to be comprehensive and the need to be parsimonious.

Deriving the importance of diagnostic measures

The importance of events is derived using multiple regression, with customer satisfaction as the dependent variable and customer experiences as the independent variables. This statistical modeling process discloses a number of things:

1. The relative rate of change in customer satisfaction that is associated with each event, circumstance, or condition;

2. The maximum score they can achieve within the model if all the important problems were eliminated; and

3. The total amount of satisfaction that can be explained exclusively on the basis of the model.

Deriving impact scores

We now have two measures: the frequency of a problem (as stated by the customer) and the importance of the problem (as derived by the model). The items with the highest impact are those that occur frequently and cause dissatisfaction (also called penalty) when they occur. An impact score for each variable is derived by weighting the frequency score with the derived importance score and dividing the resultant value by the sum of the scores, so that the impact score is expressed as a relative percentage. Thus, each impact score represents the percentage of potential improvement that is attributable to the elimination of that problem. It provides a relative measure of the impact of each problem and points out which problems represent the greatest potential opportunity for improving satisfaction. Exhibit 20.4 shows the model as applied to student satisfaction with a university course in anthropology.

Why model satisfaction?

As mentioned previously, it is important to have a model. Such specifications should be explicit and should be hidden in a "black box." A model does not automatically make the measurement and interpretation superior. Many models are poorly conceived and are difficult to defend. However, a clearly specified model provides several advantages, which can be illustrated with the use of this model. For example, why use a numeric scale for satisfaction? Why use a binary scale for events? Wittink and Bayer (1994) provide the rationale for the use of these two scales. Again, the assumption that satisfaction is a function of events can be tested. Because a clearly specified model is amenable to tests and modifications, it can help us adapt to a changing marketing environment.

Exhibit 20.4

OVERALL SATISFACTION MODEL

Model Statistics

Cases: 456
R-square: .76
Standard Error: .53
Overall F Value: 50.35
Level of Significance (p-value): .001

Penalty (beta coefficient) is the average reduction in satisfaction scores reported by students who indicate the occurence of each problem.

Impact Index is a combination of the penalty and the % reporting the problem. It represents the percent of potential improvement that can be realized if the occurrence of the problem is reduced to zero.

	% with Problem	Penalty	IMPACT INDEX
Instructor available to discuss graded exams?	32%	1.27	29%
Readings/sessions complemented each other?	29%	1.03	21%
Positively challenged/learned more than expected?	23%	1.01	17%
Instructor demonstrated expertise in material?	10%	1.90	14%
Instructor enthusiastic about course?	12%	0.88	8%
Instructor well organized/prepared?	16%	0.60	7%
Instructor respected students' opinions?	6%	0.90	4%
Course lived up to its description?	39%	0.06	2%

Improvement Possible

☐ Current Grade
■ Max. Possible Score

Satisfaction Score

10
8
6
4
2
0

8.0   9.2

This graph shows the current student mean rating for overall satisfaction, along with the maximum possible score.

Courtesy: Gordon S. Black Corporation. Used with permission.

Part V

Toward a Philosophy of Quality

21

A System of Profound Knowledge

R ecent articles in business magazines such as *The Economist* and *Fortune* inform us that many companies that have implemented service quality programs have been disappointed with the results. Although such programs were expensive, they did not result in either higher sales or higher profitability. So, is providing service quality a passing fad or an enduring way of doing business? Why have good intentions, hard work, and best efforts not paid off? Here is Deming's answer: "Hard work and best efforts, without guidance of profound knowledge, may well be at the root of our ruination. There is no substitute for profound knowledge."

What is profound knowledge? Profound knowledge is the framework for applying the best efforts to the

Profound knowledge is the framework for applying the best efforts to the right tasks.

right tasks. It is needed for a quality program. We do not have to be eminent or brilliant to understand and apply profound knowledge, which consists of four aspects: appreciation of a system, theory of variation, theory of knowledge, and understanding of psychology.

APPRECIATION OF A SYSTEM

Every organization has goals. A system is a series of different processes and subprocesses that work together to achieve the goals of the organization. The components of the organization work together to achieve the objectives. Therefore, it is important for management to make the objectives of the organization clear to everyone within that organization. Optimization of an organization cannot be achieved through an independent optimization of the components of an organization. If the organization is a total system, then what a component (such as the marketing department) does has a direct bearing on other components (such as manufacturing and sales departments). When optimization of one department is carried out without an understanding of the system as a whole, it may adversely affect the entire organization. Thus, when an organization is understood as a system, departments are not judged against one another, employees are not in adversarial positions, and blame is not passed on. They all work together toward a common goal.

THEORY OF VARIATION

Variations in performance are a universal reality. Responding to variations in performance without any understanding of the causes is destructive. Every manager should have the following:

- An understanding that there will always be variations among people, in service, in product, and in output;

- An understanding of the stable system and the difference between a stable system and a capable system;

- An understanding of the difference between common and special cause variations;

- An understanding of the two basic mistakes: treating common cause variations as special cause variations and vice versa. Both these mistakes result in misplaced efforts and poorer quality.

THEORY OF KNOWLEDGE

To be successful, management should be able to predict the future with some degree of success. To do this, it should have some theory as to why a certain course of action would lead to a given outcome. For example, if an organization that has instituted a service quality program has a theory behind it, then it can test this theory by the results. If the results are not in the predicted direction, then it can revise its theory or look for possible lapses: Did we confuse common and special causes? Are the processes under control?

A theory of knowledge provides the framework for hypothesizing why a certain course of action would lead to a given outcome.

If management does not have a theory of knowledge, it has no way of knowing why what works does work and why what doesn't does not. Without a proper theory of knowledge, management can only be in a trial-and-error mode, with no understanding to guide its efforts.

UNDERSTANDING OF PSYCHOLOGY

By constant rewards and punishments, management ignores psychological principles. People are driven by two kinds of motives: intrinsic and extrinsic. The desire to contribute and take pride in one's work arises out of intrinsic motivation. Those who are not familiar with the existence of intrinsic motivation immediately try to link behavior to extrinsic motivators, such as rewards and punishments. This linking (called *overjustification*) destroys intrinsic motivation. Any reward program should be such that it neither pits one component of the system against another nor kills people's intrinsic motivation.

IMPLEMENTING A QUALITY PROGRAM

When a decision has been made to subscribe to the service quality philosophy, we must consider several elements that go with such a commitment. A few of these points are mentioned here.

Internal customers. Service quality must be delivered not only to external customers (those we traditionally view as customers), but also to people within the organization who deal with us. These are our internal customers. When quality is a way of life, there is no distinction between external and internal customers.

Internal marketing. The concept of service quality must be marketed within the organization, so that it becomes a part of every employee's orientation.

Hiring and training. An organization must hire people who are fully qualified to do the job and provide them with suitable training.

Team skills. Working at cross-purposes, or working to maximize individual efficiency, is likely to hinder overall quality. To deliver quality, team skills are required and their development should be a part of any training program.

Single supplier. Service quality depends not only on us, but also on our suppliers. If we work with many suppliers, we cannot instill in them our philosophy of service quality. Working with a single supplier enables us to work more efficiently. Quality can be controlled much more effectively.

Measurement. As psychologist Reymond B. Cattell once observed, "Anything that exists, exists in some quantity; anything that exists in a quantity can be measured." Unless we measure constantly, we will not get the input we need to monitor our performance. We need to measure our performance to

- reduce service variability,

- improve the service level,

- monitor our progress, and
- identify our weak spots.

Delivering quality. Although quality needs constant monitoring, it should not be viewed as an onerous undertaking. Delivering quality adds meaning to a person's work and, thus, increases job satisfaction. Job satisfaction, in turn, increases productivity, and productivity increases profits. Delivering quality is an easier and more pleasant way to make more profits.

22

Deming's 14 Points

Most philosophers of the quality movement—such as Deming, Juran, and Crosby—have created lists that can serve as blueprints for success. Because these lists have much in common, there is little point in presenting more than one. I have chosen to present Deming's 14 points. But why Deming?

Deming, an eminent statistician, was one of the first to recognize the importance of service as a vital component of quality. He is credited with having taught the Japanese how to create and deliver quality. While much of his work centers around products, his vision of quality is broad in scope and extends beyond statistical quality control, making his ideas relevant to any area of service quality.

One of the major objectives of this book is to focus on the shortcomings of using standard methodologies to measure service quality. Discussion has centered on several themes that focus on how standard methods can show high service quality ratings (even though there might be serious customer dissatisfaction) and how even standard qualitative research can be ineffective in identifying the underlying problems.

So far, we have not focused on whether what is being measured is worth measuring. For example, many companies link managerial compensation to customer satisfaction. It may be innovative, but is it a good way to ensure service quality? We have not discussed the relevance of the aspect being measured, but only whether a given methodology will achieve the stated research objectives.

In this context, it might be worthwhile to review the ideas of Deming, whose views are somewhat at variance with those who seem to be climbing on the bandwagon of "service quality"—as if it were a secret incantation, the mere repetition of which will bring profits with little effort. His views on quality differ somewhat with what many organizations appear to believe. For example, he believes that quality does not add to the cost of doing business, but instead reduces it. The following are some of his other views:

- Eliminate slogans, exhortations, and targets for the workforce.
- Eliminate management by objective.
- Eliminate management by numbers and numerical goals.

These and other pronouncements by Deming run counter to many current practices.

Deming developed 14 points that outline what an organization has to do to achieve quality. A review of these 14 points shows that many assumptions that underlie current service quality research can be challenged as being destructive and running counter to the spirit of providing genuine service quality.

The major themes of Deming's method are presented here with comments, followed by questions and suggestions for measurement. Answering the questions may lead to insights on what needs to be done and the research procedures that may be relevant to achieving the stated goals. It may even make us wonder whether we are researching the right areas, whether we are asking the right questions, and whether our assumptions about service quality are tenable. These 14 points also focus on the need to carry out internal research as vital input for providing service quality.

1. CREATE CONSTANCY OF PURPOSE

Create constancy of purpose toward improvement of product and service, with the aim to become competitive, stay in business, and provide jobs.

How many organizations that profess a belief in quality support employees who provide quality, even if it is not profitable to the organization? For example, if an insurance company employee spends 30 minutes with a customer who is not particularly profitable but who has a problem, will the manager appreciate the employee's efforts? Many organizations that talk about service quality fail to provide it because they use the concept selectively, without constancy of purpose.

Questions: Do all employees know the purpose? How do you know whether it is understood by all? What is the mechanism for determining customer needs? What prevents a new president from changing the philosophy of the company?

Suggested measurement: Internal research to assess the depth and breadth of understanding the organization's mission in terms of service quality; an evaluation of the strength of commitment to the mission at various levels of the organization; identification of the weaker links in the chain. Research techniques, such as force field analysis and proactive tracking, could be used to support constancy of purpose.

> **Create constancy of purpose toward improvement of product and service.**

2. ADOPT THE NEW PHILOSOPHY

Adopt the new philosophy. We are in a new age. Western management must awaken to the challenge, must learn their responsibilities, and take on leadership for change.

Quality is not a cost-added component of a product. The assumption of many organizations is that quality costs money and that someone has to pay for it. If we cannot charge more, we cannot afford quality. Deming suggests otherwise. Effort expended to improve the process increases the uniformity of output (e.g., consistency of service) and reduces waste of manpower.

Questions: Do you know the cost of not meeting your customers' needs? Do you know how to make your customers brag about your company?

Suggested research: An analysis of the cost of meeting customer needs; an analysis of the cost of not meeting customer needs. We can use the cost-benefit analysis technique to understand the benefits of adopting the new philosophy. However, this point really relates to management assuming the leadership role, rather than to any specific analysis.

> **Adopt the new philosophy. We are in a new age. Western management must awaken to the challenge.**

3. MANAGE THE PROCESS, NOT THE OUTCOME

Cease dependence on inspection to achieve quality. Eliminate the need for inspection on a mass basis by building quality into the product in the first place.

In many organizations, there is an emphasis on managing the outcome (handling service-related complaints), rather than on managing the process (identifying the source of the problems and managing it in such a way as to prevent the complaints from arising in the first place). When an organization manages the outcome, it tends to brag about how far it goes to keep customers happy. When an organization manages the process, customers brag about the organization. The latter is the real measure of service quality. It is this aspect that retains your current customers and attracts new ones.

Questions: How many problems are handled simply to satisfy customers? What mechanism is in place to connect problems to processes? When they are connected, what mechanism is in place to ensure the processes that generate service quality are maintained and improved upon?

Suggested measurement: A continuous elicitation and assessment of customer complaints, with a view to reduce the variability in service. Relate the complaints to the processes that give rise to problems, with a view to streamlining the processes. The use of the complaint-elicitation mechanisms and proactive tracking techniques can be useful in managing the processes rather than the outcomes.

Eliminate the need for inspection on a mass basis by building quality into the product in the first place.

4. LOOK AT THE TOTAL COST, NOT PRICE TAGS

End the practice of awarding business on the basis of price tag. Instead, minimize total cost. Move toward a single supplier for any one item for a long-term relationship of loyalty and trust.

If we are to meet our customers' needs in the long run, we need suppliers that are consistent and reliable. Suppliers are more likely to invest in improving quality when they have a long-term relationship with us and are not constantly worried about someone underbidding them and taking away the business. What is relevant to a business is the total cost of the product (service), not the cost of individual components. An organization may be able to buy each (comparable) individual component at a lower cost, however, doing so may affect the organization's ability to deliver quality in the long term. The main point here is that, for an organization to deliver quality, it is important that its mission is understood and followed by its suppliers, as well as its employees. Modern organizations have several suppliers, all of which indirectly affect the quality of products and services offered by the organization. When we change suppliers every year in our quest for the lowest cost, we are indeed looking at the price tag. What about the cost of briefing potential suppliers? What about the cost of evaluating new suppliers? What about the cost of teaching our new suppliers about the standard we expect of them? These costs are not reflected in the price tag, and we should make sure that these factors are taken into consideration.

Questions: How many single-source suppliers do we have? How frequently do we change suppliers? How important is price in making buying decisions? What effort has been expended to encourage suppliers to adopt a service quality philosophy?

Move toward a single supplier for any one item for a long-term relationship of loyalty and trust.

Suggested measurement: Research programs in this area should measure buyers' and suppliers' understanding of the organization's mission. Here again, the cost-benefit analysis that includes the total cost, rather than the price quoted for a task, could be illuminating.

5. IMPROVE SERVICE QUALITY AND THUS DECREASE COSTS

Improve constantly and forever the system of production and service to improve quality and productivity and, thus, constantly decrease costs.

Deming's theme directly contradicts a widely held assumption (especially among neophyte converts to quality), namely, that providing quality means decreased profitability. It is a common assumption among many organizations that if customers do not complain and if service objective specifications are met, no further improvement is necessary. But one of the main components of cost is variability. A service that is less variable results in lower costs in the long run. This approach minimizes the costs associated with remedial action as well as the false economy associated with using the wrong tools or people for the job.

Questions: What aspects of your service are not considered to be problematic? How many of those are on the active agenda for improvement?

Improve constantly and forever the system of production.

Suggested measurement: Formal tracking and recording of steps taken to improve service quality in areas in which research has shown no specific deficiency; brainstorming sessions to continuously improve service quality.

6. INSTITUTE TRAINING ON THE JOB

Institute training on the job.

In many North American companies, training consists of attending a seminar or workshop. However, when the employee returns to his or her job, systems are not in place for the employee to put into practice what he or she has learned. In other words, current systems usually have inhibitors already built in. Such inhibitors make the new knowledge marginally useful at best, or totally irrelevant at worst. Many Japanese firms provide at least one year of training before giving anyone the sole responsibility for a job. According to Genichi Taguchi, a Japanese manager "faces much the same pressures to reduce cost that his [or her] American counterparts do. He [or she] has flexibility to cut costs in many areas, but one area that cannot be reduced is the training budget, because training and education are the cornerstones of greater consistency" (Scherkenbach 1986). *Questions:* What training is provided to employees? Is there on-the-job training in the company? Do current procedures make it difficult for employees to implement what have they learned? Is management committed to quality, or is quality put on the back burner because current systems dictate that there are other, more important priorities?

Institute training on the job.

Suggested measurement: Internal research to identify the courses the employees have been exposed to and their objectives; specific details of the outcome in terms of concrete steps taken to implement what was learned; research on a continual basis to identify the possible impediments to implementation.

7. INSTITUTE LEADERSHIP

Institute leadership. The aim of leadership should be to help people, machines, and gadgets do a better job. Supervision of management is in need of overhaul, as well as supervision of production workers.

This point refers to empowering workers to do the job effectively. However, Deming also notes that many leaders do not necessarily participate in the processes that they are supposed to manage. If they do not participate in the processes, how are they supposed to teach others and help them achieve productivity? It is important that leaders be familiar with the functional aspects of the processes they manage.

Questions: Is the manager aware of and proficient in the processes that are being carried out by others? Can he or she teach and/or help people make the processes more efficient? What steps can the organization take to ensure that managers not only manage, but also provide leadership through teaching and helping those they supervise?

The aim of leadership should be to help people, machines, and gadgets do a better job.

Suggested measurement: Internal research to identify the functional processes that a manager manages but does not know the details of; research on processes that typically require help from other people, especially the supervisor.

8. DRIVE OUT FEAR

Drive out fear, so that everyone may work effectively for the company.

This is one of the most important of Deming's 14 points.

Exhibit 22.1

The Importance of Driving Out Fear

Driving out fear is not only one of the 14 principles. Fear affects — and is affected by — 9 other principles listed here:

In North America, fear is used as a prime motivator. Fear is highly leveraged. Knowledge of any punishment or threat meted out to an employee travels fast. Unfortunately, fear immobilizes, and as long as an employee is paralyzed, no innovation is likely to happen. Fear has a bearing on nine other principles (see Exhibit 22.1). Thus, when this principle is violated, it may affect many other initiatives taken to bring about quality.

Drive out fear, so that everyone may work effectively for the company.

Questions: Do employees believe that they cannot really say what they think about a situation for fear of offending their superiors? Do senior people deliberately foster a nonthreatening work environment?

Suggested measurement: Internal research to ascertain how secure employees are about their jobs, taking initiative, expressing a different point of view to their superiors, and possibly making mistakes.

9. BREAK DOWN BARRIERS BETWEEN DEPARTMENTS

Break down barriers between departments. People in research, design, sales, and production must work as a team to foresee problems of production and in use that may be encountered with the product or service.

Suppose a bank has just completed a survey regarding service quality. Let us examine one aspect of this survey. Customers might have indicated that the most important factor while waiting in a lineup is that they be served quickly. Yet, if we analyzed their responses, we might find that they would like all their banking needs to be taken care of once it is their turn at the counter. Thus, their primary and secondary needs are not necessarily compatible. There also might be tertiary requirements. Customer requirements cannot be implemented satisfactorily unless different departments—in this case, the computer department, personnel who are not directly at the counter, and others—work together to satisfy the apparently conflicting customer expectations. Whether the customer is satisfied might depend not only on the people behind the counter, but also on whether they have a good computer system and whether they can count on people who do not work at the counter. As long as there are barriers between departments, customer expectations can be fulfilled only partially. The "It's not my department!" attitude is not only an insult to the customer but a deterrent to eventually delivering what he or she wants.

Break down barriers between departments.

Questions: How frequently are customer expectations described in terms of involvement of several departments? How are communications and cooperation among departments managed?

Suggested measurement: Desk research to identify the departments needed to participate in implementing a specific strategy; research to identify the barriers to instant cooperation to achieve the objectives.

10. ELIMINATE SLOGANS

Eliminate slogans, exhortations, and targets for the workforce that ask for zero defects and new levels of productivity.

Slogans and exhortations often are used in place of the training and tools needed to deliver quality. A plaque that loudly proclaims "Customers First!" or "Toward Excellence" is meaningless to an employee and an irritant to the customer if no procedures are in place to deliver what is proclaimed. When quality is really delivered, there is no need for slogans.

Eliminate slogans, exhortations, and targets for the workforce.

Questions: Does your company have slogans and exhortations for its employees? What procedures are in place to make the slogans a reality? Can actions be substituted for slogans?

Suggested measurement: Desk research to assess slogans and exhortations used by the company; secondary or primary research to determine training and equipment needed to implement the message of the exhortations.

11. ELIMINATE QUOTAS (WORK STANDARDS)

Eliminate work standards (quotas). Substitute leadership. Eliminate management by objective. Eliminate management by numbers and numerical goals. Substitute leadership.

Numerical goals inhibit long-term improvement. When emphasis is placed on the outcome and not on the upstream process, management limits its ability to deliver what customers want at a price they are willing to pay. Employee concentration shifts from long-term customer satisfaction to short-term target practice.

Questions: What are the work standards currently in place for employees? What are your targets? What plans are in place to achieve your targets?

Eliminate work standards (quotas). Substitute leadership.

Suggested measurement: Desk research and internal interviews can be undertaken to identify the existence of quotas and work standards within the organization. If there is some resistance to eliminating these quotas and standards, nominal group techniques and force field analysis can be used to find common ground.

12. REMOVE BARRIERS

Remove barriers that rob the worker of his or her right to pride of workmanship. The responsibility of supervisors must be changed from stressing sheer numbers to stressing quality. This means, inter alia, abolishment of the annual merit rating and of management by objective.

Although it may not be readily apparent, performance evaluations and management by objective can destroy teamwork. Performance evaluations are carried out usually within specific departments and often are related to numerical goals. Let us consider the performance evaluation in which a person is judged on how fast he or she can serve customers. The emphasis put on efficiency may work against taking time to serve the customers properly. Again, a customer may be shunted from one person to another or from one department to another so that a person or a department can meet the objectives (or the numerical goals) of management. The performance appraisal system also fosters mediocrity. When goals are set for appraisals, the employee either negotiates with the employer to lower the standards, so that they can be met, or, alternatively, may just do enough to exceed the standards. By doing just enough, the employer keeps the difference between what is achieved and what is achievable "in reserve," to be used the following year. Yet another problem is that, no matter how excellent the performance of each employee is, some employees' performances will be above average, and the performances of others will be

Remove barriers that rob the worker of his or her right to pride of workmanship.

below average. This is a statistical certainty. In addition, in many cases, the visible performance aspects are directly related to the type of job handled by the employee.

Questions: What barriers to pride and quality exist within the organization? Is performance evaluation contributing to quality in any way?

Suggested measurement: Structural and functional analysis of the organization can be helpful here.

13. INSTITUTE PROGRAMS OF EDUCATION AND RETRAINING

Institute a vigorous program of education and self-improvement.

It is Deming's view that a program of education and self-improvement reduces the need for all incoming resources. This, in turn, reduces waste. Consequently, the cost of doing business will go down. A company must make it clear to its employees that it is not only investing in them, but also making a lifetime commitment to them. This will increase the cooperation between management and employees because the employees will feel reassured that, by spending time in educational and self-improvement programs, they will not be working themselves out of a job.

Questions: How many educational programs did management attend? How many did the employees attend? What plans are at hand to retrain employees in the near

Institute a vigorous program of education and self-improvement.

future?

Suggested measurement: Gap analysis research can be undertaken, with a view to identifying the difference between knowledge required to do the job and the current level of knowledge. This can be used to assess the training needs of the organization.

14. ACCOMPLISH THE TRANSFORMATION

Put everybody in the organization to work to accomplish the transformation. The transformation is everybody's job.

This is a global dictum. Management has to communicate

to the outside world and its employees that it is not business as usual. This is a call to identify middle managers (and others) who may thwart the new direction and frustrate the organization.

Put everybody in the organization to work to accomplish the transformation. The transformation is everybody's job.

Questions: Is everyone in the organization working toward similar goals? Are there still impediments to transformation? If so, how can these impediments be removed?

Suggested measurement: A wide variety of techniques, such as nominal group techniques, can be used to assess where we stand and what the obstacles are to achieving transformation.

DEMING'S 14 POINTS AND SERVICE QUALITY AND RESEARCH

Deming's 14 points challenge conventional wisdom. They directly contradict the practices of several organizations. In addition, they emphasize internal transformation to a much greater degree.

Deming versus conventional thinking

Many of Deming's 14 points are at variance with what is being practiced today to achieve quality. Many companies are violating several of his principles on a regular basis. The following are some examples:

Drive out fear. Many organizations use fear as a strategy to achieve service quality. They believe that fear is what keeps employees in line and attempt to achieve service quality by using fear as a leverage device.

Eliminate work standards and numerical goals. Again, many organizations attempt to achieve service quality by specifying a standard for the employee by which he or she will be evaluated.

Eliminate slogans. Many organizations that have discovered service quality appear to believe that slogans and exhortations are the way to achieve service quality. It is not uncommon to find such slogans proudly displayed in many organizations.

Another critical assumption made by many organizations is that delivering quality is a cost-incurring activity. This is obviously a disincentive to delivering quality. Deming, on the other hand, believes that quality brings the cost down and is, therefore, a cost-reducing activity.

Thus, when we review current management practices and analyze the extent to which they conform to Deming's 14 principles, it becomes fairly evident that most organizations simply have different views on how to achieve quality. It is not my intent to suggest that Deming's approach is superior. However, given his track record in helping Japanese firms achieve quality and profitability, it may be worthwhile to give serious attention to his ideas.

Quality: Internal and external forces

Another difference between Deming's approach and conventional approaches is the focus. Deming is much in favor of research. Yet, his 14 points emphasize improvement within a company. The alternative approach adopted by many companies is to assess what the customer wants and then attempt to deliver it, if it is cost-effective, without much regard as to how the organization must transform itself to cater to customer needs. When the organization does not align itself with the philosophy of quality, what is delivered to the customer is individual behavioral acts that simulate quality. Anytime the company makes a loss or there is a change in senior management, quality may be sacrificed if it is not part of the current management philosophy. Again, this can be observed easily in many organizations.

Although Deming is primarily a statistical quality control expert, it is surprising to note that most of his principles can be applied (almost without modification) to any area that emphasizes quality.

DEMING'S 14 POINTS AND MEASURING SERVICE QUALITY

Throughout this book, we have discussed a number of techniques to measure service quality. How do they relate to Deming's 14 points? Although I have provided a partial answer to this question by mentioning relevant research techniques that could be used for each point, to relate the techniques rigidly to each is counterproductive. It is more likely that, when an organization starts implementing Deming's 14 points, it will come across problems such as

- How to elicit and analyze problems faced by customers.
- How to track the interconnectedness of different activities.
- How to find out when the system breaks down.

The techniques discussed in this book provide answers to such questions and are expanded in the final chapter.

Part VI

Putting It All Together

23

Choosing the Right Technique

My exposition of service quality and customer satisfaction measurement techniques follows the P3D3 matrix. The matrix was designed for pedagogical purposes and to provide a conceptual framework for understanding the techniques. As I have mentioned throughout this text, once the techniques are understood, they can be used in other contexts as well. For example, the matrix puts complaint tracking at the diagnostic stage. Yet, there is no reason why it cannot be used for tracking purposes at the delivery stage. Similarly, the nominal groups technique discussed in the delivery stage can be used equally effectively at the diagnostic stage. Once the technique is clearly understood, the reader should be able to use a given technique wherever it is appropriate.

We also can view these techniques as providing answers to commonly asked questions. Such a framework is provided here:

Question	Technique	Chapter
Where do we stand as an organization?	Structural analysis	10
Where is the problem?	Check sheets	10
How do customers see us?	Mystery shopping	10
How to explore with limited prior knowledge?	Internal focus groups	10
How to summarize and understand quickly?	Graphic techniques	11
How to uncover hidden relationships?	Stratification	11
How to understand the patterns of activity?	Run charts	11
How to get a picture of the system as a whole?	Flow charts	11
How to elicit complaints?	Complaint elicitation	12
What are underlying customer beliefs?	Belief system analysis	12
How to identify the most frequent problems?	Pareto chart	12
How to analyze customer complaints?	Content analysis	12
How to track customer complaints?	Content tracking	12
How to elicit uninhibited opinions and ideas?	Nominal group technique	13
How to model after the best companies?	Benchmarking	13
How to have a fresh perspective?	Dimension reduction	13
How to find creative solutions?	The as-if frame	13
How to understand the customer perspective?	Video-camera technique	13

How to identify stable systems?	Control charts	14
How to explore customer needs?	External focus groups	15
How to assess the first dimension of service?	Survey research	15
How to explore customer motivations?	Laddering	15
How to identify service attribute groups?	Factor analysis	15
How to generate ideas to deliver the unexpected?	Wish lists	15
How to identify service gaps?	Gap analysis	15
How elicit the best ideas?	Brainstorming	16
How to neutralize forces opposed to change?	Force field analysis	16
How to decide among alternative courses of action?	Cost-benefit analysis	16
How to pinpoint the problem source?	Fishbone diagram	17
How to follow a process to effect changes?	Process mapping/evaluation	17
How to monitor your progress?	Tracking	18
How to interpret two aspects simultaneously?	Quadrant analysis	20

MEASURING CUSTOMER SATISFACTION

Although many of these techniques also can be used in studying customer satisfaction, I believe that proper customer satisfaction measurement depends more on an understanding of the pitfalls of measurement than on the use of specific techniques. We note that measuring the wrong things, using internal measurements that are detrimental to external customer satisfaction, using rearview measurements, measuring things the wrong way, having no key measures of satisfaction, and the use of CSIs are some of the reasons why customer satisfaction measurements turn out to be ineffective. The following are some courses of action that might improve customer satisfaction measurements.

Area of concern	*Sources/concepts*
Gathering background data	Qualitative research, customer complaints
Choosing attributes to measure	Mission statements, derived importance scores
Choosing the right audience	Focusing on the "vital few"
Deciding on the basic questions	Incidence, frequency, importance, performance, criterion
Choosing the right metric	Some metrics can mislead, no universal answer
Making analysis action-oriented	Even simple techniques can illuminate/mislead
Segmenting customers	Group customers with similar needs
Interpreting measures correctly	Separate common causes from special causes
Using CSIs with caution	The inappropriateness of using CSIs to guide our actions

A FINAL WORD

Techniques are important. They provide us with a quick and tested way of solving a problem. But, to effectively implement a service quality or a customer satisfaction program, we must go beyond techniques. We need to understand where and how we can go wrong. For those of us who are in the business of measuring service quality and customer satisfaction, the rewards are many. But so are the pitfalls. I hope this book presents a balanced view of the power and the pitfalls of measurement techniques.

General References

Band, R. (1991), *Creating Value for Customers.* New York: John Wiley and Sons.

Barlow, J. and C. Moller (1996), *A Complaint is a Gift.* San Francisco: Berrett Kohler.

Berry, L.L., V.A. Zeithaml, and P. Parasuraman (1985), "Quality Counts in Service Too," *Business Horizons*, 28 (3), 44–52.

Brown, M.G. (1996), *Keeping Score: Using the Right Metrics to Drive World-Class Performance.* New York: Quality Resources.

BusinessWeek (1991), Quality Imperative. New York: McGraw-Hill.

Campenella, J., ed. (1990), *Principles of Quality Costs.* Milwaukee: ASQC Quality Press.

Carlzon, J. (1987), *Moments of Truth.* New York: Ballinger.

Chakrapani, Chuck (1996), "Customer Satisfaction Index: The Emperor with no Clothes," *Imprints*, (October), 11–14.

Chang, R.Y. and M.E. Niedzwiecki (1993), *Con-tinuous Improvement Tools*, Vol. 1. Irvine, CA: Richard Chang Associates.

Clemmer, J. (1990), *Firing on All Cylinders.* Toronto, ON: McMillan Canada.

Cortada, J. and J. Wood (1995), *McGraw-Hill Encyclopedia of Quality Terms and Concepts.* New York: McGraw-Hill.

Crosby, P.B. (1979), *Quality is Free.* New York: Mentor.

Deming, W. E. (1986), *Out of the Crisis.* Cambridge, MA: MIT CAES.

——— (1993), *The New Economics for Business, Government and Education.* Cambridge, MA: MIT CAES.

Devlin, S., H.K. Dong, and M. Brown (1993), "Selecting a Scale for Measuring Quality," *Marketing Research*, 5 (Spring), 12–18.

Dey, I. (1993), *Qualitative Data Analysis.* London: Routledge.

The Economist (1992), (April 18), 42.

Eureka, W.E. and N.E. Ryan (1995), *Quality Up, Costs Down.* Burr Ridge, IL: Richard D. Irwin.

Feigenbaum, A. (1956), *Total Quality Control.* New York: McGraw Hill.

Fortune (1987), (December 7), 78.

——— (1995), "After All You Have Done for Your Customers, Why Are They Still Not Happy?" (December 11), 178–82.

——— (1995), "Americans Can't Get No Satisfaction," (December 11), 186–94.

Garvin, D.A. (1987), "Competing on the Eight Dimensions of Quality," *Harvard Business Review*, (November/December), 101–09.

Hayes, B.E (1992), *Measuring Customer Satisfaction: Development and Use of Questionnaires.* Milwaukee: ASQC Quality Press.

Ishikawa, Kaoru (1986), *Guide to Quality Control*, 2d Revised Edition. Tokyo: Asian Productivity Organization.

Lithwick, D. (1995), "A Survival Guide to Mystery Shopping," *Imprints*, (November), 8.

McConnell *(1991), Safer Than a Known Way*. Manly Vale, New South Wales: Delaware Books.

Mears, P. (1995), *Quality Improvement Tools and Techniques*. New York: McGraw-Hill.

Naumann, E. and K. Giel (1995), *Customer Satisfaction Measurement*. Cincinnati, OH: Thomson Executive Press.

Ontario Public Service (1992), *Best Value for Tax Dollars: Improving Service Quality in the Ontario Government*. Ontario: Ontario Public Service.

Parasuraman, A. (1987), "Customer-Oriented Corporate Cultures are Crucial to Services Marketing Success," *Journal of Services Marketing*, 1 (Summer), 39–46.

Reichheld, R.F.(1996), *The Loyalty Effect*. Boston: Harvard Business School Press.

Scherkenbach, W.W. (1986), *The Deming Route to Quality and Productivity*. Washington: CEEP Press.

Schwarz, R.M. (1994), *The Skilled Facilitator*. San Francisco: Jossey-Bass.

Stewart, T. (1997), "Another Fad Worth Killing," *Fortune*, (February 3), 119–20. (Argues that the concept of internal customers is outdated and counterproductive and therefore should be scrapped.)

Tenner, A.R. and I.J. DeToro (1992), *Total Quality Management*. Reading, MA: Addison-Wesley.

Terra (1995), *Catpac 4 for Windows*. Birmingham, MA: Terra.

Treacy, M. and F. Wiersema (1995), *The Discipline of Market Leaders*. Reading, MA: Addison-Wesley.

Whiteley, R.C. (1991), *The Customer Driven Company*. Reading, MA: Addison Wesley.

Wittink, D.R. and L.R. Bayer (1993), "The Measurement Imperative," *Marketing Research*, 6 (4), 14–22.

Yoshida, S. (1989), "Quality Improvement and TQC Management at Calsonic in Japan and Overseas," paper presented at the Second International Quality Symposium, Mexico (November).

Zeithaml, V.A., P. Parasuraman, and L.L. Berry (1990), *Delivering Quality: Balancing Customer Perceptions and Expectations*. New York: The Free Press.

Index

MEASURING SERVICE QUALITY: WHEN TO USE WHAT

Question	Technique	Chapter
Where do we stand as an organization?	Structual analysis	10
Where is the problem?	Check sheets	10
How do customers see us?	Mystery shopping	10
How to explore with limited prior knowledge?	Internal focus groups	10
How to summarize and understand quickly?	Graphic techniques	11
How to uncover hidden realtionships?	Stratification	11
How to understand the patterns of activity?	Run charts	11
How to get a picture of the system as a whole?	Flow charts	11
How to elicit complaints?	Complaint elicitation	12
What are underlying customer beliefs?	Belief system analysis	12
How to identify the most frequent problems?	Pareto chart	12
How to analyze customer complaints?	Content analysis	12
How to track customer complaints?	Content tracking	12
How to elicit unhibited opinions and ideas?	Nominal group technique	13
How to model after the best companies?	Benchmarking	13
How to have a fresh perspective?	Dimension reduction	13
How to find creating solutions?	The as-if frame	13
How to understand the customer perspective?	Video-camera technique	13
How to identify stable systems?	Control charts	14
How to explore customer needs?	External focus groups	15
How to assess the first dimension of service?	Survey research	15
How to explore customer motivations?	Laddering	15
How to identify service gaps?	Gap analysis	15
How elicit the best ideas?	Brainstorming	16
How to neutrailze forces opposed to change?	Force field analysis	16
How to decide among alrenative courses of action	Cost benefit analysis	16
How to pinpoint the problem source?	Fishbone diagram	17
How to follow a processes to effect changes?	Process mapping/evaluation	17
How to monitor your progress?	Tracking	18
How to interpret two aspects simultaneously?	Quadrant analysis	20

MEASURING CUSTOMER SATISFACTION: BASIC CONCEPTS

Area of Concern	Sources/concepts
Gathering background data	Qualitative research, customer complaints
Choosing attributes to measure	Mission statements, derived importance scores
Choosing the right audience	Focusing on the 'vital few'
Deciding on the basic questions	Incidence, frequency, importance, performance, criterion
Choosing the right metric	Some metrics can mislead. No universal answer.
Making analysis action-oriented	Even simple techniques can illuniate/mislead
Segmenting customers	Group customers with similar needs
Interpreting measure correctly	Seperate common causes from special causes
Using CSI with caution	The inappropriateness of using CSI to guide cations